THE ESSENTIAL BOOK OF
HOME IMPROVEMENT TECHNIQUES

THE ESSENTIAL BOOK OF
HOME IMPROVEMENT TECHNIQUES

*All you need to make
the home you've got
the one you want*

DAVID HOLLOWAY   MIKE LAWRENCE   JOHN MCGOWAN

CONSULTING EDITOR
TONY WILKINS

A New Burlington Book
Conceived, edited and designed by Marshall Editions
The Old Brewery, 6 Blundell Street, London N7 9BH

First published in the UK in 1999 by Marshall Publishing Ltd

This edition printed in 2006 by Bookmart Ltd
Blaby Road, Wigston, Leicester LE18 4SE
registered number 2372865

ISBN-10: 1 84566 085 4
ISBN-13: 978 1 84566 085 7

10 9 8 7 6 5 4 3 2 1

Originated by PICA Colour Separation Pte
Printed and bound in China by Midas Printing Ltd

Project editor Theresa Lane
Editorial assistance John Plowman
Art editor Amzie Viladot Lorente
Design assistants Karen Kloot, Philip Letsu
Technical coordinators Stephen Corbett, Mike Trier
Picture research Zilda Tandy, Elaine Willis
Copy editor Mike Stocks
DTP editor Lesley Gilbert
Editorial assistant Dan Green
Indexer Susan Cawthorne
Managing editor Clare Currie
Managing art editor Helen Spencer
Editorial director Ellen Dupont
Art director Sean Keogh
Editorial coordinator Becca Clunes
Production Mary Osborne, Nikki Ingram

Note: Every effort has been taken to ensure that all information
in this book is correct and compatible with national standards
generally accepted at the time of publication. This book is not
intended to replace manufacturers' instructions in the use of their
tools or materials – always follow their safety guidelines.
The authors and publisher disclaim any liability for loss,
injury or damage incurred as a consequence, directly or indirectly,
of the use and application of the contents of this book.

FOREWORD

At some time, and in one way or another, every room in the house will require some attention. This could be only a new coat of paint to freshen up the walls, or it could mean a complete overhaul from ceiling to floor. Whatever the scope of your project, *The Essential Book of Home Improvement Techniques* shows all the relevant techniques to get the best results, as well as provides all the necessary details on choosing the materials to decorate your home. By taking the time to follow the instructions carefully – and without skipping the preparation work – you can redecorate you home with professional results. In fact, you may find the most difficult part of the job is deciding on the colours, patterns and textures for each room.

ABOUT THIS BOOK

At the start of each chapter a "directory" section gives a brief summary of the information you'll find in the subsequent pages, a guide to how long it may take to complete the job and a recommended level of skill. Within each chapter you'll find pages filled with "options" to help you choose the materials for the job and to give you design ideas. Having decided on the decoration for your room, follow the step-by-step pages to master the techniques. Clear photographs illustrate each of the steps, and lists are supplied of all the materials and tools you'll need for the job. You'll also find helpful hints from the professionals and ideas for alternative treatments. Cross-references to other pages will guide you to pertinent preparation instructions or to additional techniques to help finish a job. Whether you want to complete a single task or combine techniques to come up with your own ideas, all the help and advice you need is at hand.

Stewart Walton

CONTENTS

Chapter 4
FLOORS 172

Chapter 5
SHELVING AND STORAGE 218

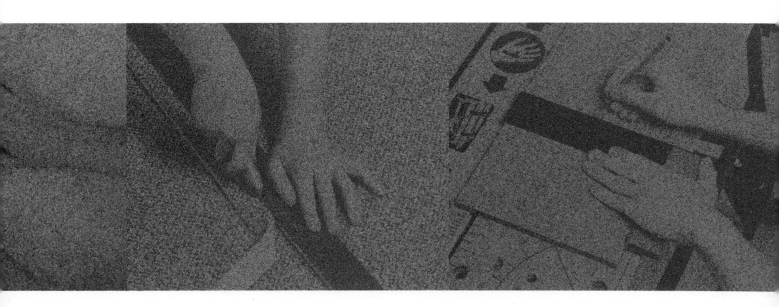

ASSESSING YOUR SITUATION

There is no straightforward answer to how much time and effort will be required to redecorate a room from ceiling to floor. There are a number of factors to consider, including the present condition of the room, your experience and ability to use tools and the amount of free days you have in which to tackle the work.

A room in good condition in a new house may simply need painting to suit your personal tastes – potentially, a simple job of two or three days' work if the walls only require a washing down and a sanding of any old gloss paint before applying the new paint. Even the novice do-it-yourselfer would not find the job daunting. However, in an old house where the room may have been poorly decorated many times over, or where there is dampness, rotting wood or numerous cracks in ceilings and walls (see pp.12–13), you are looking at the worst case scenario; it may take months before the room can be completely redecorated.

DOING THE JOB RIGHT

Preparation – in which the surfaces are made clean, smooth and even and any repair work is undertaken – is the key to successful decorating. Unfortunately, preparation must be done thoroughly, which can take considerable time. How much time is difficult to gauge because, although you can estimate how long the obvious problems will take to fix, you have no idea what might be lurking behind old wallpaper, flaking ceiling paint or a damp patch. Wood cladding might have been fixed to disguise uneven walls, and thick wallcovering might have been hung as a quick, less expensive solution to repairing badly cracked plaster walls.

This wall was stripped of peeling wallpaper with the plan of painting the room. However, the wall needs extra preparation before it will be ready for painting. The mantlepiece also requires work before it will be ready for decoration.

Lifting up an old floor covering may expose one or more cracked or damaged floorboards. You may have to repair or replace several boards before you lay down the new floor covering.

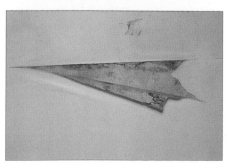

Moisture has stained this wallpaper and caused it to peel – the cause of the moisture must be resolved before attempting any redecoration.

Often there is no way of knowing the condition of the walls, ceilings and floors until whatever material is hiding the surface has been removed – but there are some clues. For example, a wet patch on wallpaper in the middle of a chimney breast is a sign of dampness in the flue caused by a lack of ventilation or rainwater ingress. Inspect the areas around windows and external doors, which are subjected to wet conditions. They could be affected by wet rot – clues include cracked paint and dark wood (see pp.60–61). If you take up a floor covering (see pp.40–41), examine the floorboards for signs of rot or woodworm (see pp.12–13). In each of these cases, any problems will require some remedial work before you redecorate.

Deeply indented, chipped paint on wood trim indicates that many coats of paint have been applied over the years. It is probably time to strip off the lot back to bare wood; however, if there is just the odd chip and the rest of the surfaces are sound, then it makes more sense to leave the paint alone as it will provide a sound, flat surface to paint on. You don't want to make unnecessary work and expense for yourself. The same goes for lining paper on the ceiling; if it's flat to the surface, it may be better to leave it there because it could be covering a lot of cosmetic repair work.

Because there are so many corners in this kitchen, additional time was allocated to allow for the cutting of all the wall tiles. The worktop also required more time to custom fit it.

OTHER CONSIDERATIONS

Apart from the basic aspect of straightforward decorating, you may want to make changes to the room such as removing an old fireplace mantelpiece or putting one in. Cupboards or shelves may need removing, replacing or installing, or you may want to replace a door. Don't forget that old plumbing and electrical wiring might be factors.

The size and shape of the room also come into the equation. The bigger the room, the longer it will take to hang wallpaper. If the room has more than its fair share of alcoves, arches, windows and doors, then hanging wallpaper is going to take far longer than in a simple rectangular room.

The vital thing is to calculate for the worst, then you won't be frustrated by unexpected delays. It is very upsetting to think you can decorate a room in a weekend, only to find that on Sunday evening you're still doing the preparation work. Don't be tempted to cut corners – it may create more work in the future.

Dark, pulpy soft wood is a sign of wet rot, which is found in damp areas. You can test for it by inserting a screwdriver, bradawl or sharp knife into the wood.

PLANNING THE CAMPAIGN

When decorating just a single room, other rooms in the house can be affected by becoming temporary storage space for furniture and ornaments. Few people like living in clutter, so it's best to tackle the work in a continuous session. If you only have a weekend to spare, consider waiting until you can take time off from work.

Summertime is the best time for decorating: days are warmer and longer and open windows won't create cold working conditions. Painting in a cold temperature can adversely affect the finish. It's also not a good idea to paint in poor or artificial light, because it can be difficult – especially when using white paint – to see which areas have been painted or whether the paint has dripped. If you must decorate in winter, plan to do all your painting while there is natural light. You can always do the other jobs with artificial light.

BEFORE THE DECORATION

If you're doing major renovations that involve changing the use of a room, you may need to seek planning permission from your local council. For example, a bathroom must have a source of ventilation and a bedroom must have a window.

If you want to install new electrical sockets, switches or wall or ceiling light fixtures, then make sure the work is done before you start decorating. Plan the positions of these items carefully – repositioning them can mean having to redecorate a complete wall. The same applies to plumbing, gas and water fittings. If you employ professionals to do the work, make sure it is completed before you take time off to decorate. It can be frustrating to start your holiday while tradesmen are still finishing a job. You should remember they can get it wrong when it comes

Preparation for this room included stripping wallpaper from below the picture rails and removing the floor covering. Plasterboard was fixed on one wall to create a smooth surface, and a new skirting board was fixed to it. Moulding was added to the other skirting boards to match the styles.

Damaged floorboards were replaced in this room. The ceilings and walls will be redecorated before the new floor covering is installed.

The kitchen above was transformed (see right) with careful planning. An electrician changed the track lighting to down lights and a plumber fitted a new sink and oven before any decoration began, including installing new worktops and painting the ceiling and walls.

to time estimates – sometimes through no fault of their own, but because of an unexpected problem.

Make a check list of all the materials and equipment you'll need and make sure you have everything before you get started. This may mean waiting for a delivery of a custom-ordered kitchen worktop or visiting a DIY centre to pick up abrasive paper, PVA adhesive or additional screws. When you're ready to start the work, have everything at hand, including stepladders and plastic bags for disposing of any rubbish.

ORDER OF WORK

If you are decorating a whole house, work from the top downward. By doing so, the inevitable dust will make its way downstairs to the unfinished ground floor rooms. However, if you do choose to decorate the downstairs first, make sure that any upstairs room to be decorated is kept as dust free as possible. This may mean taking occasional breaks when sanding a floor, for example, to clean up the debris.

Once you decide where to start, clear away as much furniture from the room as possible. Whatever has to remain should be piled in the centre of the room, then completely covered up – paint splashes have a way of ending up in the unlikeliest places.

The first job is to tackle any structural work or major repairs. Dealing with rot or woodworm (see pp.12–13) may mean replacing a number of floorboards. Putting in shelves or cupboards can be left until last, provided there is no risk of damaging new decorations.

Generally speaking, a room should be prepared and decorated from the ceiling downward. Clearly you wouldn't paper a wall before painting the ceiling, because you would almost certainly get paint splashes on the new wallpaper below. So the order is ceiling, walls, woodwork (such as doors, architrave and skirting boards) and metalwork (such as radiators). The exception is when hanging wallpaper – you should paint the woodwork and metalwork beforehand.

THE BIG ISSUES

Some problems in a house are best treated by an expert, including rising damp and dry rot. In fact, some mortgage and insurance companies may insist on a guarantee from a professional.

RISING DAMP

Moisture coming up from the ground causes rising damp and, if it is not stopped, it will rise to about 1000 mm (40 in) on a wall. Because of this, a house has an impermeable layer, called a damp-proof course (DPC), built into the walls 300 mm (12 in) or so above ground level. Solid concrete floors have a damp-proof membrane (DPM) laid in them. The DPC and DPM keep the house dry. If a part of the DPC or DPM fails, rising damp can develop. The symptoms are damp patches low on the wall, often accompanied by a "tidemark", which shows the level the dampness has risen to.

If you think you have rising damp, check first that the DPC has not been bridged by earth piled against the wall outside or a pathway built too high. There are do-it-yourself treatments, but most people opt for a professional company to install a new DPC where needed. Rising damp in solid floors can be treated by digging up and re-laying the floor to incorporate a DPM, but applying several coats of a liquid DPM is an easier solution.

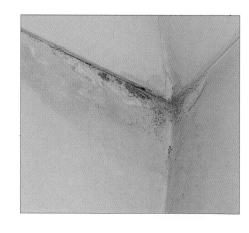

The mould in this corner may be caused by either penetrating damp or condensation. Before redecorating, the cause of the damp must be isolated and treated, and the mould must be removed.

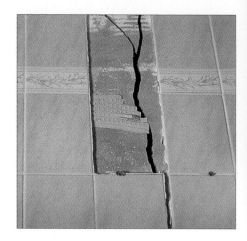

Ceramic tiles removed from this bathroom wall exposed the tell-tale wide cracks created by subsidence. This is a situation that should be rectified only by specialists.

PENETRATING DAMP

Water creeping from the outside to the inside is called penetrating damp. Wet patches on walls or ceilings or near a window frame are signs of this, but they may be a distance away from where the damp is getting in. Cavity walls in houses are comprised of two leaves of brick or block with a 50 mm (2 in) air space between them. Damp shouldn't be able to cross the gap; but if mortar was dropped during building on the wall ties holding the leaves together, it creates a bridge for damp to cross the gap. Older houses with solid walls rely on the thickness of the masonry to keep out the damp, but it doesn't always do so for various reasons. The signs of penetrating damp are often worse after it has rained.

You can treat penetrating damp by correcting the structural fault – replacing a missing roof tile or leaking gutter, for example – then applying a silicone water repellent. Or you can paint the wall with a good quality exterior masonry paint.

CONDENSATION

Although a different problem, condensation is sometimes wrongly diagnosed as structural damp. It occurs when warm, moist air meets a cold surface, such as an outside wall or window pane,

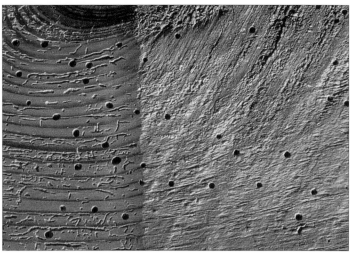

The underside of the floorboards is host to the fruiting body of dry rot. *The rust-coloured spores can spread rapidly.*

The main sign of a woodworm attack is the exit holes. The dark section *has been planed to show the tunnels inside the wood.*

and is cooled. Cold air holds less water vapour than warm air, and the difference is deposited on the cold surface as water droplets – the "misting" on windows on a cold morning is an example. The symptoms of condensation are random damp patches on walls, which become worse in cold weather, and black mould. To distinguish between damp and condensation, dry the damp area with a hair dryer, then place a piece of glass over it, bedded down on putty around its edges. Moisture should form on the glass after a few days. If it is on the room side, the problem is condensation; on the wall side, penetrating damp.

Treatment for condensation depends on the cause. It may simply be a matter of heating a cold room, adding ventilation in a bathroom or kitchen (or a blocked chimney breast) or insulating a loft or cold water pipes.

INFESTATIONS

Woodworm is a type of insect that will attack all structural wood in a house, including roof rafters, floor joists and floorboards. However, the exit holes are easy to spot, and it is easy to treat if caught early. You can buy liquids to both prevent woodworm attack and kill off a current outbreak.

Wood can also be attacked by wet rot (see pp.8–9) and dry rot, which are types of fungi. Wet rot only occurs in damp wood and can be found in window frames and exterior wood. After treating the cause of the damp wood, dig out and replace the damaged wood (see pp.60–61).

Dry rot is more serious. Once established, it can transfer from wet wood to dry wood. It can cause severe structural damage and should be treated only by a specialist. Signs of its presence are cracks across the wood grain, a musty smell and growths like cotton wool and mushroom on the wood. It is often discovered in poorly ventilated areas such as cellars or under floorboards.

SUBSIDENCE

Two of the causes of subsidence are the ground below a house drying out in a drought and the roots of a nearby tree draining water from the ground. The signs are wide cracks in the walls, especially near windows and doors, and splitting bricks. You must call in professional help. A "tell-tale", two pieces of glass or plastic with a grid pattern, will be fitted over a crack to monitor for continual movement. If the house has subsidence, its foundation must be underpinned to support it.

1

PREPARATION

PREPARATION DIRECTORY

STRIPPING A ROOM

SKILL LEVEL Low
TIME FRAME ½ day
SPECIAL TOOLS Circuit tester
SEE PAGES 18–19

Remove items from a wall or ceiling, including shelves and curtain rail brackets. Wall sockets, switches and light fittings can be pulled forward after turning off the electricity.

DEALING WITH CRACKS, DENTS AND STAINS

SKILL LEVEL Low
TIME FRAME Under 2 hours
SPECIAL TOOLS Flexible filler knife, cartridge gun
SEE PAGES 20–21

Repair small cracks and dents with filler; use mastic sealant for cracks at skirting boards or a door or window frame. Cover stains with a sealer before painting.

PATCHING HOLES IN WALLS

SKILL LEVEL Medium
TIME FRAME Under 2 hours
SPECIAL TOOLS Plasterboard knife, hawk, trowel
SEE PAGES 22–23

Repair small holes in plasterboard with a one-coat plaster on a backing material; patch a larger hole with a piece of plasterboard and a coat of plaster filler. Fill holes in a plaster wall with plaster.

REPAIRING DAMAGE TO A CEILING

SKILL LEVEL Medium
TIME FRAME Under 2 hours
SPECIAL TOOLS Flexible filler knife, cartridge gun
SEE PAGES 24–25

Repairs include fixing a popped nail in plasterboard ceilings and filling holes in plaster and plasterboard ceilings. Larger holes in plaster ceilings have to be reinforced with expanded metal mesh.

STRIPPING OLD WALLPAPER

SKILL LEVEL Low
TIME FRAME 2 hours to ½ day
SPECIAL TOOLS Wire brush, steam stripper
SEE PAGES 26–27

You should remove an old wallcovering before hanging a new one. Some wallcoverings peel away from the wall; others must be scored, soaked and scraped off or removed with steam.

REMOVING OTHER WALL DECORATIONS

SKILL LEVEL Low to medium
TIME FRAME ½ to 1 day
SPECIAL TOOLS Bolster chisel, club hammer, heat gun, crowbar
SEE PAGES 28–29

You may have to prise ceramic tiles off a wall or lever off cladding. Remove textured finishes with a textured paint remover.

WASHING DOWN AND PREPARING SURFACES

SKILL LEVEL Low
TIME FRAME Under 2 hours
SPECIAL TOOLS None
SEE PAGES 30–31

Paintwork may need attention such as scraping off flaking paint, filling and sanding. Wash walls with sugar soap. If wallpapering, scrape off any remaining paper after stripping the walls. Eradicate any mould with a fungicide.

STRIPPING PAINT FROM WOOD TRIM

SKILL LEVEL Low
TIME FRAME 2 hours to 1 day
SPECIAL TOOLS Shavehook, narrow scraper, heat gun
SEE PAGES 32–33

Paintwork that is flaking, badly chipped or cracked must be stripped off by using a heat gun or chemical stripper. Chemical strippers are preferred for mouldings, where heat can cause scorching, and near windows, where heat can crack glass.

STRIPPING AND PREPARING METAL

SKILL LEVEL Low
TIME FRAME Under 2 hours
SPECIAL TOOLS Wire brush, power drill plus wire brush attachment, safety glasses, dust mask
SEE PAGES 34–35

Clean a rusty cast iron fireplace or baluster with emery paper or by wire brushing. Fill pitting with an epoxy-based filler. To remove paint in intricate areas, use a chemical stripper.

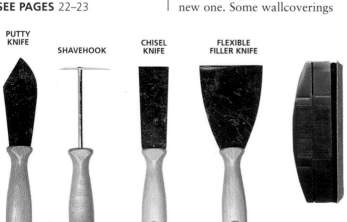

PUTTY KNIFE

SHAVEHOOK

CHISEL KNIFE

FLEXIBLE FILLER KNIFE

SANDING BLOCK AND ABRASIVE PAPER

WALLBOARD KNIFE

CROWBAR

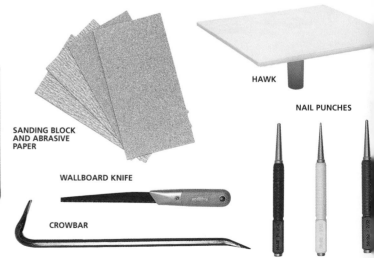

HAWK

NAIL PUNCHES

REMOVING SKIRTING BOARDS AND MOULDINGS

SKILL LEVEL Medium
TIME FRAME ½ day
SPECIAL TOOLS Bolster chisel, club hammer, crowbar
SEE PAGES 36–37

Repair old skirting boards. To remove a board, prise it away from the wall. You may need to remove other mouldings such as picture and dado rails.

REPLACING SKIRTING BOARDS

SKILL LEVEL Medium
TIME FRAME ½ to 1 day
SPECIAL TOOLS Coping saw, mitre frame and saw (or tenon saw and mitre box), block plane
SEE PAGES 38–39

Fix new skirting boards by using panel adhesive or screws. If on a plaster wall, buy a new board of the same depth or greater.

REMOVING FLOOR COVERINGS

SKILL LEVEL Low to medium
TIME FRAME 2 hours to 1 day
SPECIAL TOOLS Tack lifter, crowbar, heat gun, bolster chisel, club hammer
SEE PAGES 40–41

Prise away a fitted carpet from gripper strips that have been fitted around the room; these can be reused. Pull foam-backed carpet away from double-sided tape. If sheet vinyl or vinyl tiles are stuck down, use a heat gun and scraper to remove the adhesive. Prise up ceramic tiles and wooden floors.

MAKING MINOR REPAIRS TO A WOOD FLOOR

SKILL LEVEL Low to high
TIME FRAME 2 hours to 2 days
SPECIAL TOOLS Metal detector, mallet, block plane
SEE PAGES 42–43

Knock down protruding nails. If boards are loose, secure them with screws (this usually cures a squeaking board). Repair any split boards and fill in large gaps with a piece of wood. Check for a pipe or electrical cable below the boards before inserting screws or nails through them.

REPLACING A DAMAGED FLOORBOARD

SKILL LEVEL Medium
TIME FRAME 2 hours to 1 day

SPECIAL TOOLS Bolster chisel, circular saw (or floorboard saw), jigsaw
SEE PAGES 44–45

Replace a damaged floorboard before laying down a new flooring material; the technique for removing the board will depend on whether it has square edges or is tongued and grooved. Fit a new floorboard of the same thickness.

LAYING A HARDBOARD OVERLAY

SKILL LEVEL Medium
TIME FRAME ½ day
SPECIAL TOOLS None
SEE PAGES 46–47

Hardboard is a suitable underlay for many types of flooring such as carpet and sheet vinyl. Condition the boards to the room's atmosphere, then start laying them in one corner of the room; stagger the boards to avoid joints aligning.

MINOR CONCRETE FLOOR DEFECTS

SKILL LEVEL Low to medium
TIME FRAME 2 hours to ½ day

SPECIAL TOOLS Bolster chisel, club hammer, trowel
SEE PAGES 48–49

Deep cracks should be inspected and repaired by a professional. Prime minor cracks with diluted PVA adhesive before filling with mortar. If a concrete floor is dusty, apply a coat of concrete floor sealer. Dampness can be cured in a modern house by brushing on a coat of waterproofing emulsion.

LEVELLING A CONCRETE FLOOR

SKILL LEVEL Medium
TIME FRAME ½ to 1 day
SPECIAL TOOLS Trowel, steel float
SEE PAGES 50–51

First clean the floor and fill any cracks with the compound. Level out hollows with a self-levelling screeding compound, which is spread out with a trowel – it should find its own level as it is left to dry. For a large area or a complete room, apply the self-levelling compound in small batches (it dries quickly). If you are not successful the first time, sprinkle water on the compound and try again.

RUBBER GLOVES

FLOAT

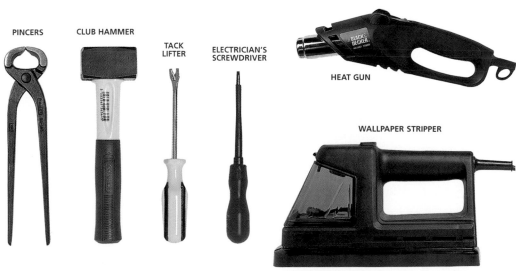
PINCERS
CLUB HAMMER
TACK LIFTER
ELECTRICIAN'S SCREWDRIVER
HEAT GUN
WALLPAPER STRIPPER

STRIPPING A ROOM

You should never be tempted to try decorating around items that are fitted to a wall or ceiling. These include shelves, light switches and light fixtures. The end result will be poor, the fitting may become smeared with paint and the whole process will take much longer than it would if the object were simply removed and replaced afterward. The exception is with some electrical fittings – sockets, switches and ceiling roses. With these, it is usually possible to pull forward the cover plate, decorate, then put the plate back.

When stripping a room, the best way to work is to go around the room and systematically remove anything that can interfere with the decoration. Keep each fitting and its screws in a separate polythene bag so they are easily found when the time comes to replace them. Always turn off the electricity to a fixture before working on it (see box, opposite page).

LIGHT FIXTURES

After turning off the power (see *Helpful hints)*, remove any wall light fixtures, standard ceiling light fixtures, spotlights or fluorescent striplights. You can usually release a fixture by unscrewing the body of the light and pulling it forward to expose the wiring. Disconnecting an electrical fitting is the simple part – the difficult part is replacing it afterward. Before releasing anything, label the wires and their terminals or make a sketch of the wires as a guide to replacing them. Or employ a qualified electrician to both remove and replace the fitting or to simply replace it after decorating.

Any bare wires from the ceiling or walls must be protected by covering them with insulating tape. You may have to restore power to the circuit while decorating takes place, or all the house lights on that circuit will be out of action. Arrange for additional lighting from lamps for the decoration.

PULLING OUT A SWITCH OR SOCKET

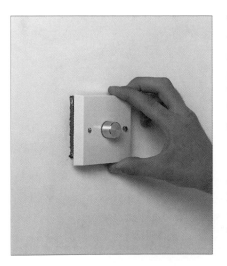

With the electricity turned off, release the mounting screws and pull the plate away from the wall. You can leave the switch or socket in this position until the decoration has been completed. As further protection, you should apply masking tape to the edges of the switch.

REMOVING A DOWNLIGHT

This light fixture simply drops down from its hole in the ceiling. If it isn't heavy and you're painting the ceiling, tape a polythene bag around the body. If you're covering the ceiling with lining paper or wallpaper, detach the body from the wires (see *Removing a standard ceiling light fixture).*

REMOVING A STANDARD CEILING LIGHT FIXTURE

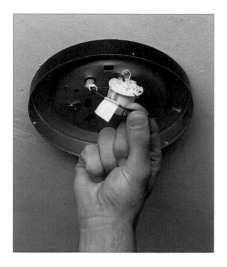

1 With the electricity for the fixture turned off, remove any shade or covering and any light bulbs. Mark corresponding wires and terminals with tape and label them. This simple wiring arrangement required only one wire to be marked – yours may require more.

2 Release each wire from its terminal by undoing the small grub screw. Remove the mounting screws to pull away the back plate and fixture. Cover the exposed portions of the wire with electrical tape.

STRIPPING OTHER WALL FIXTURES

1 You may have shelves, towel racks, mirrors, curtain rails and so on to remove. This will simply be a question of unscrewing their supports such as one or more brackets. You may want someone to help you handle large, cumbersome items such as curtain rails.

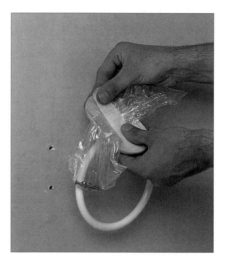

2 The best way to avoid losing the screws and other items that normally hold the fixtures in place is to seal them in a polythene bag, then tape the bag to the fixture.

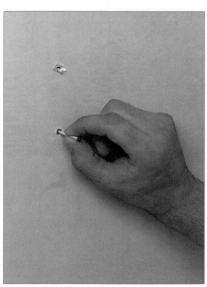

3 To avoid wiring and pipes buried in the walls (see pp.228–229), try using the original mounting holes to rehang the fixtures once you finish the decoration. Because wallpaper will cover the holes, insert into them toothpicks or matchsticks trimmed to protrude slightly from the wall – they will poke through the wallpaper.

Helpful hints

The most important rule when working with electricity in the home is safety. It might be tempting to think that you can wallpaper around a switch by simply pulling the cover plate forward because you're unlikely to touch any wiring – but you could touch an exposed wire, with disastrous consequences.

It takes just a few seconds to go to the consumer unit and isolate the switch, socket or light fixture by turning the power off at the fuse or circuit breaker for that circuit. Then use a circuit tester to check that the switch, socket or light is "dead". This ensures you have isolated the correct fuse.

DEALING WITH CRACKS, DENTS AND STAINS

Superficial cracks and small dents can be repaired quickly with a cellulose or acrylic filler. If there are a lot of fine hairline cracks, cover a plaster surface with lining paper.

Fillers come in powder form, which must be mixed with water, or in ready-to-use form in tubes and tubs. The powder type is more economical. Follow the instructions on the packet for mixing the filler and for how quickly it must be applied before it starts to become too hard to be usable. If you're inexperienced, it is best to mix up only small quantities at a time so none is wasted.

DIFFICULT CRACKS

Not all cracks should be filled with cellulose fillers. Normal seasonal movement of the house structure can cause cracks at joints. Filling them usually fails because the movement creates additional cracks. If they are where the walls meet the ceiling, the real answer is to hide them by fixing coving (see p.148). Cracks above a skirting board or around window and door frames need a different treatment. You can use a cellulose filler if you first squeeze strips of damp newspaper into the gap as a base, but the best solution is to use a mastic sealant. It remains flexible, so it keeps the gap closed despite any movement.

Minor damage in an ordinary plaster cornice or ceiling rose can be repaired. However, most ornate repairs are best left to the professional.

TREATING STAINS

Most stains are due to water damage (from dampness or a plumbing leak) or tobacco smoke. Stains seep through paint, but you can prime a water stain. For a room stained by tobacco smoke, try a strong sugar soap solution on painted surfaces. If it doesn't work, you'll have to remove the paint (see pp.28–29). Wallpaper must be stripped.

REPAIRING A CRACK

1 Using the edge of a pointed putty knife, "undercut" the crack – the idea is to widen the crack below the surface, forming an inverted V cavity, with the point of the V exposed to the surface. This will help the filler stay in place.

2 Remove any loose debris from the work area with an old paint brush. Using a square-edged flexible filler knife, firmly press the filler into the crack, forcing it into the cavity.

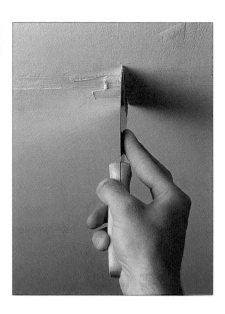

3 Hold the filler knife at an angle perpendicular to the work and scrape away the excess filler, but leave it slightly proud of the surface. The more experienced person can smooth the filler level to the surface. Leave the filler to dry.

4 A wood or cork sanding block will help you achieve a smooth finish. Wrap a piece of fine wet and dry abrasive paper around the sanding block and, holding it flat against the work, sand the filler until it is flush with the surface.

APPLYING A MASTIC SEALANT

For a crack above a skirting board or around a window or door, squeeze a bead of mastic sealant along it, making sure the sealant contacts both surfaces. A slow, continuous movement will avoid creating ripples in the bead; you can use a wet fingertip to smooth the sealant.

TREATING A WATER STAIN

You can apply a coat of aluminium primer sealer, available in large cans or small aerosols, over a water stain. However, first deal with the cause of the problem and allow the ceiling to dry before applying the sealer. The sealer will seal the surface and form a good base for the paint.

FILLING CHIPPED MOULDING

1 If the damage to a plaster moulding is small, you can make the repair yourself. Carefully remove any loose sections or debris with a small paint brush.

2 Fill in the damage with a cellulose filler, using a small artist's clay modelling tool or a similar device. Try to match the profile of the surrounding pattern.

PATCHING HOLES IN WALLS

YOU WILL NEED

Patching a plasterboard hole

Padsaw **or** plasterboard knife
Spirit level
Pencil
Hammer
Fine-tooth saw
Nail punch
Flexible filler knife
Sanding block
Fine abrasive paper

Filling a hole in plaster

Hawk
Trowel
Wood straightedge
Fine sandpaper

MATERIALS

Patching a plasterboard hole

50 mm x 25 mm (2 in x 1 in) wood batten
Oval nails
Galvanized plasterboard nails
Plasterboard

Filling a hole in plaster

One-coat plaster

SEE ALSO

Dealing with cracks, dents and stains pp.20–21
Repairing damage to a ceiling pp.24–25

Holes in plasterboard often occur as a result of physical damage or by the removal of a fixture. If the hole is more than 87 mm (3½ in) wide, it requires patching with plasterboard. Before making the repair, locate the vertical studs (wood battens) on either side of the damage. You can do this by either tapping the plasterboard until you hear a dull thud (instead of a hollow sound) or by using an electronic stud detector (see p.229).

DAMAGED PLASTER WALLS

Holes in plaster develop for the same reasons as for plasterboard, as well as because of dampness. In the latter case, deal with the dampness before making a repair. There are different types of plaster available, but the best one for the do-it-yourselfer is one-coat plaster.

A condition known as blown plaster occurs when the plaster loses contact with the bricks and bulges out. You should tap the bulge with a bolster chisel and club hammer to remove all loose plaster, working back to a sound edge around the damage. Brush away all dust, dampen the repair with clean water and fill the hole with plaster.

LATH-AND-PLASTER WALLS

Repair a hole in a lath-and-plaster wall in the same way as for plasterboard. If you cannot find plasterboard of the same thickness as the plaster, nail new, thicker laths to the studs so that a thin piece of plasterboard lies flush with the surface or just below it.

Helpful hints

Plaster walls are often damaged at external corners. Use a filler knife to fill and smooth the plaster on one wall, then on the flanking wall. After the plaster stiffens, run a wet fingertip down the corner to blunt the edge – a pointed edge is more susceptible to damage.

To patch a hole in plasterboard less than 87 mm (3½ in) wide, use a flexible filler knife to press in a one-coat plaster; once dried, sand it flush to the surface. Use cellulose filler in a small dent (see pp.20–21).

PATCHING A PLASTERBOARD HOLE

1 Using a padsaw or plasterboard knife, cut back the damaged area flush with the edge of the stud; then extend it a further 25 mm (1 in) to the centre of the stud – use a spirit level to draw a vertical guide line on the stud. Repeat the procedure on the other side of the damaged area.

2 The top and bottom edges of the repair also need to be cut to create a rectangular opening. Use the spirit level to draw horizontal guide lines, making sure you extend them beyond the damage.

3 To serve as fixing points for the top and bottom edges of the plasterboard, use oval nails to secure 50 mm x 25 mm (2 in x 1 in) wood battens between the studs. Position the nails at a 45° angle (this is called skew-nailing), driving them through the battens and into the studs.

4 Using a fine-tooth saw, cut a piece of plasterboard to an exact fit. With the grey side of the patch facing outward, secure it with galvanized plasterboard nails 12 mm (½ in) from the edge (so they will be fixed to the studs behind), at 150 mm (6 in) intervals. Use a nail punch to set the nail heads into the surface of the board.

5 Finally, sand the edges to make them neat before filling the joints with cellulose filler. Use the flexible filler knife to remove any excess filler, and once the filler dries, sand the repair for a smooth finish (see *Repairing a crack,* pp.20–21).

FILLING A HOLE IN PLASTER

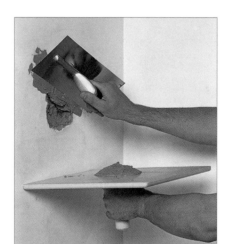

1 Hold a hawk loaded with plaster close to the wall at a 45° angle. Scoop up some of the plaster with a trowel and sweep it into the bottom of the repair area. Don't press the trowel flat against the wall or the plaster will fall away. Continue, working up the repair area, until it is filled.

2 To level the plaster with the wall, use a true piece of wood batten (one with planed straight edges) that is wider than the repair. Working from the bottom, rest the wood on the wall and zig-zag it from side to side as you move it up.

3 To create a fine surface for painting, leave the plaster to dry, then sand it smooth with fine abrasive paper wrapped around a wood batten.

REPAIRING DAMAGE TO A CEILING

YOU WILL NEED

Fixing a popped nail
Screwdriver
Nail punch
Hammer
Flexible filler knife

Patching plasterboard
Plasterboard knife
Drill plus a twist bit
String plus a galvanized nail
Flexible filler knife

Repairing lath and plaster
Safety goggles
Dust mask
Old paint brush
Tinsnips (if required)
Bloster chisel
Club hammer
Float

MATERIALS

Fixing a popped nail
Plasterboard screw
Cellulose filler

Patching plasterboard
Plasterboard
Cellulose filler

Repairing lath and plaster
Expanded metal mesh **or**
PVA adhesive
Plaster filler

SEE ALSO

Dealing with cracks, dents
and stains pp.20–21

A ceiling can suffer the same wear and tear as a wall, but it may also be damaged by a leak. Make sure you repair the cause of the leak and let the ceiling dry before making a repair to the ceiling.

PLASTERBOARD CEILINGS

A fairly common, minor defect in a plasterboard ceiling is a protruding nail head – this is often referred to as a "popped" nail. The boards are nailed to the ceiling joists above them, and sometimes a nail can work its way loose. It is easy to repair, and you can follow the same procedure if a nail has popped from a stud on a wall.

A small hole can be covered with plasterer's glass-fibre patching tape and covered with a cellulose filler, but a hole larger than 87 mm (3½ in) in diameter requires a backing piece to serve as a base for the filler. You'll need an offcut of plasterboard slightly longer and wider than the hole.

LATH-AND-PLASTER CEILINGS

Most older houses were constructed with lath-and-plaster ceilings. This type of ceiling was formed by nailing thin battens to the joists above and then adding horsehair plaster. This was forced through the small gaps between the laths so that, when set, the plaster was anchored in place.

How a hole is filled depends on its size and the condition of the laths. If the laths are not broken, coat them with diluted PVA adhesive (follow the manufacturer's instructions) to make them less absorbent before filling the repair. If the laths are broken and the hole is less than 75 mm (3 in) across, simply push scrunched up newspaper into it to serve as a backing before plastering the hole. Where a hole is more than 75 mm (3 in) across, you'll need to use fine expanded metal mesh as a backing piece for the plaster. Expanded metal mesh can be bought at a builder's merchant.

FIXING A POPPED NAIL

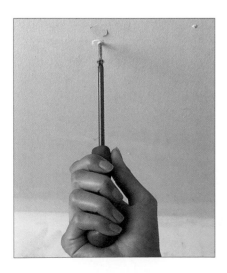

Insert a plasterboard screw 50 mm (2 in) away from the nail, ensuring that it goes into the joist above. Carefully remove any debris covering the protruding nail, then use a nail punch and hammer to knock it below the surface. Cover the hole with a cellulose filler (see pp.20–21).

PATCHING PLASTERBOARD

1 Cut a plasterboard patch 25 mm (1 in) larger than the damaged area, and drill a hole through the middle. Slip a length of string 150 mm (6 in) long through it, and tie a nail to the string on the ivory side of the board. The nail will prevent the string exiting the hole.

2 Apply plaster filler around the edges of the grey side of the plasterboard, then slip the piece through the hole – the grey side of the board should face outward. Use the string to pull the plasterboard against the hole, then pull the string taut and allow the filler to set.

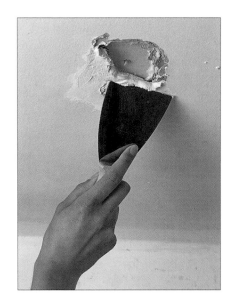

3 Apply plaster filler to bring the patch almost flush with the surface. Allow the filler to almost set before cutting off the string and adding a final layer of filler flush with the surface. If you don't succeed in getting a flush finish, allow the filler to dry and sand it smooth later (see pp.20–21).

REPAIRING LATH AND PLASTER

1 Use an old paint brush to remove any dust and debris from the areas to be repaired, wearing safety goggles and a dust mask.

2 If the laths are damaged, use tinsnips (a metal-cutting tool) to trim the expanded mesh to size. Then fit it in place by curling its edges around the back of the laths. The mesh is flexible, so this should be easy to do.

3 Use a bolster chisel and club hammer to undercut the edges of the hole so that the plaster will have a better grip (see pp.20–21). Make sure you do this gently to avoid creating any further damage. Once again, use the old paint brush to remove any debris.

4 Place an excess of plaster filler onto a float and push it up into the repair until it is flat against the ceiling, forcing the filler through the holes in the mesh; slide the float over the repair. Scrape off as much excess filler as you can and, if necessary, sand smooth when the filler is dry (see pp.20–21).

STRIPPING OLD WALLPAPER

YOU WILL NEED

Using water to strip
Stiff wire brush **or** serrated scraper
Bucket
Water
Wallcovering adhesive
Sponge
Wallcovering scraper
Detergent

Using a steam stripper
Steam stripper
Water
Wallcovering scraper
Detergent

Peeling away vinyls
Utility knife (if required)
see *Using water to strip* above

SEE ALSO

Dealing with cracks, dents and stains pp.20–21

There are various forms of wallpaper or, more correctly, wallcoverings. Apart from straight-forward paper, there are washables, vinyls and woodchips, among others. One thing they all have in common is that they must be stripped off before hanging a new wallcovering. Hanging new wallcovering on top of an old one can cause both coverings to bubble.

STRIPPING THE WALL

How difficult it is to strip a wall depends on the wallcovering material and on the paste used – an over-diluted paste may hold a wallcovering in place but is not strong enough to withstand a soaking with water. The wall may be damp, which is fine for helping you get the wallcovering off; however, it is not a surface on which you should hang a wallcovering.

Water is an essential ingredient in stripping wallcoverings. Vinyls and washable wallcoverings are designed to withstand water, so they must be scored before they are soaked (unless you have a peelable vinyl). The same applies to a painted wallcovering.

If the covering isn't loose after a first soaking, try a second soaking. Or add a liquid detergent to the water to act as a wetting agent, plus some cellulose paste to hold the water in place.

Another choice is to use an electric steam stripper, which can be bought or hired locally. It has a tank to hold water, which takes from 30 seconds to 10 minutes to heat up before running for a couple of hours, depending on the model used. Never leave it sitting on an unprotected floor.

Helpful hints

Avoid soaking wallcovering around switches and sockets. If you can't remove the covering by peeling it away while dry, turn off the electrical power at the consumer unit, unscrew the face plate and ease it away from the wall. Use as little water as possible.

USING WATER TO STRIP

1 Use a wire brush or serrated scraper to scratch the surface of non-peelable vinyls and other washable coverings. This allows the water to penetrate through the covering to reach the adhesive. Do not allow the wire bristles to reach the plaster. Tiny pieces of metal from the brush can cause rust spots.

2 To hold the water to the wall, add some wallcovering adhesive to a bucket of warm water. Start in one corner of the room and work your way around it, soaking the walls with a sponge. By the time you get back to the starting point, the water should have done its job.

3 Using a scraper, carefully work the wallcovering loose – it should bunch up and come away easily. If it doesn't, soak it with more water. Don't scrape too hard; this can gouge the wall. Leave small pieces for later. If you're stripping from plaster-board, bear in mind that this has a paper face that you don't want to strip off.

4 After removing most of the wallcovering, go around the room to soak and remove any small pieces or stubborn sections left behind. Once all the wallcovering has been removed, wash down the walls with a little detergent in a bucket of warm water.

USING A STEAM STRIPPER

1 Score washable coverings (see step 1, opposite page). Place the plate of the stripper (it has perforations through which the steam passes) against the wall; hold it in place from a few seconds to a minute, depending on the model and the thickness of the wallcovering.

2 Reposition the steam stripper onto the next section of wallcovering. At the same time, scrape away the loosened covering with the scraper as in step 3 above. Continue until all the paper is removed, and wash down the walls as in step 4 above.

PEELING AWAY VINYLS

1 Some modern vinyls have been designed to simply peel off the wall. Try using your fingernail or the blade of a utility knife to lift a corner. If it comes up, simply pull the covering upward. If you're unlucky, you'll have a problem paper that requires scoring before you can strip it.

2 When you pull up a peelable vinyl, you'll discover a thin paper backing left behind. Simply soak and scrape it as for other wallcoverings – it will easily come off. If well stuck, it can be left in place and used as a lining paper.

REMOVING OTHER WALL DECORATIONS

There are materials other than wallpaper (see pp.26–27) attached to walls as decoration. Whatever the type of decoration, it can be removed, but some may be difficult and the walls may need repairing afterward.

TEXTURED PAINTS

There are two types of textured paints: textured emulsion paint and the Artex group. Emulsion types need a brush-on textured paint remover (normal emulsion paints are also removed with a paint remover). For the Artex group, use a steam stripper (see pp.26–27) to soften the paint and scrape it off. Never sand off a finish; older paints contain asbestos, which must not be inhaled.

WALL TILES

Removing ceramic tiles is laborious and will create a lot of work, perhaps for a professional, to provide the flat surface required for tiling or other decoration. Provided that they are flat and well fixed, you can leave ceramic tiles on the walls and tile on top of them. Test for flatness by holding a long straightedge such as a spirit level across them vertically, horizontally and diagonally. The odd loose tile can be refixed with tile adhesive. Old ones fixed with cement mortar will be more difficult to remove. Because fragments will be flying everywhere, you must wear a dust mask and safety goggles.

It may be easy to lever off cork and expanded polystyrene tiles, depending on how the adhesive was applied: in a few blobs on older tiles or spread all over, which is common on newer tiles.

CLADDING

Individual planks are fixed to battens by pinning, screwing or with clips. Wallboards fixed to wall battens are removed in the same way as planks. If they sound solid when tapped, they were stuck to the wall with adhesive and will require being levered off.

TEXTURED PAINT

1 When using a chemical stripper to remove textured (or normal) emulsion paint, protect the floor, and wear gloves, overalls and goggles. Starting at the top of the wall, apply a thick, even coat, dabbing it well into the surface. Leave it for 3–8 hours, depending on the thickness of the finish.

2 When the textured (or normal) emulsion paint is soft, use a scraper to remove it, starting from the bottom of the wall. After you strip the wall, go over it with a stiff brush to remove any residue. Wash the wall down with sugar soap or detergent in warm water, then only water.

WALL TILES

1 Whether you want to remove only one damaged tile or a whole field of tiles, position a bolster chisel in the centre of the tile and hit it hard with a club hammer, which will shatter the tile. Insert the chisel into one of the cracks, gently tap it in further, then use it to lever off the pieces of the tile.

2 To remove additional tiles, insert the bolster chisel under one edge of an adjacent tile and gently hammer it in before levering off the tile. Some will come away whole, others in pieces. Continue to lever off the remaining tiles in the same way.

3 To remove the tile adhesive still on the wall, hold a heat gun 50 mm (2 in) from the surface. As the heat gun softens the adhesive, follow behind with a scraper to remove it.

SHEET CLADDING

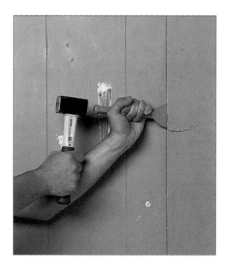

To remove sheets of cladding that were glued to the wall, insert a bolster chisel into a vertical joint, hammer the chisel in, then lever off the board. The sheets will split and come off the wall in pieces. You may have to sand off the adhesive, but first try a heat gun (see far left).

TONGUE-AND-GROOVE CLADDING

1 Start by removing the dado rail, as well as any edge trim. Position the bolster chisel behind the dado rail and tap down with a club hammer. Once it is wedged behind the rail, use the bolster chisel to lever it off the cladding.

2 Use the hook end of a crowbar to remove each length of board. Bang it between the board and batten, avoiding damaging the wall, then lever the board away from the batten. Unscrew the battens, or prise them off with the crowbar, using an offcut of wood to protect the wall.

WASHING DOWN AND PREPARING SURFACES

YOU WILL NEED

Sanding block
Wet and dry abrasive paper
Coarse-, medium- and fine-grade abrasive paper (if required)
Sugar soap **or** detergent and warm water
Bucket
Sponge
Lint-free cloth
Pointed stick
Methylated spirit **or** white spirit
Scraper (if required)
Putty knife (if required)
Tacky rag (if required)

MATERIALS

Cellulose, acrylic **or** wood filler (if required)

SEE ALSO

Dealing with cracks, dents and stains (pp.20–21)

Whether a wall, door or wood trim has been stripped or is to be repainted, it must be washed down to ensure that all dirt, grease or remnants of old wallpaper adhesive is removed. A dirty surface can lead to wallpaper lifting or paint flaking.

Use plenty of newspaper on top of the dust sheets near the skirting boards to soak up the water running down the walls. If you intend to repaint over old paint, wash walls from the bottom up so that dirty water will run down the wet wall and not leave dried streak marks. These can show through a new coat of emulsion paint. Stains will also show through and require treatment (see pp.20–21). Always let a wall dry before redecorating.

Distemper, an old-fashioned casein-based paint, can be found in older homes; use a coarse cloth and water to rub it off, then follow with a coat of stabilizing fluid to bond any remaining distemper to the surface.

SANDING AND FILLING

Gloss paint, which is normally used on woodwork but sometimes on walls, has a sheen that prevents new paint from adhering to it. Sanding it down will remove the sheen and leave the surface with a "key" so that the new paint will stick to it properly. Sanding can be done by hand, but you may prefer a power sander for a large surface. Whether you are sanding by hand or machine, always wear a dust mask and safety goggles. After you sand, clean all the surfaces thoroughly: any dust will be picked up in the brush or roller and leave a pimpled surface when the new paint has dried.

The final job is to remove flaking paint and fill any minor blemishes. Use a cellulose or acrylic filler, which comes in a tube or tub ready for use or, if the surface is to be painted, as a powder to be mixed with water. Where wood will show, use a wood filler in the same way as a cellulose filler.

1 To take the sheen off gloss paint, wrap abrasive paper around a sanding block and use a circular motion to roughen the surface. Work methodically, starting at the top and working down, to ensure the whole surface is sanded. If the surface is pitted, start with a coarse paper and finish with a fine-grade paper.

2 Whether or not you have sanded, wash the surface with sugar soap or detergent and warm water. If you plan to repaint the surface, work your way from the bottom to the top; otherwise, you can start from the top if you wish, as long as the surface isn't too dirty.

3 To clean the nooks and crannies of intricate mouldings, wrap a piece of lint-free cloth around a pointed stick, dip it in methylated spirit or white spirit and clean the debris from these places. Don't forget to clean the top edge of doors and windows, as well as the exterior edges so that dirt is not picked up on the brush.

4 If old paintwork has bubbled or is flaking off, push the scraper under the loose paint and lift it off, and scrape away any surrounding areas of loose and flaking paint.

5 Only mix up enough filler for the job in hand. Load up the putty knife with the filler and push it down into the damaged area. Press down and draw the knife across the repair before lifting it off.

6 Allow the filler to dry, then sand the filled area level with the surrounding paintwork, using fine abrasive paper wrapped around a wood or cork sanding block.

7 Finally, use a lint-free cloth (cheese cloth is ideal) soaked in white spirit or methylated spirit to clean off the dust from the filled area. Or use a tacky rag – a resin-coated duster designed to collect fine dust.

Helpful hints

Mould, recognizable as a covering of dark specks, can develop on a damp surface. Treat the cause of the dampness (see pp.12–13) before treating the mould. To eradicate mould, sterilize the surface with a fungicide bought from a builder's merchant. Allow six hours for the sterilizer to do its work before rubbing off the mould. Treat the area again and leave it for a few days. Before redecorating, coat the wall with a stabilizing primer. If wallpapering, use an adhesive that contains a fungicide.

STRIPPING PAINT FROM WOOD TRIM

YOU WILL NEED

Using a chemical stripper
Overalls with long sleeves
Heavy-duty rubber gloves
Safety goggles
Dust mask
Plywood, hardboard or
newspapers
Chemical stripper
Old paint brush
Glass jar
Wide scraper
Shavehook
Polythene sheet
Sponge
Bucket and water **or** white
spirit
Wire wool
Medium wet and dry
abrasive paper

Using a heat gun
Overalls with long sleeves
Plywood or hardboard
Bucket filled with water
Heat gun
Shavehook
Medium wet and dry
abrasive paper

SEE ALSO

Removing other wall
decorations pp.28–29
Washing down and
preparing surfaces pp.30–31

When paint or varnish on wood trim is in poor condition – flaking, badly chipped or cracked, or so thick that a door or window won't close easily – then strip it to the bare wood before washing down and redecorating. You can sand small areas, but the more practical ways to strip paint are to use chemicals or heat. Always wear protective clothing: gloves, long sleeves, safety goggles and a dust mask, and open windows or use fans to ventilate the room.

CHEMICAL STRIPPERS

Although powerful, chemical strippers are not economical for large areas, so they are best used for intricate work such as mouldings and cornices. These strippers are also used around glass because of the risk of heat cracking it.

The chemicals come either as a gel, paste or liquid, and most strip both paint and varnish. How many coats of paint or varnish will be removed in one go depends on the product; some require several applications. Always read the instructions carefully before using a chemical stripper.

USING HEAT

By far the easiest and most economical way to strip paint or varnish is by using an electrically powered heat gun. It may look like a hair dryer, but a heat gun gets very hot and must never be used for anything other than its intended applications. When using a heat gun, never put your hand into the air stream, and switch off the gun when it is not being used.

Helpful hints

Avoid using a heat gun around an open window on a blustery day – the wind may dissipate the heat before it softens the paint. Remove curtains to keep them out of the way.

Using a heat gun on paint can cause the paint to burn, so keep a bucket filled with water below the work area and drop the paint peelings into it (never use newspapers).

USING A CHEMICAL STRIPPER

1 The stripper can damage the floor, so make sure it is well protected: you can use a sheet of plywood or hardboard, or several layers of newspaper. Decant the paint stripper into a glass jar. Use an old brush to lay on a thick coat of stripper, starting from the top and moving down.

2 Follow the instructions from the manufacturer for how long to leave the stripper in place, which can be a few minutes to hours. When the paint has softened, use a wide scraper on the flat areas of the work to remove the paint, taking care not to dig into the wood.

3 To scrape the paint from mouldings, corners and other intricate areas, use the most suitable part of the shavehook, pulling it along the work to remove the paint.

4 Protect the floor with a polythene sheet. Wipe off the excess stripper with a sponge and water or white spirit. Use wire wool to get into the crevices of the mouldings. If some paint still remains in a crevice, you can use a folded edge of medium wet and dry abrasive paper.

USING A HEAT GUN

1 Always protect the floor, using a sheet of plywood or hardboard. When switched on, the heat gun quickly produces a constant flow of hot air, so handle it with extreme care. To remove the paint, hold the gun 50 mm (2 in) from the surface of the work until the paint starts to bubble.

2 Before the paint congeals, use a shavehook to scrape off the softened paint. Continue to hold the heat gun over the work, but don't concentrate the heat on one spot as this can scorch it; instead, keep playing it across the surface.

3 Some types of heat gun have an integral scraper attachment, allowing you to heat and scrape off the paint in one movement. Some heat guns are equipped with metal deflectors to keep heat off sensitive surfaces such as glass panes in windows.

4 Whatever method used to remove the paint, there will always be traces remaining. Remove them with medium wet and dry abrasive paper: fold the paper, insert an edge into the crevice, then sand back and forth.

STRIPPING AND PREPARING METAL

YOU WILL NEED

Safety goggles
Dust mask
Emery paper
Wire brush
Power drill plus wire brush attachment
Cork **or** wood sanding block
Putty knife
Abrasive paper (if required)
Old, small paint brush
Small brush
Heavy-duty rubber gloves
Bucket and water
Soapy detergent (if required)
White spirit **or** water
Steel wool

MATERIALS

Expoxy-based filler
Gel-type paint stripper
Rust-inhibiting primer

SEE ALSO

Painting windows
pp.66–67

Paintwork on metal that is in good condition – whether a cast iron fireplace surround, steel window frame or a radiator – may need only a wash with sugar soap or detergent to clean off grime and a sanding to provide a key for the new paint. Additional preparation for a few paint drips is only a matter of sanding down the drips flush with the surrounding area. However, a build-up of paint that obscures any details requires stripping.

TREATING RUST

Sadly, cast iron fireplace surrounds and steel-framed windows are often neglected. Rust can form in iron and steel where paint is chipped away and, if left alone, the rust can eventually eat away at the metal, causing it to become pitted.

The metal doesn't have to gleam, just be free of rust with no loose material remaining. A small area of rust can be removed with emery paper, but larger areas may demand using a power drill with a wire brush attachment. Always wear safety goggles and a dust mask as protection against flying particles.

To remove old paint and rust in detailed areas, use a gel-type chemical stripper (a heat gun doesn't work well on metal); it is peeled off after a few hours, bringing all the paint with it.

If the rust has caused pitting in the surface, then fill this with an epoxy-based filler. After you remove the rust, apply a coat of a rust-inhibiting primer to the patches straight away – rust can return in less than a day.

Helpful hints

Aluminium used in window and door frames is not affected by rust, but a dull grey coat and white crystals can form on the surface. To restore it to a bright metal finish, use a fine wet and dry abrasive paper lubricated with white spirit; then wipe the metal with a cloth and white spirit to remove any debris such as metal particles. After the metal dries, apply a coat of a zinc-phosphate primer.

1 To remove a small patch of surface rust, or rust near a moulded area, fold a piece of emery paper and rub the rust away.

2 Where there is a large patch of chipped paint or rust, a hand-held wire brush is a more efficient tool to use.

3 For large areas of loose, flaking paint and rust, you can use a power drill fitted with a wire brush attachment. A cup-shaped brush is best for detailed moulded areas; a wheel-shaped one allows you to hold the drill at an angle. Remember to wear safety goggles and a dust mask.

4 To sand down paint drips, use emery paper wrapped around a wood or cork sanding block until the paint surface is flush with the surrounding area.

5 Fill in any pitted areas with an epoxy-based filler. (Removing old paint and rust will expose these.) Simply apply it with a putty knife; then use the blade of the knife to scrape off any excess until it is smooth with the surface, or leave it slightly proud of the surface and rub it down with abrasive paper once it is dry.

6 To remove paint in detailed areas, use an old paint brush to apply a thick layer of chemical stripper, and leave it in place the amount of time recommended by the manufacturer.

7 Once the paint has softened, it is ready to be removed. Use a small brush – an old toothbrush is ideal – to scrub away the paint from nooks and crannies. Some manufacturers suggest using soapy water.

8 Finish the work by cleaning the metal with water or white spirit (depending on the brand of stripper used) to neutralize any remaining traces of the chemical. Use steel wool in intricate areas.

REMOVING SKIRTING BOARDS AND MOULDINGS

In older houses, skirting boards can be elaborate and up to 300 mm (12 in) high, but a plain 100-mm-(4-in-) tall moulding is more likely to be used in newer homes. Skirtings are either nailed to wood blocks set into the brickwork behind them or into the studs behind a plasterboard wall. New ones may be fixed with panel adhesive.

One option when putting down a new flooring, such as laminated floorboards, is to remove the skirting boards, install the flooring, then replace the boards. Especially with old boards, avoid this if you can because you can damage them. However, if you do remove the boards with the intention of refitting them, make sure you number them so that you can put them back in their original position. If the boards are already damaged, it is worthwhile trying to do repairs or even removing a damaged section to see if you can find a match at a local architectural salvage yard.

OTHER MOULDINGS

Coving is used to cover a crack at the joint between the ceiling and walls. Because this is the only way to hide the crack, think carefully before you remove it. The method will depend on the way is was fixed to the walls. Hack off plaster coving with a bolster chisel and club hammer, or lift off polystyrene coving with a flexible scraper, then use a heat gun to soften and scrape away the old adhesive.

Picture and chair rail mouldings were fixed to the wall with cut nails in older houses. Use a claw hammer against scrap wood (to protect the wall) to prise off the moulding. Pull out cut nails that remain in the wall with pincers – if you leave them, rust will stain the wall. Newer types of mouldings are installed with screws – dig out the filler hiding the screw heads to remove the screws – or with a clip system in which mouldings slip onto clips fixed to the walls.

REMOVING A SKIRTING BOARD

1 Run a utility knife along the joint of the wall and skirting board to break a seam with wall paint or the wallpaper. Starting at an external corner or door, place a bolster chisel behind the board and hit it with a club hammer. Wedge a piece of wood into the gap and remove the chisel.

2 Insert a crowbar into the gap, with a piece of scrap wood behind it to protect the wall. Gently pull the crowbar back; as the board comes away, move the crowbar and wood along about 1 m (3 ft) and repeat the process. Keep moving along until the board comes off the wall.

3 If the skirting board is proving difficult to loosen, hammer in a wedge of wood, then use the hook end of the crowbar to lever the board away from the wall.

4 To remove a piece of board with an internal scribed corner, prise it away from the wall with a bolster chisel and hammer and insert a wedge into the gap. Rest the crowbar on a piece of wood and bang it in under the skirting board, then press down on the crowbar to lift up the skirting board away from the corner.

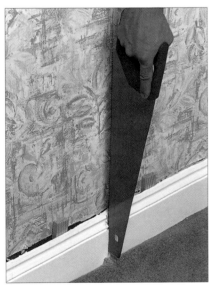

5 For a long board with ends covered at internal corners, use the bolster chisel and hammer to open a gap between the wall and board; place a wedge at each side of the chisel. Use a panel saw to cut through the board at a 45° angle, drawing the saw upward. If you're not used to handling a saw, use a tenon saw with fine teeth.

6 If you plan to refit a skirting board, always remove the nails by pulling them through from the back to avoid damaging the front of the board. Clamp the skirting board onto a work surface. Grip the nail with pincers and firmly pull the nail down toward the board to lever it out.

FILLING A DENT OR HOLE

To fill in a dent or hole in a skirting board, mix up a small amount of acrylic filler, load up the filler knife and push it into the damaged area. Press on it, pulling the knife toward you and away from the skirting board. After the filler dries, sand it level with the board.

REPLACING A DAMAGED SECTION

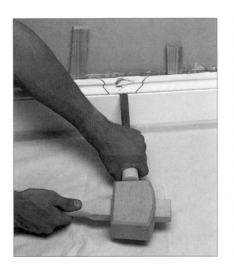

With the skirting board prised away from the wall (see step 5 above), make two diagonal cuts on either side of the damaged area with a tenon saw. Using a chisel and mallet, cut out the damaged piece. Glue a piece of wood into the area, then use a plane and chisel to shape it.

REPLACING A DAMAGED FLOORBOARD

YOU WILL NEED

Bolster chisel
Hammer
Crowbar
Circular saw, floorboard saw
or padsaw
Power drill plus twist bit
(if required)
Jigsaw **or** padsaw
Screwdriver
Block plane **or**
woodworking chisel
Nail punch (if required)
Flexible filler knife

MATERIALS

Floorboard
50 mm (2 in) floorboard
nails **or** No. 6 screws
Acrylic filler **or** wood filler

SEE ALSO

Making minor repairs to a
wood floor pp.42–43

There are two types of floorboard: square edged and tongued and grooved. A square-edged board, as the name implies, has square edges, which simply butt up against the adjoining boards. A tongue-and-groove board has a tongue on one edge and a groove on the other; the tongue of one board slides into the groove of its neighbour.

Before removing a floorboard, you'll have to know what type of board it is because the procedures to remove them are different. If you don't know, slide a knife down between the long edges of two boards. If the knife goes straight down, they have square edges; the knife will be stopped by the tongue of a tongue-and-groove board.

The ends of the board are nailed or screwed down to the joists below, as well as at intermediary stages to joists between the ends. A square-edged board can be prised up. However, tongue-and-groove floorboards present a problem; the tongue of the first

board will have to be cut off before the board can be prised up. Afterward, the other boards will lift up easily. If the board is screwed down, first remove the screws.

Nails in floorboards are likely to be rusty. To avoid the risk of someone treading on a nail, remove the nails from the damaged board immediately and dispose of them safely. Unless the board is replaced right away, cover any gap with hardboard to prevent someone putting their foot into it.

A NEW BOARD

If you can't buy boards of the correct thickness, get thinner ones and fix plywood packing pieces to each joist with panel pins. You can use either nails or screws to fix the board, but screws are preferred where boards may have to be taken up in future to gain access to pipes or wiring and in upstairs rooms where hammering may cause damage to the ceiling below.

1 To prise up a square-edged board, insert a bolster chisel near one end of the board – if necessary, carefully force the chisel in with a hammer. Lever up the board until the nails are released. Repeat on the other side of the board. Slip a crowbar under the board, then move to the next section and repeat the procedure.

2 Once you have lifted enough nails to get good leverage, with the crowbar under the board, step down on the free end of the board to release the next few rows of nails still secured to the joists. Move the crowbar along and repeat the process until the board is free.

3 To remove a tongue-and-groove board, set a circular saw to cut 12 mm (½ in) deep. After checking for cables and pipes (see step 1, p.42), saw alongside the board to cut the tongue. You can now lever up the board in the same way as a square-edged board, as well as any successive boards.

4 Alternatively, you can cut through the tongue using a special hand-held floorboard saw, which has an adapted nose with teeth to allow you to start the cut from above. You can also use a padsaw, but you will have to first make a start hole with a suitably sized drill bit.

5 To replace a short section of board, cut across it before you lever it up. Find the first joist beyond the damage (look for a line of screws or nails); drill a 10-mm-(³⁄₈-in-) diameter hole close to it. Insert a jigsaw or padsaw into the hole; cut across the board. Repeat at the other end at the first joist after the damaged area.

6 Because the damaged board has to be sawn off flush with the joist, you'll have to create a fixing point for the new board. Cut a piece of 38 mm (1½ in) wood batten just wider than the board, and fix it with screws to the side of the joist. Make sure that the top of the batten is flush with the top of the joist.

7 While a square-edged board will slot neatly into the opening, a tongue-and-groove board won't. The simple solution is to use a block plane or chisel to remove the tongue.

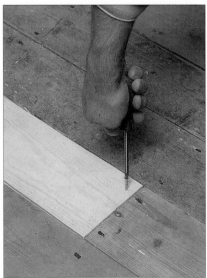

8 Position the board with its ends resting on the joists. Fix the board along the end joists and at any intermediary ones (look for lines of nails across neighbouring boards), using 50 mm (2 in) floorboard nails or No. 6 screws. Drive nail heads below the surface with a nail punch or countersink screw heads.

LAYING A HARDBOARD OVERLAY

YOU WILL NEED

Bucket
Brush
Hammer
Wood block
Utility knife
Straightedge
Profile gauge **or** compasses
(if required)
Pencil
Tenon saw **or** jigsaw
(if required)

MATERIALS

Water
Hardboard
Annular ringed nails,
hardboard pins **or** staples

With the exception of ceramic and quarry floor tiles, which require a thick plywood underlay, the wearing power and appearance of any floor covering will be improved by first laying hardboard. It can provide a level surface where floorboards curl up at the ends, and it is useful for creating a smooth surface over slightly damaged floorboards that may have gaps between them. Hardboard is inexpensive and easy to lay.

Standard hardboard is 3 mm (⅛ in) thick and is ideal for most rooms. Use oil-tempered boards on ground floors because they won't be affected by any damp below. If a floor is more uneven than usual, use sheets that are 6 mm (¼ in) thick. Hardboard sheets can be 2440 mm × 1220 mm (8 ft × 4 ft) or 1220 mm × 610 mm (4 ft × 2 ft).

If the hardboard is not oil-tempered, it must be conditioned to the room's moisture content before being laid, otherwise it can buckle later on. To form a perfect surface for the floor covering, make sure the boards are butted up snugly before you secure them. The boards are usually laid rough side up to provide a gripping surface for the adhesives used to lay the finished floor. To avoid a narrow strip at the edge of the room, lay out a dry run of the boards along two adjacent walls of the room and adjust the starting point of the first board.

You can fix the boards using 19 mm (¾ in) annular ringed nails, hardboard pins or staples, or you can use panel adhesive. Avoid longer nails, which can pierce any plumbing or cable under the floorboards.

Helpful hints

To ensure that a sheet of hardboard is in perfectly flat contact with the floorboards below it, kneel on the board before inserting the fixings. You should start the fixings at the centre of one edge of the board and work your way out to the ends and to the opposite side of the board in a pyramid fashion.

1 To condition the boards, simply brush water onto the rough side of each one. Use about 1 litre (1¾ pt) of water for each 1220 mm sq (4 ft sq) of board.

2 Stack the boards rough side to rough side in the room in which they are to be used. Make sure that they are lying flat and leave them for 48 hours.

3 Secure the first board in a corner, using fixings 100 mm (4 in) apart along the edges of the board and 150 mm (6 in) apart in rows across the board. Butt the second sheet against the first one and fix it in place. Continue fixing the boards until you reach the last full one in the row – do not secure it until the end one is trimmed.

4 To fit an end board, first use a wood block to scribe a line (see pp.200–201) along the end that will fit against the wall if the wall if uneven; trim it with a knife and straightedge (see step 8). Position the board, then place the neighbouring one on top of it to act as a guide. Score along the bottom board with a utility knife.

5 Depending on the thickness of the hardboard, make several scores along the original one. Stand on one half of the board and briskly raise the other half to snap the board along the score line. Secure the the previous board in place with the fixings, then the end one.

6 Continue to secure the following rows of boards, but stagger them in brickwork fashion to avoid joints aligning with each other. One method (which also reduces wastage) is to use the second part of a trimmed board from a previous row to start the following one.

7 If you have to make a notch to fit around a pipe, simply use a utility knife to make a series of scores. For a larger obstacle, such as a basin pedestal, make a paper template to transfer the shape to the hardboard (see pp.200-201). Then use the utility knife to make a series of scores.

8 At a doorway, roughly trim the board to the shape of the architrave. You can use a profile gauge (see p.195) or compasses to transfer the shape to the board. To cut out the shape, use a utility knife to make a series of scores along a metal straightedge. An easier way to cut hardboard is to use a tenon saw or jigsaw.

MINOR CONCRETE FLOOR DEFECTS

YOU WILL NEED

Filling in a minor crack
Brush and dustpan
Work gloves
Safety goggles
Club hammer
Cold chisel
Small paint brush
Bucket
Trowel
Wood batten (if required)

Sealing in dust
Paint roller and thick-pile
sleeve

Treating dampness
Bucket
Large disposable paint brush

MATERIALS

Filling in a minor crack
PVA adhesive
Cement and sand **or**
dry-mixed mortar

Sealing in dust
Concrete floor sealer

Treating dampness
Waterproofing emulsion

SEE ALSO

The big issues pp.12–13
Levelling a concrete floor
pp.50–51

Cracks in a solid floor are usually superficial, affecting only the thin screed covering the concrete slab. However, if you find a deep crack or a long crack runs across the room, call in a professional for advice.

If you have sand and cement left over from a previous job that is in good condition – not hard or lumpy – you can use it to make a mortar mix. Sand and cement are not available in small quantities. If you don't have a supply on hand, then buy a bag of dry-mixed mortar, which simply requires mixing with water.

A DUSTY SURFACE

Sometimes a concrete floor will continually give off dust no matter how often it is swept. The problem is often caused by the screeding layer of the floor being mixed with too much water, leaving it weak. The dust must be sealed in or any adhesive used to lay a floor covering will not adhere.

DAMPNESS

A wet patch on a concrete floor may be attributed to condensation or to dampness rising from the ground below. The two conditions are treated differently. To test for and cure condensation, see pages 12–13.

If rising damp is the enemy and the house is old, then it is likely to have a brick-on-earth construction. Here the only answer for a builder is to dig it up and construct a solid concrete floor containing a damp-proof membrane (dpm). The membrane – either heavy-duty polythene sheeting or a bitumen emulsion – is laid between the concrete slab and the top screed covering. The membrane will be linked to the damp-proof course in the walls to form an effective barrier against rising damp.

If there is rising damp in a modern house, the dpm was breached in some way – usually because a tear in it was not noticed when it was laid. Treat the floor with a damp-resisting liquid.

FILLING IN A MINOR CRACK

1 To inspect the damage, first sweep away any dirt and debris with a brush. To ensure a good repair, also brush away any new debris created by following step 2.

2 Wearing work gloves and safety goggles, use a club hammer and cold chisel to "undercut" (open up) the crack by forming an inverted V-shape – with the point of the V at the top surface of the crack. This provides a better gripping surface for the mortar.

3 Prime the crack with a coat of PVA adhesive. Follow the manufacturer's instructions for diluting the adhesive and use an old paint brush to apply it. The adhesive will also help the mortar to grip the surfaces of the crack.

4 Use a trowel to mix one part of cement with three parts of sand mixed with diluted PVA adhesive (again, follow the manufacturer's instructions). The mix should be buttery, not weak – it is better to err on the dry side rather than having a runny mixture.

5 Using the trowel, press the mortar into the crack. Level it off with the surface of the floor, using the edge of the trowel. Skim off any excess before it dries. Leave the mortar to dry overnight, then brush away any loose dust.

6 To fill a wide crack, instead of using the trowel to level the repair as in step 5, use a wood batten – move it from side to side as you pull it toward you.

SEALING IN DUST

To bind the dust layer and seal it in, simply roll or brush diluted PVA adhesive or a proprietary concrete floor sealer from a builder's merchant over the floor. Follow the manufacturer's recommendations for the drying time necessary before laying a floor covering.

TREATING DAMPNESS

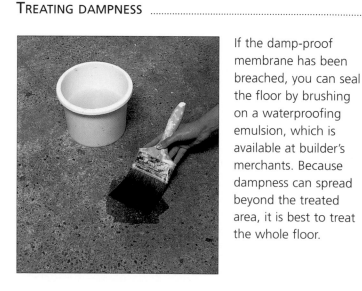

If the damp-proof membrane has been breached, you can seal the floor by brushing on a waterproofing emulsion, which is available at builder's merchants. Because dampness can spread beyond the treated area, it is best to treat the whole floor.

LEVELLING A CONCRETE FLOOR

YOU WILL NEED

Paint brush
Bucket
Roller with extension handle
Trowel (if required)
Steel float
Watering can (if required)
Hammer (if required)

MATERIALS

Water
Sugar soap
Self-levelling screeding
compound
Threshold strip (if required)
Nails (if required)

SEE ALSO

Minor concrete floor defects
pp.48–49

A slab of concrete forms the bulk of a concrete floor. When it is covered with a layer of a sufficiently strong mixture of a cement mortar screed, it should remain flat. Hollows in a concrete floor are usually caused by an excessively weak layer of screed. Sometimes there is a disparity in the floor, with some areas flat while others are hollow. This can occur because the screed has to be mixed in batches; as the work proceeds, too much water may be used in some of the batches, which weakens the mixture. The hollows can be as much as 12 mm (½ in) deep at the centre.

SCREEDING

The best material for levelling the floor is a self-levelling screeding compound. Because it is easy to mix and apply, it's suitable for anyone to use. The term "self-levelling" is exact. The compound is spread over the floor and levels itself after some assistance with a trowel – all float marks will disappear as the compound dries.

Although minor holes, cracks and ridges in the screed can be attributed to poor workmanship, cracks can also be caused by shrinkage. Any holes or cracks deeper than 6 mm (¼ in) should be filled with mortar (see pp.48–49). Shallow dents can be filled with the same compound used to level the floor.

You may need to screed only part of the floor. For a complete floor, start away from the door by which you will be leaving the room. The reason for this, of course, is that you don't want to be trapped by a carpet of wet compound between you and the door when the floor is completed. If there is no raised threshold at the door and the compound is to be levelled there, you'll have to add a threshold.

A floor covering can usually be laid after 12 hours, but check the time recommended by the manufacturer of the compound that you are using.

1 First, sweep or vacuum the floor clean. Then scrub it with sugar soap, diluted according to the manufacturer's instructions. Rinse it off with plenty of water and leave it to dry for a couple of days. If the room is cold, put in temporary heating to ensure the floor dries completely.

2 Dents are best filled with a small amount of the self-levelling compound, which must be allowed to dry for 12 hours before you lay the all-over coat of compound.

3 Follow the manufacturer's directions for mixing the compound with cold water. A trowel is a good tool for mixing. Because the compound will start to dry after 10 minutes, at first mix only about an average-sized bucket for each batch. As you start to work more quickly, you can make larger batches.

4 Just prior to using the compound, dampen the floor with water. This prevents the compound from drying out too quickly and possibly cracking at a later date.

5 Pour the mixture onto the floor, a bucket at a time. It will start to spread out in a puddle, so allow space for it to spread to any neighbouring walls.

6 You can assist the compound in spreading by using a steel float. Hold the float parallel to the floor and move it in a semicircular motion. You should notice the float marks disappearing as the compound dries.

7 Should you not – at first – be able to use the float with complete success, then immediately sprinkle water onto the compound to prevent it from drying and try again.

DOOR THRESHOLD

When using the self-levelling compound at a doorway, first make sure there is a raised threshold that will prevent the compound from spreading into the adjacent room. If not, install a threshold strip, using masonry nails. A door that opens into the room may need trimming (see pp.76–77).

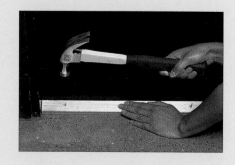

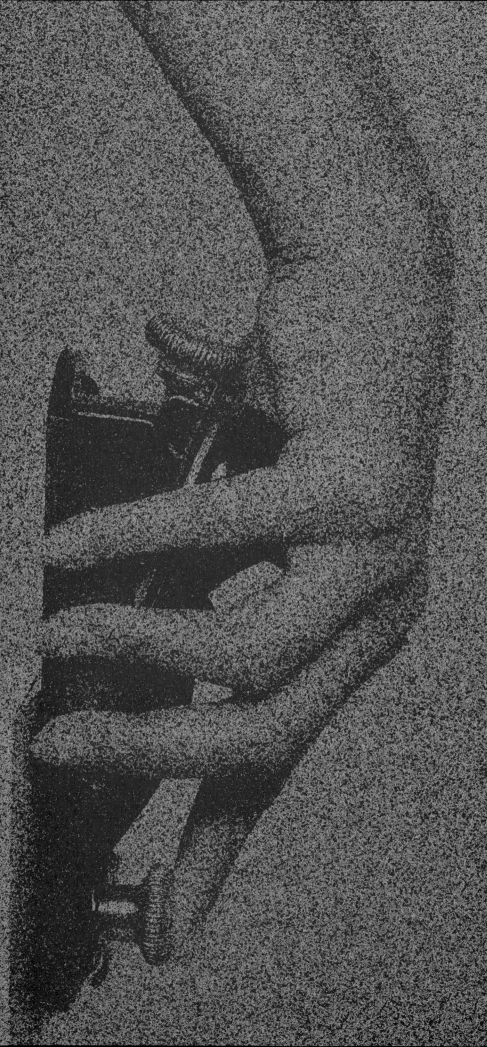

2

WINDOWS, DOORS AND STAIRS

WINDOWS, DOORS AND STAIRS DIRECTORY

TYPES OF WOOD WINDOW

SEE PAGES 56–57

A description of hardwood and softwood windows – mainly casement and sash types – and how they work, with a look at some methods of glazing.

TYPES OF METAL AND PLASTIC WINDOW

SEE PAGES 58–59

Metal (aluminium and steel) and plastic (PVC-U) are the alternatives to wood windows; they offer low maintenance, draught-proofing, double glazing and built-in locks.

REPAIRING DAMAGED WOOD WINDOWS

TIME FRAME 1 to 2 days
SKILL LEVEL Low to medium
SPECIAL TOOLS Wood chisel, router, sash clamp
SEE PAGES 60–61

How to replace wood damaged by wet rot and repair loose joints in old wood windows.

REPLACING SASH CORDS

TIME FRAME 1 day
SKILL LEVEL Medium
SPECIAL TOOLS None
SEE PAGES 62–63

How to replace the cords that normally secure the sashes to the counterbalancing weights.

REPLACING A WINDOW PANE

TIME FRAME ½ day
SKILL LEVEL Medium
SPECIAL TOOLS Glazier's hacking knife or old chisel and pin hammer
SEE PAGES 64–65

Glass is one of the most vulnerable materials in the home; if it breaks, it should be replaced immediately.

PAINTING WINDOWS

TIME FRAME 1 day per window
SKILL LEVEL Medium
SPECIAL TOOLS Paint brush
SEE PAGES 66–67

Old steel and all wood windows need regular re-coating with paint, or, for hardwood windows, preservative stain.

REPLACING OLD WINDOW FITTINGS

TIME FRAME ½ to 1 day
SKILL LEVEL Low to medium
SPECIAL TOOLS Wood chisel
SEE PAGES 68–69

Replacing handles and catches improves the appearance of a window. Replacing hinges is a more difficult job.

FITTING WINDOW SECURITY DEVICES

TIME FRAME Under 2 hours
SKILL LEVEL Low
SPECIAL TOOLS None
SEE PAGES 70–71

Burglars often gain entry to a home by breaking glass to reach through and open a window. Fitting security devices prevents them from opening the window.

TYPES OF INTERIOR DOOR

SEE PAGES 72–73

The choices for doors inside a home include panel, flush, glazed and louvre doors. There's also advice on the standard sizes.

TYPES OF EXTERIOR DOOR

SEE PAGES 74–75

Thicker than interior doors, most exterior doors are panelled or glazed, but come in other materials and styles.

MAKING REPAIRS TO DOORS

TIME FRAME Under 2 hours to 1 day
SKILL LEVEL Low to medium
SPECIAL TOOLS Door trimming saw (hired), plane, wood chisel, large clamp
SEE PAGES 76–77

How to repair a binding door, a loose joint and damaged wood, and how to trim a door to fit over a new flooring.

REPAIRING DOOR FRAMES

TIME FRAME 1 day
SKILL LEVEL Medium
SPECIAL TOOLS Mitre saw
SEE PAGES 78–79

A door frame may be loose or the hinge leaves in the frame may need repairing. You may want to replace the architrave.

CORDLESS POWER DRILL

FLAT DRILL BITS

BRADAWL

WOODWORKING CHISELS

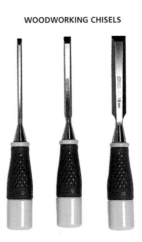

TRY SQUARE

BLOCK PLANE

PAINTING DOORS

TIME FRAME 1 to 2 days
SKILL LEVEL Medium
SPECIAL TOOLS Paint brush
SEE PAGES 80–81

As with painting a window, it is the order in which you do the work that is important.

A NEW DOOR: MEASURING UP AND FITTING HINGES

TIME FRAME 1 day
SKILL LEVEL Medium
SPECIAL TOOLS Circular saw, plane, wood chisel
SEE PAGES 82–83

Part one of hanging a door: how to measure up and fit the door to the opening and how to cut hinge recesses.

A NEW DOOR: HANGING IT AND FITTING HANDLES

TIME FRAME 1 day
SKILL LEVEL Medium
SPECIAL TOOLS Hacksaw, power drill
SEE PAGES 84–85

Part two of hanging a door: hanging the door in the frame and fitting the door latches and handles.

CHANGING THE WAY A DOOR HANGS

TIME FRAME 1 day
SKILL LEVEL Medium
SPECIAL TOOLS Tenon saw, power drill, chisel
SEE PAGES 86–87

Changing a door to open to the other side of a room or out of a room instead of into it.

CHANGING A HINGED DOOR TO A SLIDING DOOR

TIME FRAME 2 days
SKILL LEVEL Medium
SPECIAL TOOLS Spirit level
SEE PAGES 88–89

A sliding door frees space in the room into which the door previously opened. The light switch needs moving, which is best left to a professional.

FITTING A BI-FOLD WARDROBE DOOR

TIME FRAME ½ to 1 day
SKILL LEVEL Medium
SPECIAL TOOLS Power drill, clamp
SEE PAGES 90–91

A bi-fold door is hinged in the middle so it projects only half-way into a room when opened.

FITTING SLIDING WARDROBE DOORS

TIME FRAME 1 to 2 days
SKILL LEVEL Medium to high
SPECIAL TOOLS Jigsaw
SEE PAGES 92–93

Create your own built-in wardrobe by fitting sliding doors in front of a wall – either wall to wall or with an end panel.

FITTING A CYLINDER RIM LOCK

TIME FRAME Under 2 hours
SKILL LEVEL Low to medium
SPECIAL TOOLS Power drill plus flat bit, chisel, hacksaw
SEE PAGES 94–95

A common type of lock for the front door, a cylinder rim lock requires drilling to fit.

FITTING A MORTISE LOCK

TIME FRAME ½ day
SKILL LEVEL Medium
SPECIAL TOOLS Mortise chisel, brace
SEE PAGES 96–97

The most secure lock on a front door is a mortise lock fitted into a slot in the door.

OTHER DOOR HARDWARE

TIME FRAME Under 2 hours to ½ day
SKILL LEVEL Medium
SPECIAL TOOLS Jigsaw, power drill, hacksaw
SEE PAGES 98–99

How to fit extra door locks and chains, a door viewer and a letterbox.

REPAIRING STAIRS AND BALUSTERS

TIME FRAME Under 2 hours to 1 day
SKILL LEVEL Low to medium
SPECIAL TOOLS Tenon saw, power drill, sliding bevel
SEE PAGES 100–101

How to repair squeaky steps and make good broken balusters and stair nosings.

DECORATING STAIRCASE WOODWORK

TIME FRAME 1 to 2 days
SKILL LEVEL Low to medium
SPECIAL TOOLS Paint brushes, tack lifter
SEE PAGES 102–103

Preparing and painting or varnishing stair woodwork.

SANDING BLOCK

SURFORM PLANE

STANDARD SCREWDRIVERS

PIN HAMMER

HAND BRACE

CLAMP

TYPES OF WOOD WINDOW

Wood is a good insulator, so little heat escapes from the house through a wood window frame. It is also a common building material, so it blends in well with other features made of wood such as doors and eaves. There are two main types of window – casement and sash – and both are available in hardwood or softwood.

In general, hardwoods are much better at resisting rot and insect attack than softwoods. Because hardwoods have a natural beauty, hardwood windows are normally protected with an exterior varnish or a preservative wood stain; softwood windows are painted with specific paints designed for outside use, including microporous paints that prevent water getting into the wood but allow any trapped moisture to escape.

CASEMENT WINDOW
A wood frame fitted with glass is either fixed or hinged on one edge so that it can be opened. If the window opens, it is fitted with a casement stay to provide ventilation and/or a handle to hold it shut. A typical arrangement is one large fixed casement and one large side-hinged casement. A larger window has a fixed casement in the centre, with two side-hinged casements on the sides. Either may have small top-hinged casements above.

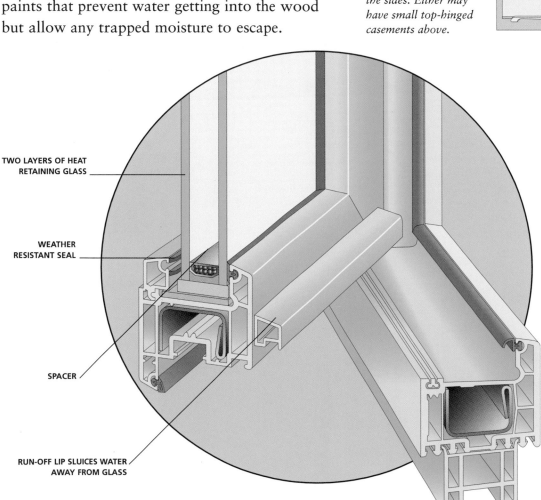

TWO LAYERS OF HEAT
RETAINING GLASS

WEATHER
RESISTANT SEAL

SPACER

RUN-OFF LIP SLUICES WATER
AWAY FROM GLASS

DOUBLE-GLAZED WINDOW
Two panes of glass with an air gap in between – a double-glazed window – reduces heat loss. Replacement windows have double-glazed sealed units (see p.59). To double glaze a window, fit a stepped sealed unit (half fits into the rebate and half fits on the frame) or secondary glazing, with a pane of glass or plastic fitted to the window or inside the reveal.

PIVOT WINDOWS

*Pivot windows – also known as
projected windows – contain a
single "sash", or piece of glass
surrounded by a frame of wood.
When opened, the top of the sash
moves back, while the bottom
moves outwards and forwards. The
hinge mechanism moves down
within channels located inside the
frame, and allows the window to
be turned entirely inside out. This
means it is easy and safe to clean
both the interior and exterior sides
of the pane from the inside. It is
common for a safety catch to be
fitted which secures the window
when opened to about 10 cm (4 in).*

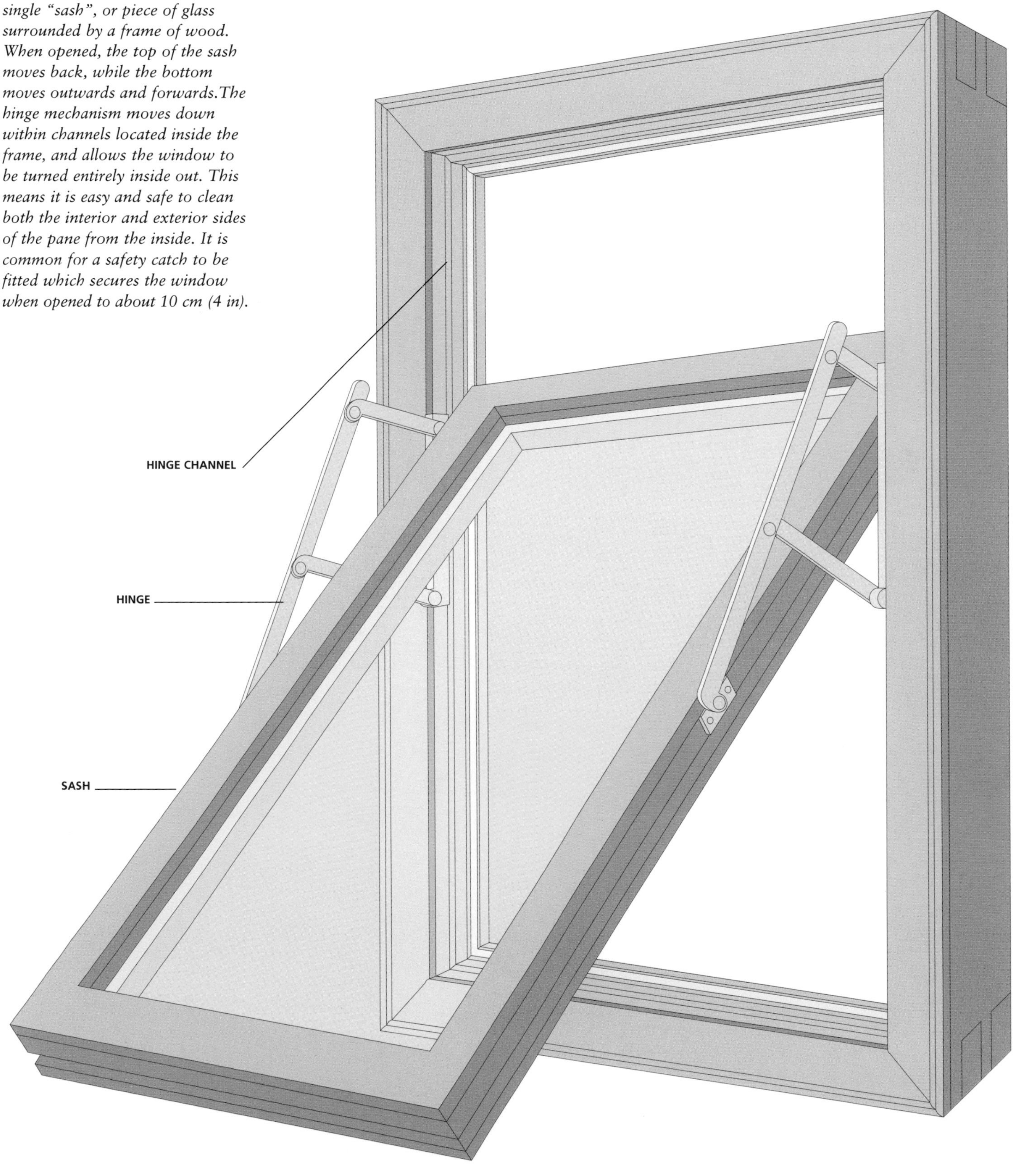

HINGE CHANNEL

HINGE

SASH

TYPES OF METAL AND PLASTIC WINDOWS

Modern metal and plastic windows are invariably double glazed and require virtually no maintenance. Steel windows were popular in the 1930s because they were relatively inexpensive, easy to install and had slimline profiles, allowing plenty of light to shine through. A huge advantage of aluminium as a window material is that it can be fashioned into almost any shape and size, making it ideal for customizing a replacement window to fit most window frames.

Unplasticized polyvinyl chloride – abbreviated to uPVC or, more commonly PVC-U – is the modern window material. It is ideal for replacing wood windows, since the window material is roughly the same thickness and is virtually maintenance-free.

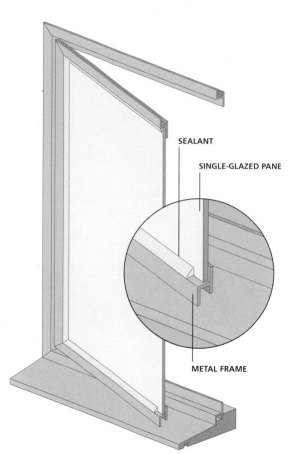

SEALANT

SINGLE-GLAZED PANE

METAL FRAME

ALUMINIUM WINDOWS
The slim profile of aluminium windows can be formed into many shapes, including octagon or hexagon shapes for bay windows and curves for bow windows. Early replacement windows had a plain anodized finish, which not only had a boring, dull grey finish, but soon became pitted. Modern windows come with a factory-applied painted finish in a range of colours, and many have insulation built into the frame. Like many steel windows, aluminium windows are fitted into a wood frame.

STEEL WINDOWS
The original steel windows have drawbacks: they can rust, steel is a poor insulator (often giving rise to condensation on the inside of the window frame) and they are difficult to secure with additional locks. Modern steel replacement windows – made in the same standard sizes as the originals – largely overcome all of these problems. They come ready-painted from the factory (which provides a degree of insulation as well as a maintenance-free finish) and usually come fitted with key-operated locks.

PLASTIC WINDOWS
White or brown PVC-U is used for plastic windows, which come in a range of styles, including a "tilt-and-turn" design – the window can be tilted inward from the bottom for easy cleaning. Once installed, maintenance is not necessary; however, the material can discolour in sunlight unless an ultraviolet (UV) light inhibitor was added to the material by the manufacturer.

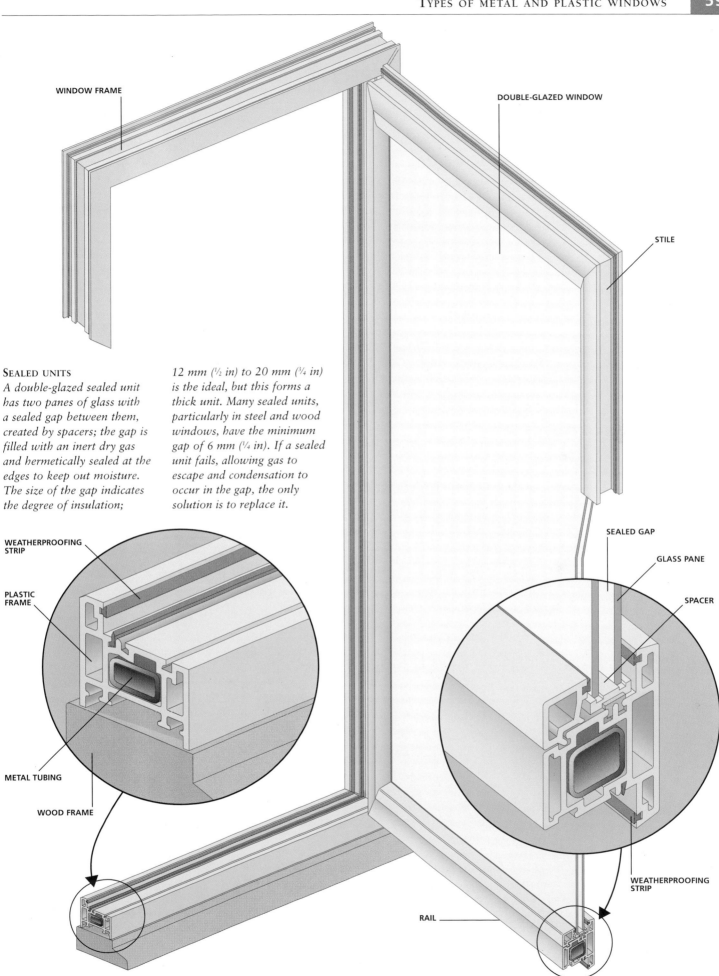

WINDOW FRAME

DOUBLE-GLAZED WINDOW

STILE

SEALED UNITS

A double-glazed sealed unit has two panes of glass with a sealed gap between them, created by spacers; the gap is filled with an inert dry gas and hermetically sealed at the edges to keep out moisture. The size of the gap indicates the degree of insulation; 12 mm (½ in) to 20 mm (¾ in) is the ideal, but this forms a thick unit. Many sealed units, particularly in steel and wood windows, have the minimum gap of 6 mm (¼ in). If a sealed unit fails, allowing gas to escape and condensation to occur in the gap, the only solution is to replace it.

WEATHERPROOFING STRIP

PLASTIC FRAME

METAL TUBING

WOOD FRAME

SEALED GAP

GLASS PANE

SPACER

WEATHERPROOFING STRIP

RAIL

REPAIRING DAMAGED WOOD WINDOWS

There are two particular problems that can affect the wood parts of windows; these are rot and failed joints in the window frame.

DEALING WITH ROT

Wet rot, which softens the wood (see pp.12–13), usually attacks window sills and the lowest frame member (rail) of softwood windows, where rainwater can collect. If the damage is serious, the only solution is to replace the frame; however, you can repair the damage by using a wet rot repair kit – which consists of a wood hardener, preservative and exterior filler – if you catch it early. Dry rot (see pp.12–13) requires specialist help.

REPAIRING JOINTS

Most joints in wood windows – both casement and sash – are mortise-and-tenon joints. A joint can shrink as the wood dries out, causing the window to sag so that it binds at the top corner farthest from the hinge on a casement window and at the bottom edge on the same side. To do a proper job of repairing this damage, you'll have to remove the window so that it can be squared up while the joint is re-glued. Use sash clamps for doing this, as shown in *Repairing a large area* (opposite page).

If "wedged" mortise-and-tenon joints were used, the simplest way to repair a dried-out joint is to cut new wedges and insert them with as much waterproof adhesive as you can force into the joint, then clamp the work while the adhesive sets.

With non-wedged joints, drill holes across the joint, passing through both the mortise and tenon, using a dowel-cutting drill bit; insert dowels plus adhesive (with more adhesive squeezed into the exposed end of the joint), then clamp and leave to set as before. Chisel off the excess length of the dowels once the adhesive has set.

TREATING A SMALL AREA

1 First determine the extent of the damage by poking the rotten area with a sharp pointed tool such as a bradawl. This will go easily into rotten areas. Use a chisel to remove all the affected wood until you reach solid wood (this ensures that all the rotten wood is removed).

2 If the wood is still damp, use a heat gun to dry it out, but keep it away from the glass to avoid cracking it. Brush on a wood hardener (follow the manufacturer's instructions); leave it to dry. If necessary, apply a second coat. Some wood hardeners contain a preservative; work it into the wood.

3 If separate preservative pellets are provided, drill holes in the sound wood. The holes should be the same diameter and slightly longer than the preservative pellets. Insert the pellets into the holes, pushing them just below the surface. Fill the holes using an exterior filler (see step 4), just proud of the surface.

4 Whether or not you use pellets, mix together the resin-based wood filler and its hardener; apply it with a filler knife, leaving it just proud of the surface. You may have to apply the filler in two layers; mix a little at a time, and wait for the first layer to set before applying the second one. When it has dried, sand it flush with the surface.

REPAIRING A LARGE AREA

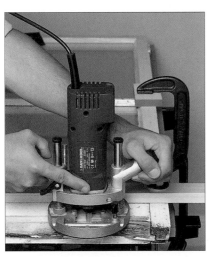

1 For a large area, draw a pencil line 50 mm (2 in) beyond the rotten area. Clamp a straightedge wood batten along this line to guide a router. Set the router's blade to a depth just greater than the rot, and hold it firmly against the guide as you cut away the rotten wood.

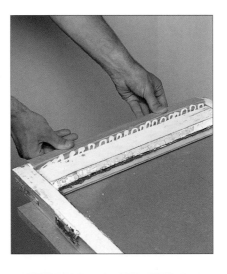

2 In the corners at each end where the router cannot reach, cut out any rotten wood with a chisel. Cut a piece of wood the correct length to fit in the gap. Use waterproof adhesive on the sides and ends of the piece, and push it into the cut-out area.

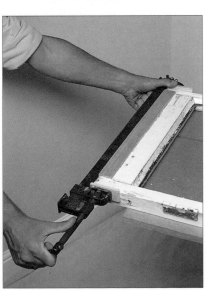

3 On a window frame, squeeze adhesive into the joints and place wedges (or dowels) at each side of the frame; clamp the frame with a sash clamp, putting blocks of wood between the clamp's jaws and the work to avoid harming the frame. Tighten the sash clamp gently – tightening it too much will break the glass.

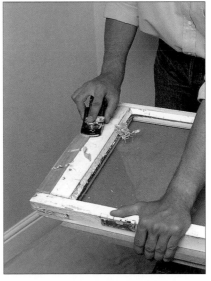

4 After 24 hours, remove the sash clamp, then use a small block plane to plane down the wood insert flush with the surrounding surfaces of the frame. Apply a finish to match the surrounding frame. Treat the repaired area with a primer and undercoat, then apply a top coat over the complete window frame (see pp.66–67).

ATTACHING WINDOW SHUTTERS

YOU WILL NEED

Paintbrush
Screwdriver
Pencil and ruler
Countersink bit
Bradawl
G-clamp
Tape measure
Filler knife
3 mm (⅛ in) drill bit
Power drill / screwdriver
Crosscut saw
Damp cloth

MATERIALS

Two shutter doors
Two 1.8 m (6 ft) lengths of
5 cm x 2.5 cm (2 in x 1 in)
wood
No. 8 screws, 4.5 cm
(1¾ in) long
Piece of scrap cardboard
4 flushmount hinges with
screws
Sliding bolt with screws
Door latch with screws
Wall plugs (optional)
Quick-drying filler
Gloss paint or matt varnish

SEE ALSO

Types of wood window
pp.56–57
Painting windows pp.66–67

This is a relatively straightforward job, the ease of which will be belied by the stunning finished effect. Typical to continental Europe, wooden window shutters add clean, uncluttered lines to your room. At the same time, they help keep the room warm in winter and cool in summer. The materials shown here apply to a 90 cm x 90 cm (3 ft x 3 ft) window reveal, but the principle may be applied to all window sizes. It is important to remember that your shutters should either fit your window perfectly or be slightly too large. You can always trim off any excess wood-surround to tailor the shutters to size. While it is always safest to use a tape measure when cutting wood – the lockable variety of tape being the best – if you have a good eye and are confident, it may actually be better to use a piece of wood to take measurements from work you already have in position as you go along.

THE RIGHT HINGES?

Flush-mount hinges allow the shutters to open fully and also do away with the need to chisel and recess the shutter doors and battens. If you have existing decorative moulding around your window which you do not wish to remove, you will require a "parliament hinge" which allows for the thickness of the moulding.

Helpful hints

If your shutters are larger than your reveal, they will ideally need to be cut to size. The battens that frame the reveal should also be set flush with the reveal for a neater finish. However, the advantage of having a frame is that it can be set back from the edge of the reveal to accommodate the size of your shutters, thus eliminating the need to cut them to size. Using the frame in this way also allows the doors to be fixed to wood rather than to the reveal, which in some cases may be made of plaster.

1 Measure along the top of the reveal, marking the centre point in pencil, to indicate the width of each shutter. Then measure the height of the reveal to give you the length of each shutter. Transfer these height and width measurements to each shutter.

2 Position the first shutter on your work surface and hold it firmly in position, or use a G-clamp. Line your saw up with the marked lines and cut it to the dimensions required. Repeat with the second shutter.

3 Position a long piece of batten next to the reveal. Mark the edge of the batten at the point where it meets the top of the reveal. For accuracy, measure and mark the second piece of batten on the other side of the reveal, then cut to size. Drill and countersink holes at 30-cm (12-in) intervals along each vertical batten.

4 Mark the wall through the drilled holes with a bradawl. Position the batten so that it is flush with the side. Drill into the wall at the marks, add wall plugs if necessary. Screw the batten into place. Repeat on the other side of the window. Measure the wood for the top batten, trim and attach as before.

5 Attach hinges to the shutters, at equal distances from top and bottom. Position the shutter flat against the wall as though it were fully open. Fold back the outer part of each hinge until it is flat against the inside edge of the vertical batten. Screw each hinge into place.

6 To keep the shutters open, attach a hook and latch to each shutter. With the shutter flat against the wall, mark a point 5 cm (2 in) up from the outermost bottom corner. Attach the eye at this point. Place the hook into the eye to establish the position of the hook plate on the wall. Secure the hook plate to the wall.

7 Fit one of the shutters with a sliding bolt. Attach the bolt on the front of the shutter on the vertical panel at the top inner corner. Then slide the bolt into the eye. Mark the correct position of the eye on the horizontal batten and attach it to the batten with screws.

8 The shutters are closed with a door latch. Measure and mark halfway down the length of one of the shutters. Attach the latch so that it is flush with the edge of the shutter. Put the latch onto the keep plate and mark the correct position of the keep plate on the edge of the opposite door. Screw the plate in place.

REPLACING A WINDOW PANE

YOU WILL NEED

Protective cloth
Old chisel **or** glaziers's hacking knife
Pincers
Thick work gloves
Safety glasses
Mallet
Narrow-blade scraper
Paint brush
Tape measure
Flixible filler knife
Wood matchsticks (if required)
Pin hammer
Putty knife
Paint brush

MATERIALS

Wood primer
Glass
Putty
Glazing sprigs **or** clips
Paint

SEE ALSO

Repairing damaged wood windows pp.60–61
Painting windows pp.66–67
Replacing old window hardware pp.68–69

Replacing cracked or broken glass is a common do-it-yourself job. It isn't difficult, but it takes time and great care is needed – particularly when removing the old glass – to avoid cutting yourself.

If you doubt your ability to do the job, have a professional glazier do it for you. Provided you can secure the opening (for example, with plywood), you can remove the window from its frame and take it to a glass merchant or glazier for replacement panes. Even if you feel capable of replacing the pane yourself, have your local glass merchant cut the glass to size for you.

THE RIGHT TYPE OF GLASS?

Normally, you should replace glass with the same type as the broken pane; for most home windows, this will be 4 mm ($5/32$ in) glass. Only small windows – or panes in, say, interior "Georgian" glazed doors with several panels – can be glazed with 3 mm

($1/8$ in) glass, while large windows need 6 mm ($1/4$ in) or 10 mm ($3/8$ in) glass.

Some glass in "vulnerable areas" (glazed exterior doors, large panels next to these doors, large "picture" windows and low-level glazing) must be glazed with safety glass, either toughened or laminated. Toughened glass is five times stronger than normal glass and breaks into harmless fragments if it is penetrated. Laminated glass consists of a sandwich of two sheets of normal glass surrounding a plastic interlayer, which holds all the glass in place if either surface is broken. It has the advantage over toughened glass of being burglar-proof.

Helpful hints

If putty has too much linseed oil in it, it can stick to your hands and be difficult to use. The answer is to roll it around on newspaper, which will absorb the excess oil, until the putty is the correct consistency. If the putty has dried out, make it more pliable by adding linseed oil. Clean putty off glass with methylated spirits.

1 Remove the window from its frame, and lay it down (exterior side up) on a worktop covered with a protective cloth. Use a chisel or a glazier's hacking knife to remove the old putty. You'll come across glazing sprigs, or clips, holding the glass in place; remove them with pincers. Wearing thick gloves, pull the glass from the frame.

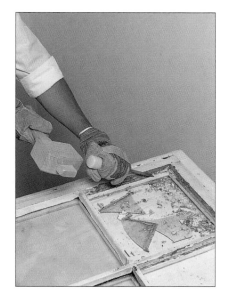

2 Wearing safety glasses to protect your eyes, use the chisel and a mallet to remove the remaining large pieces of old putty from the bottom of the rebates in the frame – make sure you avoid cutting into the wood.

3 Use a scraper to clear the thin residue of putty from the frame rebates. When completely clean, carefully gather up and dispose of the old broken glass. Give the rebates a coat of wood primer. Measure for the new pane of glass, allowing 3 mm (⅛ in) clearance on each side for both dimensions – width and height.

4 When the primer has dried, check that the new glass pane is the correct size. Knead the putty in your hands until it is pliable; run a bead 3 mm to 5 mm (⅛ in to ¼ in) thick around the bottom of the rebates. Use a filler knife to press it down flat and smooth it out, trimming off any excess putty that hangs over the edge.

5 Insert the glass into the frame, leaving a 3 mm (⅛ in) gap all around. Gently press the glass firmly into place along its edges – never the centre – until putty squeezes out of the inside of the window. If the frame is in situ (vertical), first insert matchsticks across the the lowest horizontal rebate to create an equal gap all around.

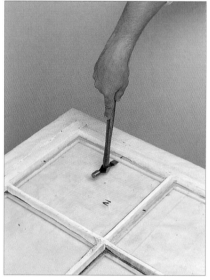

6 Use glazing sprigs (or clips on metal windows) to secure the glass in place. Slide the flat end of the hammer (or the square back of a glazier's hacking knife) back and forth across the surface of the glass to tap the sprig in place – do not hit the sprigs as you would nails.

7 Knead the putty as before and roll it into a thin sausage shape. Starting at one corner, lay the putty down and push it against the sides of the rebates in the frame. Move along the frame, laying down the putty and pushing it into place, and continue in this way completely around the frame.

8 To make a smooth bevel in the putty, hold a putty knife at a 45° angle, with its straight edge on the putty, and pull the knife along. To mitre each corner, place the knife diagonally in the centre and pull it away from the corner. Use the knife to remove any putty left on the glass. Allow the putty to dry for at least a week before painting.

PAINTING WINDOWS

YOU WILL NEED

Painting a casement window
Sanding block
Masking tape **or** window scraper
Paint brushes

Painting a sash window
See above

MATERIALS

Painting a casement window
Fine abrasive paper
Paint

Painting a sash window
See above

SEE ALSO

Stripping paint from wood trim pp.32–33
Repairing damaged wood windows pp.60–61
Replacing a window pane pp.64–65
Replacing old window hardware pp.68–69
Fitting window security devices pp.70–71

The best results were acheived on this window by removing all its fittings before it was painted.

Before painting a window, especially one made of wood, carry out any needed repairs, replace damaged glass (leave new putty to harden for a week before painting) and remove flaking paint. Sand down the surfaces with fine abrasive paper and thoroughly clean them; apply primer to any bare wood. If a window has been painted too often, it can bind on its frame. To avoid this, plane or sand back the edges before priming and painting.

If you have removed a window to repair joints or replace sash cords, it will be easier to paint it before putting it back in its frame – the frame will also be easier to paint. Whether the window is in or out of the frame, remove all window fittings, such as handles and stays, before painting.

A simple way to avoid getting paint on the glass is to apply low-tack masking tape; you can remove it once the paint has set. The alternative is to forget about getting paint on the glass and to remove it once it has dried, using a special window scraper. You may well need this anyway to remove "spots" of paint on the glass.

PAINTING A CASEMENT WINDOW

1 To paint the inside of a casement window, wedge the window slightly open. If you prefer, stick lengths of low-tack masking tape onto the glass; leave a 2 mm ($^5/_{64}$ in) gap between the glass and frame so the paint can seal the joint between the two – this helps to block moisture.

2 Using the cutting-in brush, paint the glazing bars (including the rebates). Use the brush with a dabbing motion to get paint into the corners. It doesn't matter if paint goes onto the tape, but avoid getting any paint on the glass.

3 Adjust the window to open it slightly more. Paint the top and bottom horizontal rails, then paint the vertical stiles of the window.

4 Open the window fully before you paint the inside closing edge of the window, brushing down from the top. With the window still fully open, paint the frame. Just before the paint has dried completely, carefully pull the tape away from the window – if allowed to dry, the tape can pull off paint as it is peeled away.

PAINTING A SASH WINDOW

1 To paint the inside of a sash window, push the inner sash to the top and pull the outer sash to the bottom. Using a cutting-in brush on the upper sash, paint the bottom rail, followed by the vertical stiles as far as you can reach. Paint the inside of the frame at the bottom.

2 Paint the lower rail of the inner sash, using the cutting-in brush to paint up to the glass; then paint the sections of the vertical stiles that are within reach.

3 Put the sashes back in their correct positions to reveal the parts that you haven't painted. Paint the top rail of the inner sash, followed by the remainder of the vertical stiles.

4 Slide the outer sash down, and paint its top rail and the unpainted areas of the vertical stiles. Paint the remainder of the inside of the frame and, finally, paint the window frame surround.

REPLACING OLD WINDOW HARDWARE

YOU WILL NEED

Replacing hinges
Utility knife (if required)
Screwdriver
Pencil
Chisel
Mallet
Electric drill plus twist bit

Other window hardware
Pencil
Adjustable square
Electric drill plus twist bit
Screwdriver

MATERIALS

Replacing hinges
Hinges
Dowels
PVA glue

Other window hardware
Handle, casement stay, **or** sash fastener
Dowels
PVA glue

SEE ALSO

Repairing damaged wood windows pp.60–61
Painting windows pp.66–67

One common reason for replacing old window hardware, such as handles and catches, is to create a new style – perhaps using brass or bronze in place of aluminum, or exchanging a plain design for an ornate one. You may wish to coordinate your window hardware with your interior decor – there is a huge selection of styles available, and the relative ease with which handles and catches can be replaced makes overhauling the look of your window fairly straightforward.

Another reason for changing hardware is to replace an existing handle or catch with a lockable one to make the window more secure (see pp.70–71). Unless you are very lucky, it is most unlikely that the mounting holes for the new hardware will be in the same positions as those for the old ones, so you must be prepared to fill in the old holes before beginning to drill new ones. This will make the job slightly more time consuming.

Handles and catches are available in hardware stores, DIY stores, and building supply stores; you'll also find them at mail-order and specialist suppliers, especially if you are looking for brass and wrought iron hardware in more ornate styles.

REPLACING HINGES

Ordinarily, a stiff or squeaky hinge will simply need a squirt of a general-purpose, household lubricating oil to remedy it. However, hinges may need

Helpful hints

If the screws holding a hinge in place are too stiff to remove, try holding a screwdriver in place and hitting its end with a hammer; this may shake it loose. Or you can try slightly turning the screw in the direction for tightening it (clockwise) – this may relieve pressure. Conversely, if screws are no longer holding a hinge in place, replace them with longer screws of the same diameter.

If the recess of an old hinge bed is too deep for a new hinge, you can shim it with pieces of cardboard.

CASEMENT HANDLE

To refit a handle, unscrew the old one and fill the holes with dowels (see step 3, opposite page). Hold the new handle to the window at an easy-to-reach height, mark and drill out the screw holes, and fasten the handle in place. Repeat for the catch, mounting it to the frame near the handle.

CASEMENT STAY

To replace a casement stay, fill the old screw holes (see step 3, opposite page). Fit the casement arm onto the bottom rail of the window, close the window and position the arm against the bottom rail. Mark the position of the stay, drill pilot holes, and screw it in place.

replacing if they are so old they have become worn or badly rusted, or if they are covered by so much paint that they can no longer function properly. Hinges come in standard sizes, so unless you are replacing one size of hinge with a larger one, there is a good chance that the screw holes for the new hinges will be in the same place as for the old ones.

Brass hinges may be left unpainted and can make an attractive feature when used with other brass fittings. However, steel hinges must be primed and painted to prevent them from rusting. When fitting the hinges, use screws of a matching metal.

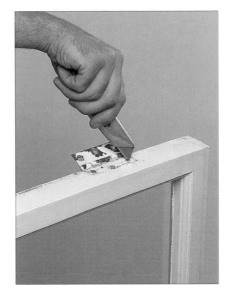

1 Unscrew and remove the old hinges, starting with the screws holding the hinges to the frame. If they are encrusted with paint, use a utility knife to remove the paint from the slots and around the sides of the screw heads.

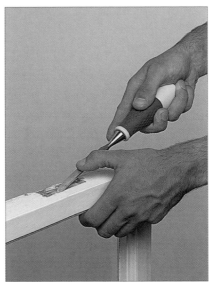

2 Check if the new hinges fit the recesses in the frame and window. To deepen, widen, or lengthen a recess, centre a new hinge over the recess, and score around it with a utility knife to mark its position. Cut along the scored line with a chisel, then pare away wood from the recess.

HOPPER WINDOWS

A hopper window opens inwards from the top, where it is secured by a latch. The window is hinged at the bottom, and the amount it opens is dictated by an arc bar, upon which the weight of the window rests while it is open.

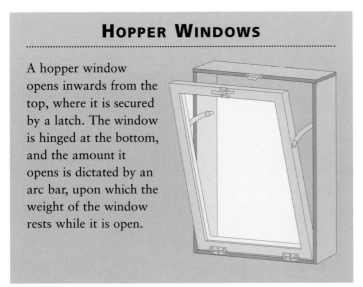

3 Fit the new hinge in the recess, then check that the holes line up. If they do, use screws a little longer than the old ones. If they are misaligned, even slightly, drill out the old holes, glue in dowels and, if needed, trim them flush to the surface. Drill pilot holes for the screws. Refit the window as you would hang a door (see pp.86–87).

FITTING WINDOW SECURITY DEVICES

Windows are the most vulnerable point of access in your home. To reduce the risk of burglary, all accessible windows in a house should have secure locks, including first floor windows, those accessible from a garage roof, all downstairs windows and any windows in partially hidden locations. In fact, some insurance companies insist on security devices before they will supply cover for your home. The most vital point to note when fitting window locks is that thay must be robust enough to resist forcing and they must be positioned in such a way that they are not compromised. Larger windows will need two locks evenly spaced to ensure they secure the whole window and complement each other.

Casement windows effectively open like doors, and should be secured either by locks which fasten to the frame, or by self-locking handles and stays. There are three main types of casement window lock: a lockable handle, which replaces the existing handle; a locking stop to prevent the existing handle or casement stay from being operated without a key; and a separate lock to hold the window shut. The two main types for sash windows are a dual screw, which holds the two sashs together, and a sash stop, which prevents the inner sash from being lifted up. There is a special lock for patio doors, which can also be used on sash windows.

Most locks require the window to be shut before it can be locked; but some have a second position, allowing the window to be left ajar for ventilation.

SECURITY CONSIDERATIONS

Few burglars will climb through a broken window – they break the window to get at the catches to open it. Locks will prevent this, but only if the key for the lock is not left on the window sill. Apart from cockspur and casement stays, always fit two locks to all but tiny windows.

If you live in an area where burglary is common, you may need to either fit laminated glass (see pp.64–65) or attach a grille to the window.

FITTING THE LOCKS

Most window locks are easy to fit, requiring only pilot holes to be made for the screws. This is simple for wood windows, but you'll have to drill holes and use self-tapping screws on metal windows. Some locks require you to drill larger holes, others need small recesses cut with a chisel. There may be a trade-off between the ease of fitting the lock and its obtrusiveness.

LOCKABLE CASEMENT HANDLE

This lockable casement handle is fitted in the same way as an ordinary handle (see pp.68–69), but has a key that enables it to be locked.

SECURED CASEMENT STAY

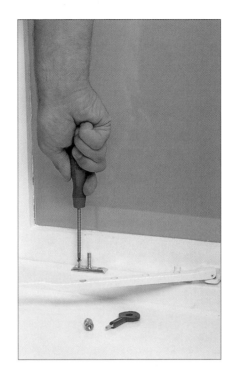

You can make a casement stay more secure by simply replacing the pin farthest away from the arm's pivot with a pin that has a threaded spindle. To lock it, place the casement arm over the pin, then use the key to screw the locking nut onto the pin.

LOCKABLE CASEMENT ARM

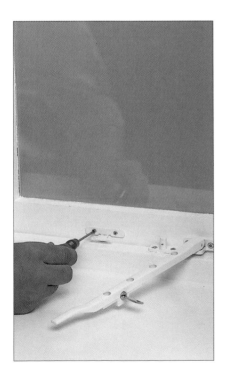

A lockable casement arm is fitted in the normal way (see pp.68–69), except the outer stay bracket is fitted to the bottom rail of the window. The casement arm should be in place so you can mark the bracket's position before screwing it in place. It can then be locked with a key.

CASEMENT LOCK

This two-part lock has a receiving bracket that is screwed to the frame and a bracket with an arm screwed to the window stile; to lock the window the arm swings over the receiving bracket. First fit the bracket with the arm, then the receiving bracket in a corresponding position.

TYPES OF INTERIOR DOOR

There are three main types of interior door for access between rooms: panel, glazed and flush. The traditional type is a panel door, which consists of a solid wood frame (hardwood or softwood) with, typically, two, four or six panels of a lighter material. A glazed door is similar to a panel door, but glass is used instead of the panels. A flush door is less expensive than a panel door, and it is lighter and easier to install. The core material may be a honeycombed paper, laminated wood, wood rails or a solid fire-resistant material.

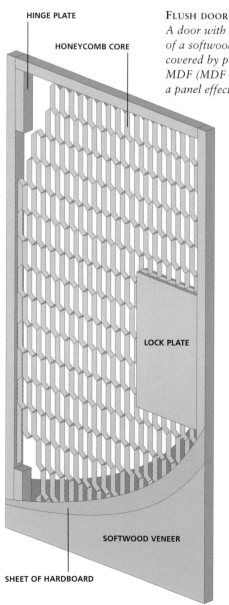

HINGE PLATE

HONEYCOMB CORE

LOCK PLATE

SOFTWOOD VENEER

SHEET OF HARDBOARD

DOOR SIZES

Interior doors are made in standard sizes, which in older houses are likely to be "imperial" (inches) and in modern houses "metric" (millimetres).

Common sizes are (by height, then width):
Imperial

6 ft 6 in × 2 ft (1981 mm × 610 mm)
6 ft 6 in × 2 ft 3 in (1981 mm × 686 mm)
6 ft 6 in × 2 ft 6 in (1981 mm × 762 mm)
6 ft 6 in × 2 ft 9 in (1981 mm × 838 mm)

Metric

2040 mm × 626 mm (6 ft 8¼ in × 2 ft ½ in)
2040 mm × 726 mm (6 ft 8¼ in × 2 ft 4½ in)
2040 mm × 826 mm (6 ft 8¼ in × 2 ft 8½ in)
2040 mm × 926 mm (6 ft 8¼ in × 3 ft ½ in)

FLUSH DOOR
A door with flush surfaces consists of a softwood frame with a core covered by plywood, hardboard or MDF (MDF may be moulded into a panel effect), then a wood veneer.

LOUVRE DOOR
Slats are fitted into the frame of a louvre door. It is ideal for a wardrobe (it allows ventilation). You can use narrow ones as a bi-fold door – a pair of doors hinged in the centre.

GLAZED PANEL DOOR
The frame is wood, but the "panels" are made of glass in this type of door. A glazed door can have from 1 to 15 glass panels, each of which fits into a rebate held in place by a glazing bead. A single-pane glazed door and the lower half of a double-pane glazed door should be fitted with safety glass (see pp.64–65).

THE ANATOMY OF A DOORWAY
A doorway between interior rooms consists of five main parts: the door frame (made of 100 mm × 25 mm/ 4 in × 1 in softwood), secured to the wood uprights of a plasterboard wall or to the masonry of a solid wall; the door stop, narrow strips of wood against which the door closes; the door itself (a panel door, below), fitted with hinges to hang it on the frame; the architrave, which covers the gap between the wall and the door frame; and the door "hardware" (handles, locks and latches) fitted to holes cut in the door and the door frame. You can replace any or all of the parts.

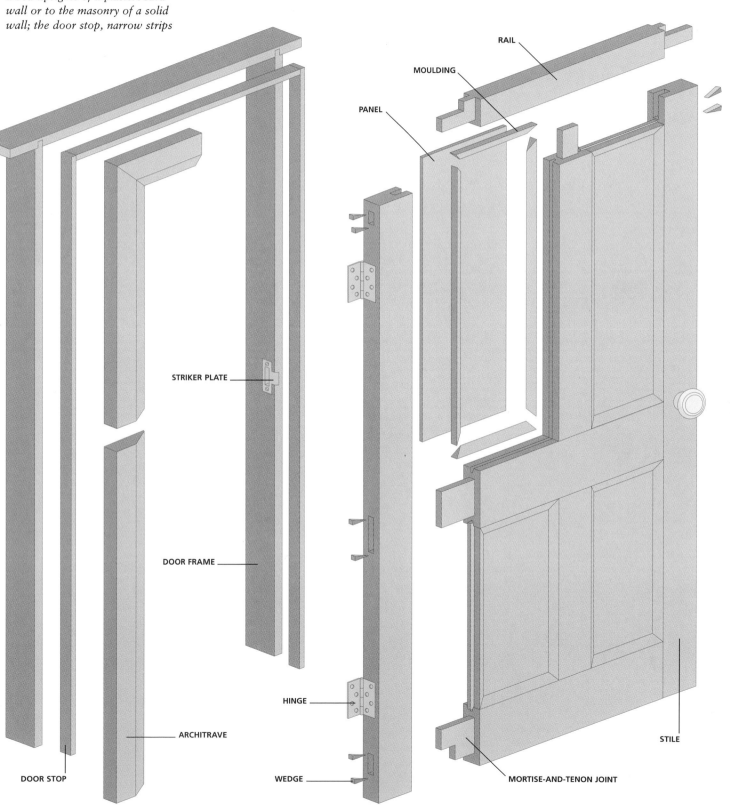

STRIKER PLATE

DOOR FRAME

ARCHITRAVE

DOOR STOP

RAIL

MOULDING

PANEL

HINGE

WEDGE

STILE

MORTISE-AND-TENON JOINT

TYPES OF EXTERIOR DOOR

Exterior doors are bigger, heavier and thicker than interior doors and come in a wider range of styles and materials. You can fit a new exterior door into the existing frame, but if you are replacing a painted softwood door with a hardwood door (to be varnished or stained), the door frame will need changing, too.

Fitting a new front or side door is similar to fitting an interior door, but it's more cumbersome to move and you'll have more work to do on the door itself – for example, fitting secure door locks.

EXTERIOR DOOR SIZES

Doors for outside use are thicker than interior doors, usually 44 mm (1¼ in) thick, and larger. They are likely to be "imperial" (inch) sizes in older houses and "metric" (mm) sizes in modern houses.

Common sizes are (by height, then width):

Imperial

6 ft 6 in × 2 ft 3 in (1981 mm × 686 mm)
6 ft 6 in × 2 ft 6 in (1981 mm × 762 mm)
6 ft 6 in × 2 ft 9 in (1981 mm × 838 mm)
6 ft 8 in × 2 ft 8in (2032 mm × 813 mm)

Metric

2040 mm × 726 mm (6 ft 8¼ in × 2 ft 4½ in
2040 mm × 826 mm (6 ft 8¼ in × 2 ft 8½ in)
2000 mm × 807 mm (6 ft 6¼ in × 2 ft 7¾ in)

SOLID CHIPBOARD CORE

FLUSH DOOR
An exterior flush door is stronger and heavier than an interior flush door. The core is of a more solid material, such as chipboard, and the door usually has an exterior-quality plywood facing.

LETTERBOX PLATE

LOCK PLATE

PLYWOOD

VENEER COVERING

FRENCH WINDOWS
A pair of glazed doors forms what are known as French windows. Each door has from 1 to 10 glazed panes. They fit into a standard frame; wider frames are available if matching side lights are fitted. The doors come in only the imperial size of 6 ft × 3 ft 10 in (1828 mm × 914 mm) or the metric size of 2000 mm × 1106 mm (6 ft 6¾ in × 3 ft 7½ in).

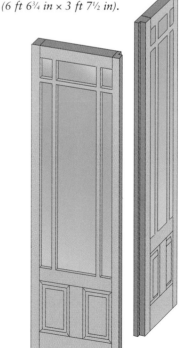

BOARDED DOOR
Softwood tongue-and-groove boards are secured to horizontal ledges and angled braces to form this door, hence its common name of "ledged-and-braced" door. It's suitable only as a door for storage areas indoors and outside.

ANATOMY OF AN EXTERIOR DOOR FRAME AND PANEL DOOR

An exterior door frame has a rebate cut in it for the door to close against and a built-in door sill (threshold). There is a huge range of exterior panel doors, made in both softwood and hardwood. Many are solid – typically with six panels – but they can also be single or double glazed. The glazing can vary from one small glazed panel to the top half divided into up to nine panels, with a range of options in between. Fanlights (glazed panels in a curved shape) are also common.

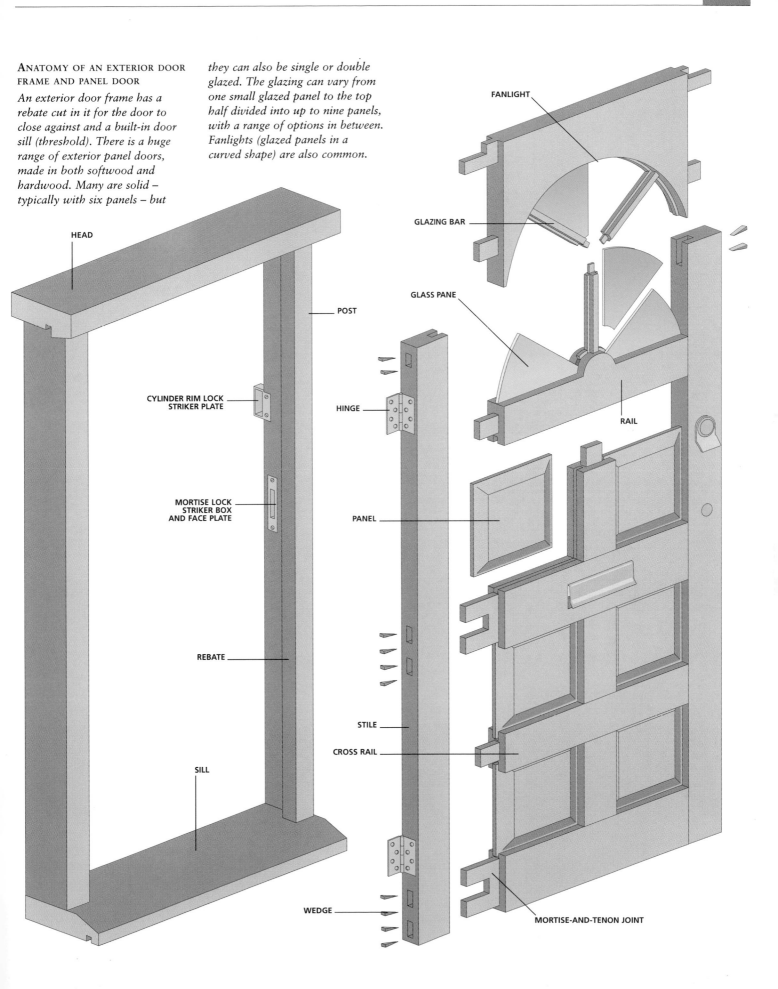

MAKING REPAIRS TO DOORS

YOU WILL NEED

Hammer
Door trimming saw
Dust mask, safety glasses
and ear protectors (if
required)
Power drill plus twist bits
Screwdrivers
Block plane
Large plane
Sash clamp **or** other large
clamp
Mallet
Chisel
Flexible filler knife
Sanding block

MATERIALS

Wood wedges
Rising butt hinges
Dowels
Softwood
Wood filler
Fine-grade abrasive paper

SEE ALSO

Stripping wood trim
pp.32–33
Painting doors pp.80–81
A new door: measuring up
and fitting hinges pp.82–83
A new door: hanging it and
fitting handles pp.84–85
Changing the way a door
hangs pp.86–87

Most door repairs are simple to do and require few tools. For a door to work, a repair may have to be made to the frame (see pp.78–79).

Too much paint on the closing edges of a door can cause it to stick. Strip off the paint and apply a thinner layer. As a wood door's moisture content changes, the door can change in size; it may bind in damp weather and go back to normal when it dries out. You may have to plane or sand it. If you can, wait until dry weather when the door is at its minimum moisture level, then paint the edges to ensure that no more moisture can get in.

A door that binds at the bottom may be caused by the door swelling or by loose hinges (see pp.78–79); or the adhesive in the mortise-and-tenon joints (which holds the rails to the stiles) may have dried out and the joints loosened. You'll have to remove the door to reinforce a joint with wood dowels.

Where you have levelled a solid floor or changed a floor covering, a door into the room may bind at the bottom, scraping on the floor as it opens. You can remove the door from the frame and plane a small amount off the bottom; use your plane from the edges toward the centre of the door to prevent the wood from splitting, or hire a door trimming saw. Or replace the existing hinges with rising butt hinges, which lift the door as it opens.

Helpful hints

To remove a door, prop it open (see below). Undo the screws holding the hinges to the frame (see pp.68–69), removing all but one of the screws from the top hinge, then taking all the screws out of the bottom hinge (and, if fitted, the middle hinge). With a helper supporting the door, remove the remaining screw from the top hinge and pull the door away. You may have to lever heavily painted hinges out of their recesses.

Fit a sprung draught strip to the bottom of an exterior door to allow the wood to expand and contract as its moisture content changes.

PROPPING A DOOR FOR REPAIRS

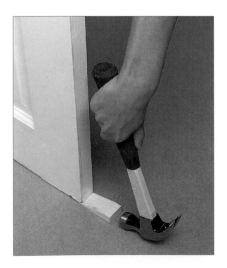

When removing, hanging or making repairs to a door, hold it firmly in position with a wedge. Open the door at a right angle to the frame. Position a wedge at the side or end of the door, and give it sharp taps with a hammer until it stops moving.

USING A DOOR TRIMMING SAW

To use a trimming saw, prop the door open with a wedge at each side and set the depth of the trimming saw. Wearing a dust mask, safety glasses and ear protectors, start cutting the door at the open end; hold the saw firmly against the door. Move the wedges as the saw cuts along the door.

FITTING RISING BUTT HINGES

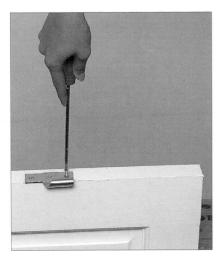

1 Choose rising butt hinges for either a lefthand or righthand door. With the door secured with the hinged edge upright, position the sleeve parts on the door and mark the screw holes. After drilling out the holes screw the hinges in place. Fix the pivot part of the hinges to the door frame.

2 Before hanging it, chamfer the top edge of the door to enable it to close into the frame, using a small plane. Make the chamfer near the hinge end of the door, and taper it down to the face of the door that opens into the room.

TRIMMING A BINDING DOOR

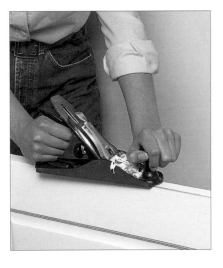

If too much paint on a its edge or a high moisture content causes a door to bind, take it off its hinges and support it with the door-latch edge upright. Remove the latch (see pp.84–85), then use a large plane to trim the edge. (Increase the depth of the recess to re-fit the latch.)

REPAIRING A LOOSE JOINT

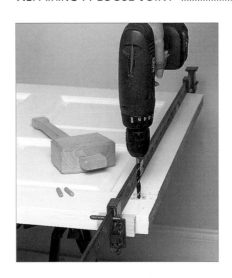

Position a clamp at a loose joint and tighten it, keeping the door square. Drill two holes the diameter of a dowel into the joint. Apply adhesive to the dowels; insert them into the holes, tapping them in with a mallet. Let the adhesive set before removing the clamp. Trim the dowels with a chisel.

REPLACING DAMAGED WOOD

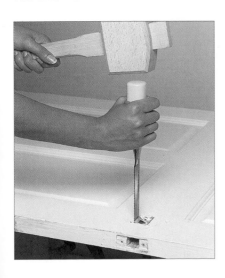

1 Lay the door flat on a worktop, then use a chisel and mallet to mark an oblong shape around the damaged area. Continue to cut out the damaged area with the chisel and mallet, going down to about half the depth of the door.

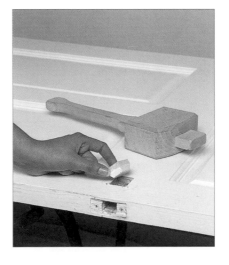

2 Cut a piece of wood to fit the cut-out area, and chamfer the bottom half of each side. Add adhesive, then push it into the hole, level with the surface of the door. Let the adhesive dry; sand the repair level with the door. Fill any gaps with wood filler; after it dries, sand and paint.

REPAIRING DOOR FRAMES

YOU WILL NEED

Replacing the architrave
Utility knife
Broad-blade chisel
Adjustable square and pencil
Mitre frame and saw **or** mitre box and tenon saw
Hammer
Nail punch
Flexible filler knife
Sanding block

Other frame repairs
Power drill plus countersink and twist bits
Screwdrivers
Hammer
Chisel
Flexible filler knife

MATERIALS

Replacing the architrave
Architrave
Panel pins
Fine-grade abrasive paper
Wood filler

Other frame repairs
150-mm- (6-in-) long screw
PVA adhesive
Dowels
Cardboard

SEE ALSO

Making repairs to doors pp.76–77

Most repairs to internal door frames are simple. For example, a rattling door can be repaired by moving its striker plate. If the frame is loose, first try tightening or replacing any existing screws; if the frame has been nailed in place, add a few screws. In a masonry wall, you could try tightening any existing screws, but you'll also need to add frame fixers (see pp.170–171).

If the hinge screws are loose, try tightening them; if they won't hold, fit bigger screws – either the same gauge but longer or, if the hinge holes are big enough, a larger gauge of the same length. If you can't get the screws tight, drill out the holes and add dowels. If too large a gauge of screw had been used, it may protrude beyond the hinge, preventing the door from closing properly; replace it with a smaller, longer screw. The recess of the hinge may not be deep enough (see pp.82–83) or it may too deep.

New architrave, with a coat or two of paint, can improve the overall look of a tired door frame.

Old architrave surrounding a door may eventually need replacing. When buying new architrave, remember to measure each length to the end of the mitred corner.

TIGHTENING A LOOSE FRAME

If the frame is fitted to a partition wall, drill and countersink a hole into the door stop. Have a helper hold the frame in place; drill a smaller diameter hole through the frame into the stud, then drive in a 150-mm- (6-in-) long screw. Cover the screw head with wood filler; once dry, sand and paint it.

REPAIRING A LOOSE HINGE

If the screws of a hinge are loose, take them out; redrill each hole the diameter and depth of small lengths of dowel. Apply adhesive to the end of the dowels and to the edge of each hole, then tap a dowel into each hole. Drill pilot holes into the dowels to take new screws for the hinges.

BUILDING UP A HINGE RECESS

A door may bind if the hinge is recessed into the door frame too deeply. To rectify this – so the door hangs farther away from the frame – remove the door from the frame (see pp.76–77). Cut a piece of cardboard the same size as the hinge leaf and insert it into the recess; then rehang the door.

FIXING A RATTLING DOOR

If the door rattles in its frame, reposition the striker plate of the door latch. Unscrew the plate; then use a chisel to enlarge the width of the recess on the side closest to the door stop. Drill out the screw holes and glue in dowels; after the adhesive dries, drill new pilot holes and screw in the plate.

REPLACING THE ARCHITRAVE

1 Insert the tip of a utility knife blade between the architrave and door frame. Slowly pull the knife down to break the skin of the paint. Repeat on the other pieces of architrave. Use a broad-blade chisel to prise off the architrave; then clean the exposed area with abrasive paper.

2 Mark a right angle 6 mm (¼ in) away from the top corner of the frame. Align a length of architrave at the vertical line, with its end above where the horizontal length will be. Make a mark on the architrave at the point where the two pencil lines meet. Repeat at the other side of the frame.

3 Use a mitre frame and saw to cut mitres at the marks – they indicate the lowest end of the mitre. Nail the lengths in place. Hold a length of architrave across their tops. With a ruler at the outside edge of one vertical length of architrave, mark the top of the horizontal length. Repeat at the other side; use these marks to cut mitres.

4 As with the vertical lengths, drive nails through the front of the horizontal length and into the frame. To hold the corners together, nail down through the top of the horizontal length into the vertical one at each side. Drive the nail heads down with a nail punch; cover with wood filler. After it dries, sand and paint the architrave.

PAINTING DOORS

YOU WILL NEED

Painting a flush door
75-mm- (3-in-) wide paint brush
25-mm- (1-in-) wide paint brush

Painting a panelled door
Cutting-in brush
75-mm- (3-in-) wide paint brush
25-mm- (1-in-) wide paint brush

MATERIALS

Painting a flush door
Paint **or** varnish
Preservative stain (if required)
Paint brush cleaner (if using solvent-based products)

Painting a panelled door
See above

SEE ALSO

Washing down and preparing surfaces pp.30–31
Stripping paint from wood trim pp.32–33
Replacing a window pane pp.64–65
Making repairs to doors pp.76–77
Repairing door frames pp.78–79
Changing the way a door hangs pp.86–87

Doors were traditionally painted white, but now there is a huge range of colours to choose from.

W hen painting or varnishing a door, choose an appropriate finish. Inside, try a low-odour, quick-drying water-based paint. Outside, use a weather-resistant paint: either a three-coat system (primer, undercoat and top coat) or a "micro-porous" paint, which may also act as a primer.

With hardwood or pine doors, you can allow the beauty of the wood to show through. Use ordinary varnish for interior doors. Exterior doors need a durable yacht varnish; a preservative stain is also a good choice.

Before you start, remove the door hardware, such as handles, and make any necessary repairs. With a new door, sand down all its surfaces; with an existing door, remove all loose and flaky paint. If necessary, strip the old paint off the door. Paint or varnish a new glazed interior door before it is glazed with beads; glaze a new exterior door (allow a week for the putty to dry) before it is painted.

PAINTING A FLUSH DOOR

1 To ensure that the paint "edge" never dries out (this will leave a line that is difficult to remove), paint the door in blocks. Start in the top left hand corner. Apply the paint horizontally until the brush is empty. Continue painting horizontally until the first block is filled.

2 To "lay off" the horizontal strokes in this first block, lightly load the brush with paint and, starting at the top, brush down in vertical strokes until the block is complete. Now quickly move on to block two – alongside the first block.

3 Start block three, picking up the bottom edge of block one. Use short vertical strokes to pick up the edge, then turn the brush around to create horizontal strokes to fill up the block. Lay off this block with vertical strokes as before. Continue painting each block in this manner until the door is painted.

4 Paint the opening edge of the door. Using a narrower brush, start at the top and paint to the bottom of the door. Paint the top and bottom edges of an exterior door. For an interior door, if the top of the door can be seen from the stairs, paint that edge. Finish off by painting the frame, working from the top down.

PAINTING A PANELLED DOOR

1 If the door is glazed, start at the top, and use a cutting-in brush to paint the glazing bars. Do not overload the brush with paint and avoid getting more than a thin band of paint on the glass (see pp.66–67).

2 Move to the topmost panel, and paint the mouldings that surround the panel before painting the panel itself. Repeat on the other panels of the door, working from top to bottom.

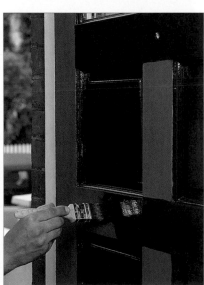

3 When all the panels are complete, paint the horizontal cross rails, starting at the top. Work down the door, painting each cross rail in turn.

4 Paint the vertical stiles on each side of the door (and in the centre, if there is one), from top to bottom. Paint the opening edge of the door, as well as the top and bottom edges if it is an exterior door or the top edge if it can be viewed from stairs above. Finally, paint the door frame: start at the top and work your way down.

A NEW DOOR: MEASURING UP AND FITTING HINGES

YOU WILL NEED

Tape measure
Square
Circular saw **or** panel saw
Block plane
Clamps (if required)
Power plane **or** bench plane
Utility knife
Chisel and mallet
Power drill plus twist bits
Marking gauge (if required)
Screwdriver

MATERIALS

Hinges (unless old ones are re-used)
New door
6 mm (¼ in) wood wedges
Screws

SEE ALSO

Repairing door frames pp.78–79
Painting doors pp.80–81
A new door: hanging it and fitting handles pp.84–85
Changing the way a door hangs pp.86–87

You might want to replace a door because the old one is damaged, or simply because you want one that is more attractive, durable or in keeping with the style of the house. Whatever your reason, new wood doors come without any hinge recesses or holes for locks, latches or door handles – you'll have to create them yourself, and make holes for the striker plates of locks and latches in a new door frame.

On these two pages are the first two stages of fitting a new door: measuring up and cutting recesses for the hinges. On the following two pages are details on how to hang the door and fit the latch. Before you start, make sure the door frame is secure and the hinge side of the frame is vertical.

MEASURING UP

Determine if your existing door is an imperial or metric size (see pp.72–75). If you're replacing a door in an old house, it could be a nonstandard size; you may have to find a second-hand door from an architectural salvage yard (which will have recesses and lock holes, but not necessarily in the correct places) or order a door to be made to your dimensions.

Measure the existing door frame (not the door); remember that you can trim most panel doors down to size. Allow for a gap of 3 mm (⅛ in) at the top and sides of the door for clearance, and 6 mm (¼ in) at the bottom.

Because the frame may not be square, check the size in at least two places for the height and at least three places for the width. Double-check the thickness, too. An exterior door must be the correct thickness to fit the rebate; with an interior door, you can move the door stop if necessary. Allow the door, unwrapped, to acclimatize for a few days before hanging it.

An interior door needs two 75 mm (3 in) hinges; an exterior door requires three 100 mm (4 in) ones.

1 Hold the door against the frame, supported on wedges (see p.67), and mark where it is larger than the frame, allowing for the correct clearance (see above). To reduce a panel door in height, divide the excess between the top and bottom, and use a panel saw or a circular saw fitted with a rip guide to cut the ends at the marks.

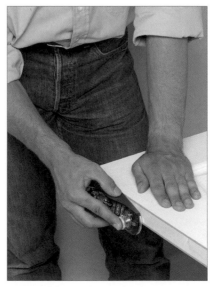

2 Each end of the door will be rough, so use a block plane to smooth the surfaces. To avoid chipping the ends, start from each edge and work to the centre. Alternatively, you can clamp a piece of scrap wood flush with the edge of the door – it will take the damage instead of the door.

3 To reduce a panel door in width, use a power plane or bench plane, working along the whole length and following your marked lines; take equal amounts off each side and ensure that the hinge side, in particular, is straight. A slight bevel on the non-hinge side will help the door close more easily.

4 Lay the door on its opening edge and clamp it in place. Mark the position of the hinges on the door (see box, below). Place a hinge at its mark; align the centre of the pin with the edge of the door. Score around the hinge with a utility knife, then score the depth of the hinge on the face of the door. Repeat the process for any other hinges.

5 Tap the chisel blade along the marked lines, bevel facing in; then chop out the wood with a series of short strokes, using a mallet. Take care not to go beyond your marked lines. Clean up the bottom of the recess, using the chisel held horizontally and bevel facing downward.

6 Check the fit of the hinge in the recess; the inner surface of the hinge should be exactly flat with the surrounding door edge and the centre line of the knuckle of the hinge should precisely line up with the edge of the door. If necessary, deepen the recess, using the chisel, bevel facing upward.

7 After making sure the hinges fit, make pilot holes for the screws and fit the hinges to the door, using just one screw per hinge.

Helpful hints

If the door frame already has hinge beds and you're re-using old hinges or the new ones fit, hold the door in place on the wedges and transfer the positions of the hinges on the frame to the door. If new hinges don't fit, fill in the recesses and make new ones (see pp.86–87). If you have a new frame, the hinges should be about 175 mm (7 in) from the top and 250 mm (10 in) from the bottom, with the third hinge for exterior doors centred between the other two.

If you have a marking gauge, it will be the most accurate tool to measure the depth of a hinge for the recess.

A NEW DOOR: HANGING IT AND FITTING HANDLES

With the door measured and trimmed and the hinges fitted on a new door (see pp.82–83), you can hang the door. Prop it up on wedges, with the hinges by their final positions, then slide it into place so that the hinges are in their recesses. With your helper steadying the door, insert one screw into each hinge in the frame, driving it home. Check that the door swings properly, without binding, and closes properly. Remove the door and reshape the hinge recesses if necessary; insert the remaining screws when it operates smoothly. You may need to refit or replace the door stop.

FITTING A DOOR LATCH

On interior doors, all you need is a simple spring latch operated by a handle on each side of the door, with a "striker plate" in the door frame. On exterior doors, you'll need a secure cylinder rim lock (see pp.94–95) or mortise lock (see pp. 96–97), or both.

Choose a door to match the style of the room that it will be most prominent in – don't forget that the style of the handles will be just as important.

1 Measure and mark the height of the handle on the edge of the door at a "lock block", or half way up the door. Use a spade bit the same diameter as the latch body, and put masking tape on its shaft to indicate the length of the latch body. Bore out the hole, keeping the bit vertical.

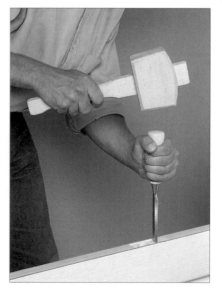

2 Insert the latch body into the hole, position the face plate parallel with the edges of the door and score around it with a utility knife; remove the latch body. Cut along the scored lines with a chisel, bevel face in, and mallet before chopping out a recess to the depth of the face plate (see step 5, p.83).

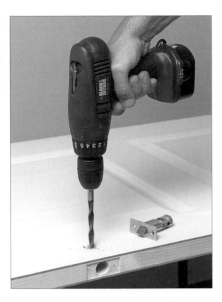

3 Place the latch body on the face of the door, with its face plate flush with the edge of the door. Use a pencil to mark the position of the spindle hole through the latch body. Repeat on the other side of the door. Using a drill bit the same diameter as the spindle, bore out the hole from both sides. Test fit the latch and spindle.

4 It may be necessary to reduce the length of the latch spindle on a thin door. After inserting the spindle in the hole and fitting on the handles, mark the amount to be cut off the spindle. Clamp the spindle in a vice or workbench, then use a hacksaw to cut it to the correct length.

5 Fit the latch body into the edge of the door and screw it in place. Insert the spindle and slip on the handle – make sure it's facing the correct way. Position the sides of the handle's face plate parallel with the door's edge. Drill pilot holes and screw the face plate to the door.

6 Turn the door over and slip the other handle over the exposed spindle. Position the face plate of the handle as in step 5, drill pilot holes and screw the face plate to the door. You can now hang the door (see main text).

7 Mark the top and bottom of the latch bolt on the door frame. Centre the striker plate at these marks, and score around it with a utility knife. Cut a recess for the plate with a chisel and mallet; use the chisel to pare the last layer. Fit the plate in the recess; mark and bore the hole for the bolt. Refit and screw the plate in place.

8 Close the door and mark the position of the door on the frame near the striker plate. Cut the door stop to length, position it against the mark and nail it in place at the plate. Use a spirit level to check it is vertical, then nail the remainder of the stop to the frame. Repeat on the other side, then nail on the horizontal piece.

CHANGING THE WAY A DOOR HANGS

A door is often hinged to swing away from the window so that when you open it you see a blank wall; but you may prefer it the other way around to show a different view of the room as the door is opened. You might also want to have the door opening outward rather than inward to create more useful space within a room. This means there are three ways you can change the way in which a door is hinged: left to right (or vice versa); in to out (or vice versa); in to out and left to right (or vice versa).

You'll have to refit the striker plate into which the door latch goes and make new hinge recesses in the door frame and door and fill in the old ones (you can re-use the old hinges unless they are "handed" such as rising butt hinges). When changing from in to out (or vice versa), you'll have to move the door stop against which the door closes. The other tasks you might have to do are refitting the door handles

and moving the light switch. When changing the side on which a door is hinged, you can avoid doing some of these by reversing the door; however, the door may have warped and might not fit, and it may need painting. The instructions here are for changing a swing from in to out. To fill recesses when changing from left to right (or vice versa), see page 88.

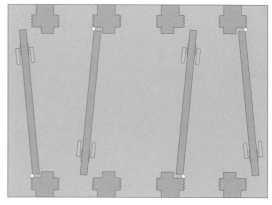

SITING YOUR HINGES
There are four positions in which a door may be hung, depending on whether you want it to swing into or out of the room and to the left or right. Most hinges can be used in any position. However, rising butt hinges are "handed", either right or left; their positions are designated by their hand.

1 To remove the door, wedge it open at the bottom (see p.76); remove all the screws from the bottom hinge and all but one from the top hinge. With a helper holding the door, remove the last screw; gently prise the hinges out of the recesses in the frame. (Fill the recesses if you move the hinges to the other side of the frame).

2 Stand the door on its opening edge and secure it in place. With a utility knife and metal straightedge, score across the door edge at the hinge recesses, then score a line along the front face to the depth of the recess. Use a tenon saw to cut along the scored lines across the edge, cutting to the line that indicates the depth.

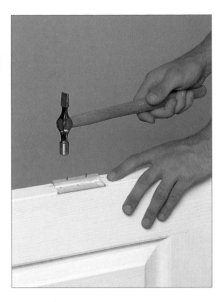

3 Chisel out the area of the new recess, bevel facing up. Fit the hinge in and mark its position. Remove the hinge and cut a piece of wood to fill the leftover recess. Glue and insert the wood into the recess; secure it with panel pins, driving them in with a nail punch. Let the adhesive dry, then plane the wood level and fit the hinges.

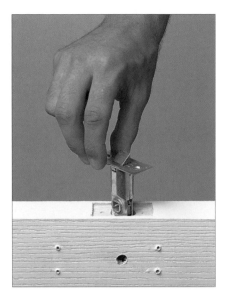

4 Rotate the door latch so its bevel will go into the striker plate. Secure the door with the latch end facing up. Remove the door handles. Unscrew the face plate of the latch, lift the latch out of its hole and turn it 180°. Push it back in the hole and screw in the face plate; drill new pilot holes if needed. Re-fit the door handles.

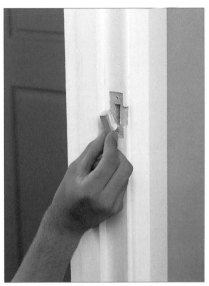

5 Remove the brass striker plate from the frame and cut a piece of wood to fit into the hole in the recess. Glue it in place and let the adhesive dry before filling the rest of the recess with wood filler. If the block of wood is proud of the surface, level it with a chisel or block plane.

6 Position the hinge side of the door vertical and at right angles to the door frame, raised on the wedges. Mark the position of the hinges on the frame. Score along these lines with a utility knife and cut out the recess with a chisel and mallet (see step 5, p.83), finishing by paring the last layer with the chisel.

7 After hanging the door (see p.84), close it and mark the position of the latch on the face of the frame. Centre the striker plate at these marks; score around it with a utility knife. Drill two holes for the latch bolt; use a chisel to finish the hole for the bolt. Cut a recess for the striker plate (see step 7, p.85), and screw it in place.

8 To reposition the door stop to ensure the door closes tightly, lever the stop away with a chisel (it may snap and need replacing). Close the door; mark the new position of the door stop on the door frame at the striker plate. Use this mark to nail the door stop back to the frame (see step 8, p.85); nail on the other pieces.

CHANGING A HINGED DOOR TO A SLIDING DOOR

YOU WILL NEED

Utility knife
Old chisel
Tape measure
Tenon saw
Pin hammer
Nail punch
Block plane
Small paint brush
Filler knife
Panel saw
Hammer
Screwdriver
Spirit level
Power drill plus twist bits

MATERIALS

Pieces of softwood
PVA adhesive
Wood primer
Plaster filler
50 mm (2 in) oval nails
75 mm (3 in) softwood
Sliding door kit
6 mm (¼ in) wood wedges
Softwood and hardwood **or** plywood (for pelmet if not supplied with kit)
Door handles

SEE ALSO

Patching holes in walls pp.22–23
Changing the way a door hangs pp.86–87

If there is room on the wall to one side of the door, converting a hinged door to one that slides can save space in the room into which the door opens.

the hinge recesses, latch recess and door handle holes; see pp.86–87), and it may be better to buy a slightly wider lightweight door so that it completely covers the door opening.

MOVING LIGHT SWITCHES

If the light switch is outside the room and the new sliding door will cover it when it's opened, the switch will have to be moved to the inside of the room or to the other side of the door. Moving the switch to the inside of the room is simple for an electrician to do if the switch is to be on a matching position on the other side of the wall; moving it to the other side of the door involves additional re-wiring.

With either method, you have the choice of filling the hole taken up by the old light switch box or simply fitting a blank cover plate over it.

You can use the existing door, but there will be a lot of work to do on it similar to that involved in changing the way a door hangs (filling

1 After removing the door from the frame (see p.86), score along the seams of the architrave and door stops with a utility knife to break the film of paint. Remove the door stop, levering it away from the frame with an old chisel; then remove the architrave, prising it off the frame with the chisel.

2 Cut pieces of wood the same size as the hinge recesses. Glue and nail them in place with panel pins, knocking the heads down with a nail punch. Once the adhesive has dried, plane the wood level with the frame and brush on a coat of wood primer.

3 Fill any gaps between the wall and the door casing with plaster and allow it to dry. Fit lengths of 75 mm (3 in) wood, the same thickness as the skirting board, to each side of the door frame, using oval nails; then fit another piece, the length of the track, across the top of the frame.

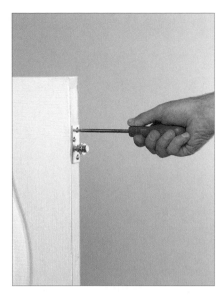

4 Secure the door on its side and position the door hangers onto the top of the door at either side, following the manufacturer's instructions; screw them in place. Hold the door against the door frame, raised 6 mm (¼ in) on wood wedges, to determine and mark the position of the track.

5 Screw the left-hand side of the track onto the top of the frame. Place a spirit level on top of the track to level it, then mark the position of the screw holes, drill pilot holes and screw it in place. Slot on the sliding piece of the track.

6 Hang the door on the track, engaging one end, then the other. Tighten the nuts at the top of the bolts to secure the door to the sliding section and level it. Then fix the door stop and door guide to the floor, following the instructions from the manufacturer.

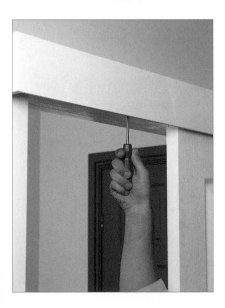

7 If a pelmet is not provided with the kit, you can make your own from softwood and hardboard or plywood. To position the pelmet, rest it on the track, then drill holes through the track – from the top or bottom – into the pelmet, and screw it in place.

8 Fit a handle on each face of the door. You can use surface-mounted handles, which are screwed through the door. Decide on their position, and drill the holes for the screws before fixing them. On a flush door, you can create blind holes in the door, using a hole saw in a power drill, then fit in recessed pulls.

FITTING A BI-FOLD WARDROBE DOOR

YOU WILL NEED

Tape measure
Hacksaw
Power drill plus twist and
flat bits
Clamp
Screwdriver
Plane (if required)

MATERIALS

Bi-fold door kit
Back-flap hinges (if not
supplied in a kit)
Door knobs

SEE ALSO

Giving storage units a
facelift pp.238–239
Making good use of
cupboard space pp.244–245

A bi-fold door consists of two narrow doors hinged together. You can buy them ready-made or make them yourself from two louvre doors.

Bi-fold doors project only a small distance into the room when open. They can be used singly or in pairs and are popular for fitted wardrobes, but you can also use them in large doorways (where double doors are normally fitted) and on free-standing wardrobes. Most bi-fold doors have a top track along which the top edge of the door slides; others are hinged at the side to the door frame. Allow 3 mm (⅛ in) clearance at each side and between the doors.

Adequate ventilation can be a problem in insulated houses; without it the result is condensation, which can lead to mould. This can be a problem in wardrobes (particularly built-in ones on an exterior wall). Bi-fold louvre doors will allow air to flow and reduce the condensation.

Multi-fold, or "concertina" doors have several sections and are fitted with a top track; they normally come in pairs. The doors are screwed to the sides of the door frame, and they need little space in the doorway or in the room when they are open.

1 Measure the width at the top of the wardrobe and cut a length of track to this size, using a hacksaw. If this involves cutting off one of the pre-drilled securing holes, you'll have to drill a hole at the cut end. Clamp the cut length securely, measure and mark the position of the new hole, then drill it out using a twist drill bit.

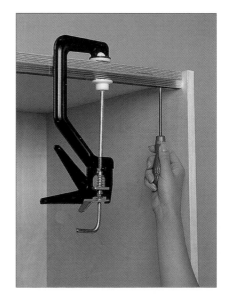

2 Clamp the track onto the under edge at the top of the wardrobe. Using the holes in the track as a guide, drill holes into the underside. Screw the track into place, then screw the receiving catch into the left hand side of the track. Check the fit of the doors – they may need trimming with a plane so they fit (see pp.76–77).

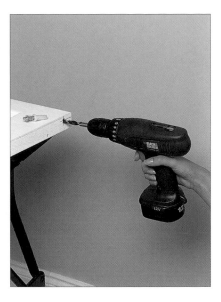

3 Mark the position of the pivot on the top, lefthand side of the door, following the manufacturer's instructions. Using a drill bit the same diameter as the pivot, bore into the end of the door to the depth of the fitting. Push the pivot into the hole, leaving its top exposed. Fit the bottom pivot in the same way.

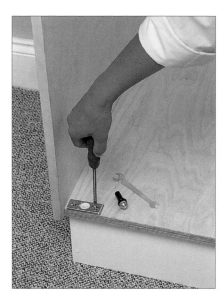

4 Screw the pivot plate into position at the bottom, lefthand corner of the wardrobe. After the doors have been hung, you can align them vertically and horizontally by using a spanner (provided with the kit) to adjust the bottom pivot and the retaining screws in the pivot plate.

5 Follow the instructions to mark the position of the guide on the top, righthand side of the door. Using a flat bit, bore out a hole the same diameter as the guide fitting, insert it into the hole and push it in, leaving the guide exposed.

6 The hinges are screwed onto the backs of the doors. Lay them down next to one another, with a 3 mm (⅛ in) gap in between. Place the three hinges equally spaced along the doors, mark the position of the screw holes and drill them out. Reposition each hinge and screw them into place.

7 To fit the doors, fold them and insert the bottom pivot into the receiving plate at the bottom of the wardrobe. Once in position, place the top pivot and guide in the top track and push the top of the door against the side of the wardrobe until the top pivot clips into the receiving catch in the track.

8 The door handle, fitted before the doors are hung (see pp.238–239), should be positioned in the middle of the righthand door – this allows the door to fold and slide along in one movement when the door handle is pulled.

FITTING SLIDING WARDROBE DOORS

YOU WILL NEED

Tape measure
Combination square
Screwdriver
Hacksaw
Metal file
Power drill plus twist bits
Hammer
Nail punch
Flexible filler knife

MATERIALS

Sliding wardrobe door kit
Oval nails
Wood fillet (if required)
100 mm x 50 mm (4 in x
2 in) wood studs (if required)
Plywood, chipboard **or**
plasterboard (if required)
Wallplugs (if required)
Wood filler

SEE ALSO

Building a partition wall
pp.170–171

In confined areas with no room for a wardrobe door to swing open, a sliding door is the answer.

You can fit sliding doors on a wardrobe, or create your own built-in wardrobe by fitting sliding doors in a frame stretching the length of a wall. The doors themselves can be normal flush doors or louvre doors –

they are fitted in the same way. A sliding door kit contains all the fittings you'll need, but you may have to create the correct opening width by fitting an end panel or spacer against one wall (see pp.234–235) or by reducing the opening height. If the size of your door kit is within 150 mm (6 in) of the distance between the two walls, reduce the width by adding a wood "fillet" on one or both sides. Screw it to the wall using wallplugs.

For a larger gap, create a side panel by using 100 mm × 50 mm (4 in × 2 in) studs to create a frame, adding a horizontal support in the middle, and covering it with plywood, chipboard or plasterboard. Secure the frame to the wall, floor and ceiling. Use the same methods for reducing the height. Where you want to stop short of a door or window, construct an end panel at right angles to the back wall.

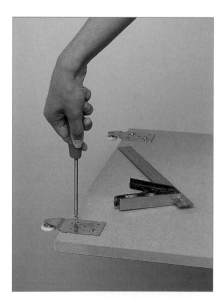

1 Use an adjustable square to position the roller plates equidistant from each side of the door. Mark the centre point of the two diagonal slots on each roller plate, drill out these marks and screw the roller plates in place.

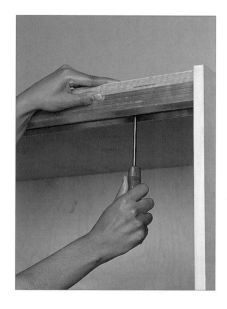

2 Measure the dimension of the wardrobe opening and cut a length of roller track to this size, using a hacksaw, then file it. If screwing it onto the underside of the wardrobe, hold the front flush with the top edge of the wardrobe. (On ceilings, make sure you screw through the plasterboard into solid wood.)

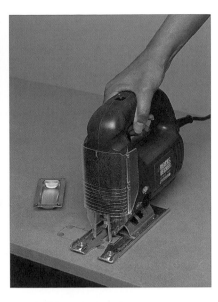

3 Measure and mark out an oblong hole for the handle. Drill a 10 mm (³⁄₈ in) hole into each corner, then insert a jigsaw into one of the holes and carefully cut out the shape. You can insert the handle after the door has been painted.

4 Hang the first door by hooking it onto the back runner track. In the same way hook the other door onto the front runner track. The doors can be aligned vertically and horizontally. Loosen the screws in the diagonal slots of each roller plate, reposition the doors and mark the new position of the plates on the doors.

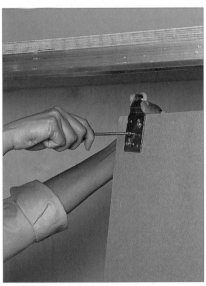

5 Take the doors down and use the new marks to reposition the plates. Screw down the diagonal slot screws, drill out the remaining holes and screw the roller plates down before rehanging the doors. Mark the position of the bottom of each door on the side of the wardrobe, then, once again, take the doors off.

6 Transfer the marks to the centre of the bottom of the wardrobe – they are for fitting the door guides in place. Follow your instructions; in general, screw the back guide down first, rehang the back door and screw down the next guide. Slot the third guide in place, rehang the second door and screw down the last guide.

7 Screw the door stop onto the bottom, lefthand side of the wardrobe. (On solid concrete floors, use wallplugs to fit the stop and door guides.)

8 Finally, fit the removable fascias to the top and bottom of the wardrobe. Use a nail punch to bang the nailheads below the surface of the fascia, then cover them with wood filler.

FITTING A CYLINDER RIM LOCK

YOU WILL NEED

Tape measure
Pencil
Combination square
Bradawl
Power drill plus twist and spade bits
Hacksaw
Mole wrench
Screwdriver
Utility knife
Wood chisel
Mallet

MATERIALS

Cylinder rim lock

SEE ALSO

Fitting a mortise lock pp.96–97
Other door hardware pp.98–99

The security provided by a rim lock can vary from a simple surface-mounted "night latch" to a cylinder rim lock that passes through the door and, if it is deadlocking, it can be as effective as a good mortise lock. The security of a rim lock is described by the number of "tumblers" it has – five is the minimum for a secure lock. Rim locks all have a "snib", which you can use to put the door on the latch when you want to walk in and out.

The effectiveness of an ordinary rim lock depends on how well it is secured to the door and, particularly, to the door frame. The lock and its keeper sit on the surface, held in place only by their screws. For extra security, use longer screws than the ones supplied, but of the same diameter.

One size of cylinder rim lock fits all the door sizes, but the lock will be "handed" – that is, suitable for left-hand or right-hand hinged doors. A deadlocking cylinder rim lock has a

Unlike an ordinary rim lock, a cylinder rim lock has a key-operated cylinder that passes through the door, making it more secure.

lock bolt that can be operated only with a key. Before installing any type of lock, make sure the door and door frame are secure (see p.96); otherwise, the door can simply be kicked in.

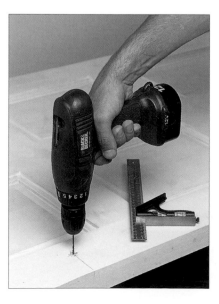

1 Measure and mark both sides of the door one-third of the way from the top. If the lock comes with a template, use it to mark the centre point of the hole for the cylinder. Or follow the manufacturer's instructions to find the centre point, using a combination square. Drill a pilot hole through the door at the centre point.

2 Bore into the pilot hole, using a spade bit the same diameter as the cylinder; however, to prevent damage to the surface of the door, drill only until the point just appears at the opposite side. Turn the work over and finish drilling the hole.

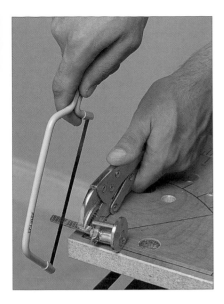

3 From the front of the door put the cylinder and the finger pull or retaining ring into the hole; hold the lock mounting plate in position. The cylinder connecting bar should project 12 mm (½ in) beyond the mounting plate. Mark the amount to be cut off; holding the bar firmly with the Mole wrench, cut it to the required length with a hacksaw.

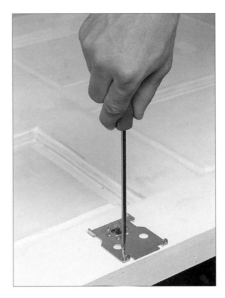

4 Reinsert the cylinder, with the retaining ring or finger pull, place the lock mounting plate over the connecting bar and use long screws to secure the plate to the cylinder. As you tighten the screws, adjust the plate so its front edge is flush with the door's edge. Drill pilot holes for the smaller screws and drive them in place.

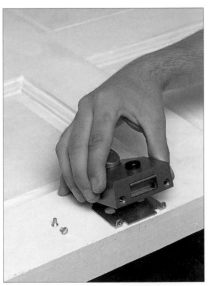

5 Push the button on the lock case to bring the latch to the unlocked position; then position it on the mounting plate, lining up the connecting bar with the slot on the back of the lock case. Slide it in place, and use the small screws to attach the lock case to the mounting plate.

6 Using the button to move the latch to its locked position, close the door toward the door frame and mark the position of the top and bottom of the latch on the frame. Place the striker plate on these pencil marks and score around its flange with a utility knife.

7 Cut along the scored lines with a chisel and mallet, holding the chisel at a right angle to the surface, with its bevel side facing in. Make cuts inside this area, then remove wood to the depth of the flange on the striker plate. To finish, use a chisel, bevel side down, to pare out the remaining wood in the recess.

8 Fit the striker plate in the recess and close the door to ensure that it receives the bolt of the lock when in the closed position – if necessary, pare out more of the recess. When the lock works efficiently, drill pilot holes for the striker plate and screw it into the recess.

FITTING A MORTISE LOCK

YOU WILL NEED

Tape measure
Try square
Pencil
Metal straightedge
Utility knife
Brace and bit **or** power drill plus twist and spade bits
Mortise **or** firmer chisel
Mallet
Wood chisel
Combination square
Padsaw
Bradawl
Screwdriver

MATERIALS

Mortise lock
Masking tape
Medium-grade abrasive paper
Packing material such as cardboard (if required)
Wood filler (if required)

SEE ALSO

Types of exterior door pp.74–75
Fitting a cylinder rim lock pp.94–95
Other door hardware pp.98–99

On a front door, a mortise lock is normally fitted in addition to a rim lock. This requires making a slot – or mortise – in the door to take the lock's body. A similar operation has to be carried out on the door frame to take the striker plate into which the lock bolt shoots. The security provided by a mortise lock is determined by the number of "levers" the lock contains; a seven-lever lock is the most secure, but five-lever locks are adequate.

Because mortise locks come in different sizes, measure the width of the door stile before you go shopping. There is no point in fitting a mortise lock to a weak door. The door itself must be at least 44 mm (1¾ in) thick and mounted in a secure frame.

Decide where you want the lock to be. If it's fitted with a rim lock, place it one-third of the way up the door; if a mortise sash lock is being fitted to a back or side door, fit it at a convenient handle height. If you positioned the

A mortise lock, which fits into the body of the door, is the best way to make a front door secure.

striker plate incorrectly, you can extend its recess and use packing pieces, such as cardboard, inside the hole to compensate. Use wood filler to make good any oversized recesses.

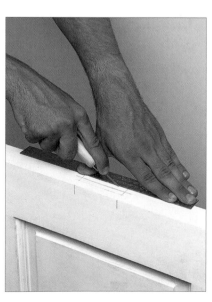

1 Hold the lock to the door and mark the position of its body on the door. Square lines across the edge of the door with a try square. Between these two lines draw a line down the centre of the door; mark out half the thickness of the lock body on each side of the centre line. Score along these two lines and the top and bottom lines.

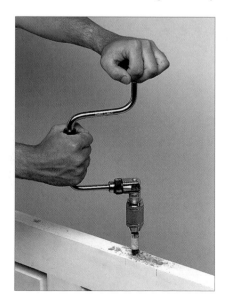

2 Using a brace fitted with a bit that fits between the marked lines (or a power drill and spade bit), start at one end and bore along the centre line within the scored rectangle to the depth of the lock's body – do not overlap the holes. Use a piece of tape on the bit as a gauge to indicate the depth of the hole.

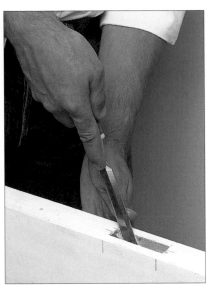

3 Make a vertical cut at each end of the rectangle with a mortise chisel – bevel side in – using a mallet. Then go along each side, carefully paring down vertically. Lever out the waste wood from the slot, and continue until the body of the lock fits snugly in place.

4 Put the lock in place, with its bolt in the locked position so it can be pulled out. Place the face plate on top and score around it with a utility knife. Remove the lock; make vertical cuts with the chisel along the scored lines. Remove enough wood to make a recess the thickness of the face of the lock's body and the face plate.

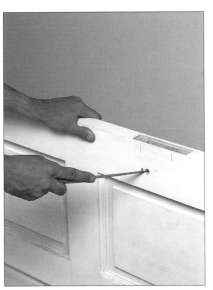

5 Measure and mark the position of the keyhole slot on either side of the door, using a combination square. Score along these lines with a utility knife. Drill a hole at each end of the slot, from both sides of the door (the top hole is bigger than the bottom hole). Use a padsaw to cut along the scored lines between the holes.

6 Sand smooth the area inside the keyhole with abrasive paper wrapped around the blade of a screwdriver. Drop the lock body into the slot, pushing it down. Ensure that the key operates smoothly from either side – if necessary, widen the keyhole before screwing the lock into the recess. Screw on the face plate.

7 With the bolt locked, close the door and mark the position of the bolt on the side of the door frame. Centre the striker plate at these marks, then mark the position of the striker box on the frame; score along these lines with a utility knife. With a brace and bit, drill to the depth of the box, then a chisel to cut out the wood.

8 Insert the box into the slot and score around its face plate with a utility knife. After cutting along the scored lines with a chisel and mallet, pare away the wood in the recess to the depth of the plate. Replace the striker box and plate, and check that the lock operates properly before screwing it in place. Fit escutcheons over the key hole.

OTHER DOOR HARDWARE

YOU WILL NEED

Fitting a letter box
Tape measure
Straightedge and pencil
Power drill plus twist bits
Jigsaw
Hacksaw (if required)
Screwdriver

Fitting a door viewer
Pencil
Power drill plus twist bits
Screwdriver

Fitting a mortise rack bolt
Pencil
Power drill plus twist bits
Utility knife
Chisel and mallet
Screwdriver

Fitting a door chain
Pencil
Screwdriver

MATERIALS

Door hardware (depending on your preference)

SEE ALSO

Painting doors pp.80–81
A new door pp.82–85
Fitting a cylinder rim lock pp.94–95
Fitting a mortise lock pp.96–97

You can fit your front door with a door chain, door viewer and letter box, or any combination of a variety of other hardware.

A mortise lock and cylinder rim lock on their own (or together) may keep the door locked, but they may not be sufficient for your safety. There are other devices you can fit on a front door where you may have unknown visitors. These include a door viewer, which allows you to see who is outside before opening the door, and a door chain (or door limiter), which allows you to open the door partially to check the credentials of the person, such as a meter reader, before you open the door completely. You may also want to fit a letter box.

Back doors and side doors can be fitted with additional door locks, such as a mortise rack bolt, that operate from inside – but these will only be effective on the front door at night or when you are in the house.

It is important that any locks you fit to your doors are not accessible from the outside. Large letter boxes (and cat flaps) may allow access to the main door lock – never hang a spare key near them on the inside. Any glazed doors, particularly French windows, are insecure if access to the locks is possible by breaking the glass.

FITTING A LETTER BOX

1 Lay the door on a work surface (remove it from the door frame if needed). Measure and mark the opening of the letter plate on the door, centred from the sides. Drill a hole into each corner; insert the blade of a jigsaw into one hole, and cut along the lines to cut out the rectangle.

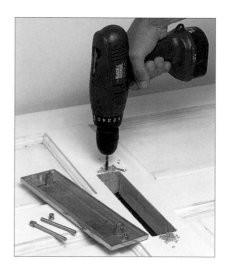

2 Check the length of the threaded rods against the door's thickness; to cut them, use a hacksaw. Mark and drill holes on each side of the opening. (Hang and paint the door if needed.) Hold the letter plate to its front, thread the rods in from the back, then add the nuts. Screw on the back plate.

FITTING A DOOR VIEWER

1 Mark the position of the peephole in the centre and at eye level on the door (unless there are steps to the door). After drilling a pilot hole, drill a hole from both sides of the door (see step 2, p.94) the same diameter as the outer sleeve of the peephole fitting. (Hang and paint a new door.)

2 Unscrew the two sections of the viewer and, from the outside, insert the lens through the hole in the door. From the inside, insert the viewing barrel and, holding the lens in place, screw the barrel part onto it. Finish off by tightening the viewer with a large screwdriver or coin.

FITTING A MORTISE RACK BOLT

1 At the centre of the door's edge, drill a hole the size of the bolt. Put the bolt in the hole; score around its face plate with a utility knife. Chisel a recess for the plate (see pp.96–97). Place the bolt on the door, aligning its face plate with the door's edge and the recess. Mark the keyhole's position.

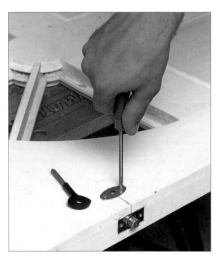

2 Drill out the hole for the key only as far as the bolt hole. (If the door is new, paint it before continuing.) Slip the bolt into the bolt hole and screw on its face plate, then attach the escutcheon plate at the keyhole by driving in screws. (Hang the door if it's not already fitted in the door frame.)

3 Close the door and operate the bolt, so it leaves a mark on the door frame. Drill a hole at the mark the same depth and diameter as the bolt. Centre the striker plate over the hole; score around it with a utility knife. Cut a recess for the plate (see step 7, p.95). Fit the plate into the recess and screw it in place.

FITTING A DOOR CHAIN

Position the chain bracket on the door frame; mark and drill screw holes. Screw the bracket in place. Insert the chain into the receiving plate, and position it on the door; mark and drill screw holes. Screw the receiving plate in place. Use the longest screws possible.

REPAIRING STAIRS AND BALUSTERS

The staircase and its accompanying balustrade is the most complex piece of carpentry in the house, and as time goes by it can develop a variety of faults, primarily caused by daily wear and tear. A step that creaks is one of the most common and annoying defects. The problem is caused by the joint between the tread (the part you step on) and the riser (the vertical part) working loose, with each part rubbing against the other as you walk up or down the flight.

The tread itself can be damaged, especially along the overhanging front edge, which is known as the nosing. This is often caused by careless movement of furniture, with heavy items being rested or dropped onto a tread as they are carried up or down the stairs. Lastly, the balustrade may be damaged and loosened by accidental impacts – a fault that needs immediate attention if the staircase is to remain safe to use.

ASSESSING THE DAMAGE

Inspect your staircase to get an idea of how it has been constructed and to assess its need for repair. The treads and risers are supported at each side of the flight by two parallel "stringers". In a closed-stringer staircase, the treads and risers fit into grooves cut into the faces of the stringers; an open-stringer staircase has the outer stringer cut in a zig-zag fashion so the outer ends of the treads can rest on the cutouts. The inner stringer against the wall is always a closed stringer. If you cannot access the underside of the stairs, remove any carpet and make the repairs from above.

Helpful hints

If you can get underneath the flight, to stop a squeak, check that the wedges holding the treads and risers into their grooves are driven home. Glue and drive in any that are loose and replace any missing ones. Glue and screw blocks of wood into the angles between treads and risers to stop them moving against each other.

FIXING A SQUEAKY STEP

1 If you cannot get underneath the flight, drill a clearance hole through the tread large enough for the shank of the screw, then drill a pilot hole slighter smaller than the screw into the top of the riser below. Countersink the top hole with a countersink bit, then drive a screw down into it.

2 You can use a store-bought wood plug to cover the screw head, or make one yourself – use a bit specifically designed to cut plugs. Dab some PVA adhesive onto the plug and tap it into place; then plane it flush with the tread. Alternatively, use wood filler to fill the hole.

FIXING A DAMAGED NOSING

1 Mark out the area to be removed, making sure the back edge is parallel with the nosing but does not reach the riser. Using a jigsaw, cut into the nosing and, to release the strip, along the back edge. Then use a tenon saw to make cuts at right angles to the back edge.

2 Cut a patch of replacement wood, with the grain running lengthwise, to fit the shape of the cut-out, then glue and screw it into place, countersinking the screws. Using a block plane or wood rasp, shape the patch to match the profile of the nosing.

SECURING A LOOSE BALUSTER

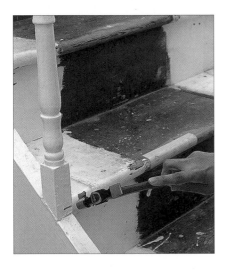

If a baluster is loose, you can tighten it by skew-nailing. Drive an oval nail into the stringer below or handrail above at a 45° angle. Use a nail punch to sink the nail below the surface. Cover the nail head with cellulose filler if the repair will be painted or wood filler if it will be varnished.

REPAIRING A SPLIT BALUSTER

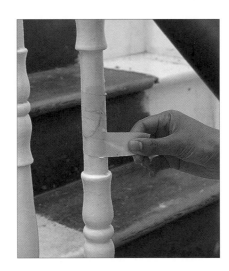

A strong impact is usually responsible for cracking a baluster. To repair it, open up the split and squirt in some woodworking adhesive. Then bind the split firmly by wrapping adhesive tape around it. Leave the tape in place for 24 hours until the glue has dried.

REPLACING A BALUSTER

1 Prise out the two broken sections. Using a sliding bevel, transfer the angles of the stringer and handrail to the new baluster. Finding one that matches can be difficult. If a mismatch will be noticeable, remove one from a less conspicuous area, but first make sure it will fit in the new site.

2 Trim the baluster along the marks with a tenon saw. Then work it carefully into place and skew-nail it to the stringer and handrail (see *Securing a loose baluster*).

DECORATING STAIRCASE WOODWORK

How you choose to decorate your staircase woodwork may depend on what decorative finish it has at present. The stairs in a relatively new house are usually finished with varnish, either clear or tinted, in keeping with recent appreciation for exposed woodwork in the home. Stairs in an older home will probably have been painted several times over the years.

You can revarnish wood that has already been varnished, perhaps in a darker shade, or paint over it. If the old finish is paint, it is usually easier to repaint the staircase – you must first strip off all the old paint if you want to varnish it. A staircase that has been covered with several layers of old paint may also require stripping before repainting. No matter the finish, the sequence will be similar.

Before painting or varnishing, inspect the balustrade to ensure that it is sound. Make sure you have good light to work in, especially if the

An ordinary balustrade is made more elegant by painting the balusters and varnishing the handrail.

stairwell normally has little light. The order of painting will depend on your staircase, but it is usually best to start at the top and work your way down.

1 If the stairs are carpeted, pull the material up, and make sure you remove any carpet tacks with a tack lifter. If you must strip off the old finish – either paint or varnish – follow the instructions from the manufacturer of the stripper for applying and neutralizing it.

2 Give the stairs a good clean to remove any loose debris. Now is the time to check for and make any repairs (see pp.100–101). As you inspect the work, fill in any small holes.

3 Key the wood by sanding it with fine-grade abrasive paper, giving it a surface to which the finish can adhere. Wipe away any sanded material with a tacky rag. Apply masking tape along wall surfaces where they meet the parts of the staircase that you plan to paint or varnish.

4 It is generally best to tackle the balustrade first. You should paint or varnish the underside of the handrail, working carefully between the individual balusters to avoid build-up of the finish, then finish the rest of the handrail. If you're using two different finishes, wait for the handrail to dry before moving on to the balusters.

5 Paint the outer stringer after the balusters. Work carefully along the stringer, painting the base rail and the fillets between the balusters first, then tackling the vertical surfaces. If the area below an open outer stringer is closed in, paint this part (which is called the spandrel) after finishing the outer face of the stringer.

6 Apply the paint to the closed stringer adjacent to the flanking wall. Instead of applying masking tape, you can use a small brush to paint near the wall if you're confident that you have a steady hand.

7 If the stairs will be covered by a runner carpet, paint the treads and risers where they will be exposed at either side of the runner and about 50 mm (2 in) beyond. Alternatively, paint the treads and risers completely if the stairs won't be carpeted. Remind the occupants that the paint is wet by placing a sign by the stairwell.

VARNISHING THE WOODWORK

To stain and varnish part of or all of the staircase, follow the steps for varnishing a floor (see pp.182–183): a coat or two of stain, then several coats of varnish. Follow the same sequence as for painting, starting with the balustrade and ending with the steps.

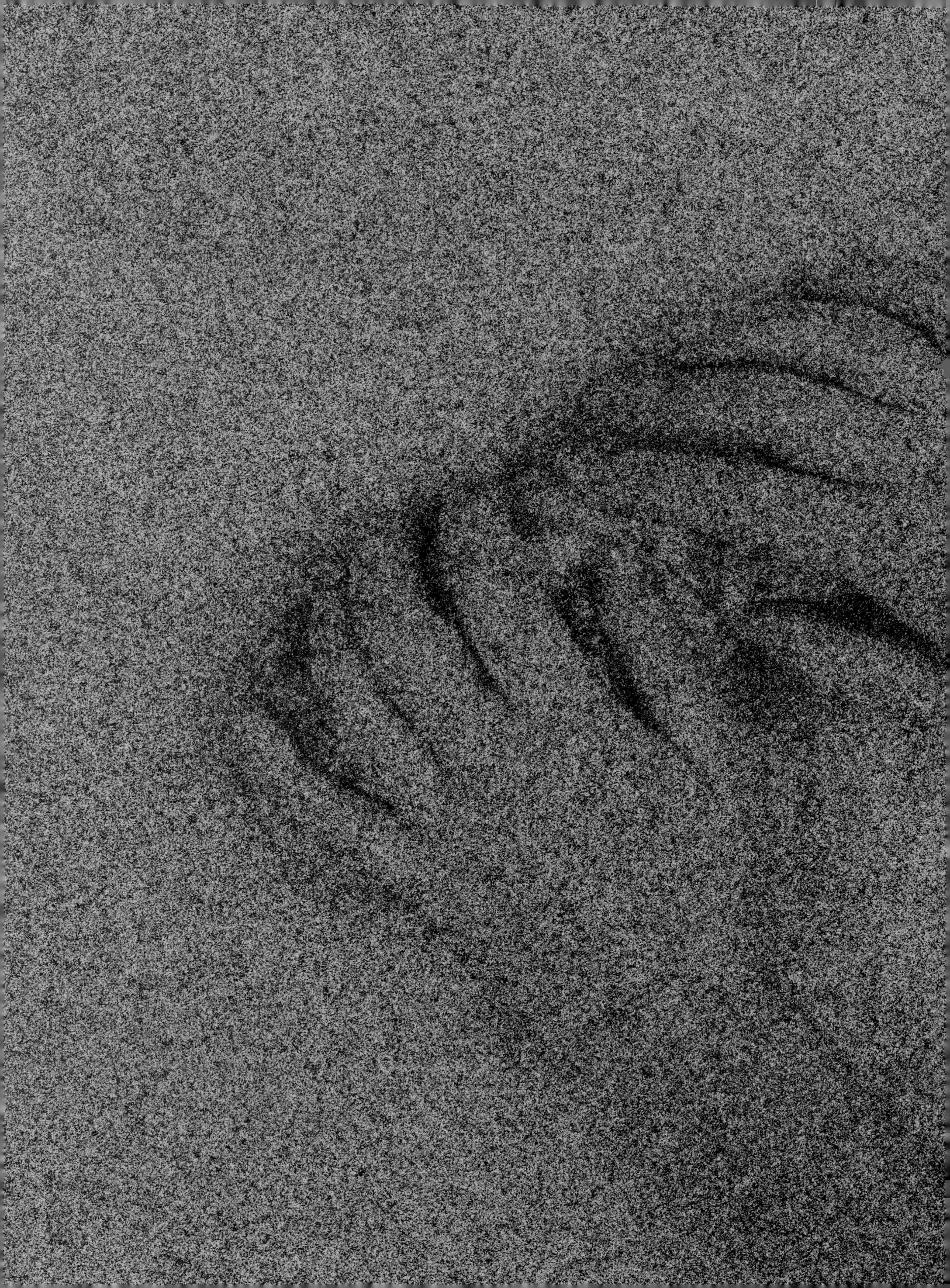

3

WALLS AND CEILINGS

WALLS AND CEILINGS DIRECTORY

INTERIOR DESIGN TRICKS

SKILL LEVEL Low
TIME FRAME ½ day
SPECIAL TOOLS Paint colour
cards, wallpaper and fabric
samples, paint test pots,
magazines for ideas
SEE PAGES 110–111

Before decorating, plan a
scheme of colour and patterns
for the room. It helps to have
an understanding of how
colour affects a room, creating
rooms that are warm and
welcoming or cool and
relaxing. Colour and pattern
can also change a room's
proportions, making high
ceilings seem lower or narrow
rooms wider.

PAINTING OPTIONS

SEE PAGES 112–113

If you choose paint as the
basic material for your colour
schemes, you can use it as a
plain colour on walls and
ceilings or create one of a
number of decorative paint
effects that can look eye-
catchingly different.

PAINTING BASICS

SKILL LEVEL Low
TIME FRAME Under 2 hours
SPECIAL TOOLS Paint kettle,
nylon fabric
SEE PAGES 114–115

How to determine the amount
of paint you'll need for a
room, and guidelines for the
order in which to apply paint
to the various surfaces in a
standard room, including the
wood trim. Also, instructions
for protecting unpainted
surfaces, ladder safety and
hints for preparing the paint.

USING PAINT BRUSHES

SKILL LEVEL Low
TIME FRAME ½ day per room
(depending on room size)
SPECIAL TOOLS Paint brushes
of various sizes, paint kettle
SEE PAGES 116–117

Paint brushes are often used
for painting walls and ceilings,
and they are the usual option
for painting panelled doors
and wood trim such as
architrave. Also included is
how to apply textured paints.

USING PAINT ROLLERS

SKILL LEVEL Low
TIME FRAME ½ day per room
(depending on room size)
SPECIAL TOOLS Paint roller,
sleeve, paint roller tray
SEE PAGES 118–119

Using a paint roller is a quick
way to apply paint to large
unobstructed areas, but it can
create messy paint splashes if
not used carefully.

USING PAINT PADS

SKILL LEVEL Low
TIME FRAME ½ day per room
(depending on room size)
SPECIAL TOOLS Large paint
pad, edging or small paint pad,
paint pad tray or paint roller tray
SEE PAGE 120

Paint pads are an alternative
to paint brushes and rollers
for applying paint.

USING A SPRAY GUN

SKILL LEVEL Low
TIME FRAME ½ day per room
(depending on room size)

SPECIAL TOOLS Airless spray
gun, strainer, safety glasses,
respirator
SEE PAGE 121
Spraying paint with a spray
gun can be considered in
rooms completely stripped of
furnishings and fittings.

PAINT EFFECTS: COLOURWASHING

SKILL LEVEL Low
TIME FRAME 1 day per room
SPECIAL TOOLS Paint kettle,
paint brush
SEE PAGE 122

A paint effect created by
applying a top coat with
random brush strokes onto a
base coat of a different colour.

PAINT EFFECTS: DRAGGING

SKILL LEVEL Low
TIME FRAME 1 day per room
SPECIAL TOOLS Paint kettle,
paint brush
SEE PAGE 123

Dragging a translucent coat of
paint over a lighter colour

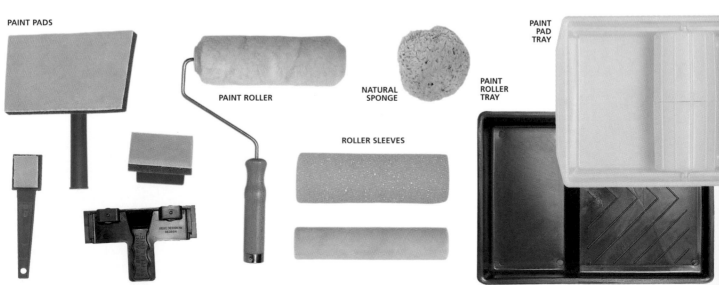

PAINT PADS

PAINT ROLLER

NATURAL
SPONGE

ROLLER SLEEVES

PAINT
ROLLER
TRAY

PAINT
PAD
TRAY

base coat creates a striped paint effect.

PAINT EFFECTS: SPONGING

SKILL LEVEL Low
TIME FRAME 1 day per room
SPECIAL TOOLS Paint kettle, paint tray, natural sponge
SEE PAGE 124

A broken effect is created by adding a top coat of glaze with a sponge, either dabbing it on or sponging it off.

PAINT EFFECTS: STIPPLING

SKILL LEVEL Low
TIME FRAME 1 day per room
SPECIAL TOOLS Paint kettle, paint brush, stippling brush or paint roller with mohair sleeve
SEE PAGE 125

Points of colour from the base coat appear through the top glaze, giving a speckled effect.

PAINT EFFECTS: RAGGING

SKILL LEVEL Low
TIME FRAME 1 day per room

SPECIAL TOOLS Paint kettle, paint brush, lint-free fabric
SEE PAGE 126

After brushing a top coat of glaze over a base coat, wads of fabric are randomly dabbed into the wet paint, creating areas of broken colour.

PAINT EFFECTS: RAG-ROLLING

SKILL LEVEL Low
TIME FRAME 1 day per room
SPECIAL TOOLS Paint kettle, paint brush, lint-free fabric
SEE PAGE 127

Similar to ragging (see above), but the fabric is crumpled into a cylinder shape and rolled.

PAINT EFFECTS: STENCILLING

SKILL LEVEL Low to medium
TIME FRAME 1 day per room
SPECIAL TOOLS Stencil, stencil brush, spirit level, palatte
SEE PAGES 128–129

A method for adding a patterned border to a room. Also included is how to use a stamp to make your own random pattern.

WALLCOVERING OPTIONS

SEE PAGES 130–131

If you prefer wallcoverings for your walls and ceilings, you have two main design elements to consider – pattern and texture – of which there is a huge variety. The covering may require pasting or it may be ready-pasted.

WALLPAPER BASICS

SKILL LEVEL Low
TIME FRAME Under 2 hours
SPECIAL TOOLS Dust cloth, wallpaper brush
SEE PAGES 132–133

Once you decide what type and design of wallcovering to use, you have to measure and estimate how many rolls you'll need for the job.

CUTTING, PASTING AND FOLDING WALLPAPER

SKILL LEVEL Low
TIME FRAME 5 minutes per length
SPECIAL TOOLS Paste table, paste bucket, paste brush
SEE PAGES 134–135

The secret to successful wallpapering lies in preparing each length correctly. After cutting a length slightly long, brush paste onto it, section by section, then fold it concertina fashion to transport it. Soak ready-pasted types in water.

HANGING AND TRIMMING WALLPAPER

SKILL LEVEL Low to medium
TIME FRAME 1 day
SPECIAL TOOLS Paperhanging brush, paperhanging scissors, seam roller
SEE PAGES 136–137

Basic techniques for hanging and trimming wallpaper for one wall, as well as details for hanging lining paper.

PAPERING AROUND CORNERS

SKILL LEVEL Low to medium
TIME FRAME 1 to 2 days
SPECIAL TOOLS Paperhanging brush, paperhanging scissors, seam roller
SEE PAGES 138–139

Additional details to help you tackle corners in rooms that are seldom perfectly square.

STAMP

PAINT BRUSHES

STIPPLING BRUSH

SPRAY GUN

SABLE PAINT BRUSH

PAINT EFFECT BRUSH

STENCIL

PAPERING AROUND DOORS AND WINDOWS

SKILL LEVEL Low to medium
TIME FRAME 1 to 2 days
SPECIAL TOOLS Paperhanging brush, paperhanging scissors, seam roller
SEE PAGES 140–141

How to paper around door and window openings to get the best results.

PAPERING AROUND OBSTACLES

SKILL LEVEL Low to medium
TIME FRAME Under 2 hours per obstacle
SPECIAL TOOLS Paperhanging brush, paperhanging scissors, seam roller
SEE PAGES 142–143

Papering around obstacles such as light switches, arches and fireplace mantles.

PAPERING A CEILING

SKILL LEVEL Low to medium
TIME FRAME ½ to 1 day

SPECIAL TOOLS Paperhanging brush, paperhanging scissors, seam roller
SEE PAGE 144–145

Once you have taken down any light fixtures, the only problem lies in handling long lengths of pasted wallpaper, and in obtaining suitable access equipment.

USING FRIEZES

SKILL LEVEL Low
TIME FRAME Under 2 hours to ½ day
SPECIAL TOOLS Pasting brush, spirit level, utility knife, metal straightedge, paperhanging brush, paperhanging scissors, seam roller
SEE PAGE 146

Friezes are wallpaper strips hung just below ceiling level or near picture or dado rails.

FRAMING WITH BORDERS

SKILL LEVEL Low
TIME FRAME 2 hours to ½ day
SPECIAL TOOLS Pasting brush, spirit level, metal straightedge, paperhanging brush, paperhanging scissors,

seam roller
SEE PAGE 147

Borders are narrower than friezes and are used to frame doors and windows or to make decorative panels on walls.

PUTTING UP COVING

SKILL LEVEL Low to medium
TIME FRAME 1 day
SPECIAL TOOLS Mitre box, tenon saw, adhesive spatula
SEE PAGE 148

Coving or cornice is a decorative moulding fitted in the angle between the walls and ceiling. Traditionally cast in plaster, modern alternatives are made from foamed plastic.

INSTALLING PICTURE AND DADO RAILS

SKILL LEVEL Low to medium
TIME FRAME 1 day
SPECIAL TOOLS Mitre box, tenon saw, coping saw, power saw plus twist, countersink and masonry bits, spirit level
SEE PAGE 149

Picture rails are wood mouldings fixed to walls above head height and used to

hang pictures; dado rails are fixed at chair height to protect walls from furniture.

TILING OPTIONS

SEE PAGES 150–151

You can choose ceramic wall tiles with plain colours or with patterns, mix the two together or finish off half-tiled areas with attractive borders. Tiles are most commonly used in kitchens and bathrooms, where their water resistance makes them ideal for splashbacks, shower cubicles and other areas likely to be in contact with water.

TILING BASICS

SKILL LEVEL Low
TIME FRAME Under 2 hours
SPECIAL TOOLS Softwood batten, tile spacers
SEE PAGES 152–153

Careful planning of the tile layout is essential for the best results. Plan to centre the tiles on each wall, then finish off with cut tiles of equal width at each side. Once you have planned the setting out, count how many tiles you'll need.

PASTE TABLE

HAMMER

WALLPAPER SCISSORS

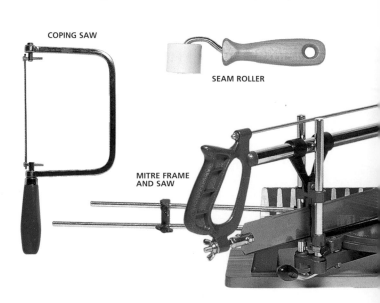

COPING SAW

SEAM ROLLER

MITRE FRAME AND SAW

TILING A WALL

SKILL LEVEL Low to medium
TIME FRAME 1 to 2 days
TOOLS Notched adhesive spreader, platform tile cutter, spirit level
SEE PAGES 154–155

Once you have fixed guide battens to the walls to help keep the tiles properly aligned, work across the wall, row by row, to position all the whole tiles. Then remove the battens and cut and fit edge tiles to complete the wall. Details are included for sheets of mosaic tiles – small tiles fixed to a backing sheet.

TILING AT CORNERS, WINDOWS AND DOORS

SKILL LEVEL High
TIME FRAME 1 to 2 days
SPECIAL TOOLS Same as for *Tiling a wall*, plus tile saw, tile nippers, tile file
SEE PAGES 156–157

Unless you are tiling just a simple splashback, you'll have to fit tiles round internal and external corners, doors and windows. Careful cutting will ensure that tiles fit neatly.

TILING IN BATHROOMS AND KITCHENS

SKILL LEVEL Low to medium
TIME FRAME 1 to 2 days
SPECIAL TOOLS Notched adhesive spreader, platform tile cutter, tile saw, tile file, tile nippers, profile gauge
SEE PAGES 158–159

Tiling a limited area in a bathroom or kitchen, such as a splashback, calls for slightly different instructions. For example, tiling over a kitchen worktop may not require using guide battens.

GROUTING AND SEALING

SKILL LEVEL Low
TIME FRAME 1 day
SPECIAL TOOLS Grout spreader, grout finisher or dowel, cartridge gun
SEE PAGES 160–161

Once the adhesive holding the tiles to the walls has dried, grout must be applied between tiles, and the joints between tiles and other surfaces must be sealed to make the area completely waterproof.

CLADDING OPTIONS

SEE PAGES 162–163

Tongue-and-groove wood boards are pinned to battens on the walls and varnished or painted. An alternative to natural wood is man-made wallboards – large sheets of hardboard or plywood with a decorative finish. These can also be fixed to battens or glued directly to the wall.

PREPARING WALLS FOR CLADDING

SKILL LEVEL Medium
TIME FRAME 1 to 2 days
SPECIAL TOOLS Spirit level, power drill, tenon saw or jigsaw
SEE PAGES 164–165

Before adding the cladding you must fix supporting battens to the wall (unless you glue sheet cladding to the walls). At the same time, add insulation for soundproofing or draughtproofing if needed.

FIXING TONGUE-AND-GROOVE CLADDING

SKILL LEVEL Medium
TIME FRAME 1 to 2 days
SPECIAL TOOLS Spirit level, try square, tenon saw or jigsaw, padsaw, plane
SEE PAGES 166–167

Details for fixing tongue-and-groove boards to battens by secret nailing through the tongues or using proprietary fixing clips.

FIXING SHEET CLADDING

SKILL LEVEL Medium
TIME FRAME 1 to 2 days
SPECIAL TOOLS Panel saw or jigsaw, profile gauge
SEE PAGES 168–169

Instructions for pinning wallboards to battens or gluing them to the wall.

BUILDING A PARTITION WALL

SKILL LEVEL High
TIME FRAME 2 days
SPECIAL TOOLS Panel saw or jigsaw, spirit level, power drill, filling knife
SEE PAGE 170–171
You can divide a room by erecting a partition wall. Build the wood frame, including a door opening, then cover it on both sides with plasterboard.

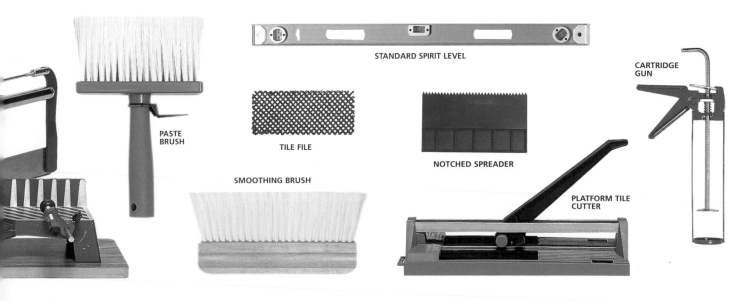

PASTE BRUSH · SMOOTHING BRUSH · TILE FILE · STANDARD SPIRIT LEVEL · NOTCHED SPREADER · PLATFORM TILE CUTTER · CARTRIDGE GUN

INTERIOR DESIGN TRICKS

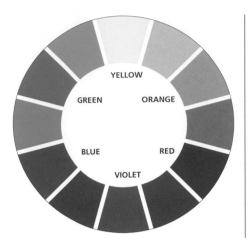

Interior designers use a host of tricks to give individual rooms distinctive moods and to alter the way they appear to the viewer. To understand how they do this, it helps to know a little about how colour works. Every colour is derived from three primary colours: red, blue and yellow. These three colours, plus black and white, can be blended together in different proportions to make an infinite range of colours. If you mix two primary colours, you get one of the three secondary colours: orange (red plus yellow), green (yellow plus blue) and violet (blue plus red). Carry on mixing, this time adding a primary colour to a secondary colour, and you'll get six tertiary colours. Mix these further to create even more colours.

▲ The colour wheel is based on the basic primary, secondary and tertiary colours. You can add white to create paler tints of these colours or black to create darker shades. Any three neighbouring colours on the wheel are referred to as "related". They work together well and create a harmonious effect in a room. Colours on opposite sides of the wheel are complementary colours – when used together, one provides contrast for the other, creating dramatic and eye-catching colour schemes.

▼ ▶ The same room has been decorated in different schemes. The complementary colours of orange and blue (right) create a warm, exciting effect; the neutral colours with touches of blue (below) create a cool, calming effect.

▶ Paint a high ceiling in a darker colour than the walls and it will seem lower. Conversely, paint a low ceiling in a lighter colour than the walls and it will appear higher, especially if you change the colour at picture-rail level.

◄ Highlight room features (such as cladding, window frames and skirting boards) by using tints of one colour or related colours for a subtle effect, or use complementary colours to create a bold look.

► Strong dark colours can provide a sense of cosiness, especially when a subtle wallpaper pattern breaks it up. Mirrors make small rooms seem larger.

◄ The neutral colours, which do not appear on the colour wheel, are white, black, grey and pale tints that contain a lot of white, including cream and beige. These colours are a perfect backdrop for stronger, more vibrant colours.

▼ The strength of a colour is important. Light-coloured surfaces reflect light better than darker ones, making rooms seem larger and more open. You can hide unattractive objects, such as a radiator, by painting them the same colour as the wall behind (use a matt or eggshell finish).

◄ Warm colours contain yellow and red. They make wall and ceiling surfaces seem to advance toward the viewer, and make rooms appear intimate and welcoming. Cool colours, based on blues and greens, have the opposite effect, making walls and ceilings recede and rooms seem cool and airy.

PAINT OPTIONS

POSSIBLE MATERIALS

MATT EMULSION

SILK EMULSION

GLOSS

EGGSHELL

ENAMEL PAINT

BLACKBOARD PAINT

STENCIL PAINTS

ARTIST'S OIL COLOURS

TRANSPARENT OIL GLAZE

SCUMBLE GLAZE

TEXTURED PAINT

Paint is the most popular decorative finish for walls and ceilings. It is inexpensive, easy to apply and simple to replace when you want a change of colour scheme. You can apply it to sealed plaster or plasterboard, or use it over a textured finish or wallcovering.

When buying paint, which comes in an almost infinite range of colours, consider the type of finish you want – for example, matt (non-reflective) or satin (a shiny sheen) – and the surface it will be covering. Water-based emulsion paint is often the choice for walls, while solvent-based paint is more appropiate for wood trim.

► Most rooms are painted in one relatively bland colour, but strong colours can be effective when used on only one wall. Here, the related colours of yellow and orange (see pp.110–111) are cleverly juxtaposed in a room where the rest of the walls are painted white.

◄ Stippling creates a delicate effect, achieved by lifting off a coloured glaze with a short-bristled stippling brush.

▼ Ragging is a variation on the technique of sponging, but uses crumpled-up cloth to remove the colour.

▲ The star motif stamped randomly around this room is an elegant way to break up the large expanse of colourwash on walls. Stencilling is another way to add pattern to walls.

▲ These dark walls provide the perfect backdrop for brightly coloured furniture, but such rooms need a lot of natural light.

▶ Textured paint is the appropriate choice for covering up less-than-perfect walls. Patterned roller sleeves designed for textured paint will help create a sophisticated but rugged look.

◀ Sponging is one of the easiest broken-colour paint effects to use. The second colour can be either sponged on or sponged off the base colour.

▶ Dragging can create a striking paint effect. If you prefer a more subtle look, choose a colour for the dragged glaze that is closer to the base coat.

PAINTING BASICS

YOU WILL NEED

Ladder **or** other access
equipment
Low-tack masking tape
Fabric dust sheet
Nylon fabric
Polythene bag **or** aluminium
foil

SEE ALSO

Preparation pp.18–35
Painting techniques
pp.116–129

*ORDER OF WORK
The numbers indicate the
order in which to paint a
room. Start with the ceiling
so that any splashes of
paint that land on the walls
can be painted over. On
a ceiling, paint in rows
1 sq m (10 sq ft) at a time.
On walls, covering the
same size areas, start at the
top and work down. If you
are right-handed, start at
the right-hand corner; if
you are left-handed, the left
one. This allows you to rest
your non-painting hand
against an unpainted
surface as you work.*

Once you have done all the
necessary preparation work on
the walls and ceilings and have chosen
the paint you want to use, your next
task is to work out how much paint
you'll need for the job and to plan the
sequence in which you'll work.

ESTIMATING QUANTITIES

On previously painted surfaces,
normal emulsion paint should cover
15 sq m (160 sq ft) per litre (1¾ pt).
Nondrip paint will cover a little less –
12 sq m (130 sq ft) per litre (1¾ pt).
However, new plaster is more
absorbent, so it is usual to dilute the
first coat of emulsion paint with
10 percent water. This makes it easier
to apply, and it acts as a sealer, which
helps prevent the top coat of paint
from being absorbed into the plaster.
The method of applying the paint –
for example, by brush or spray gun –
can also affect the paint coverage.

To work out the area of the walls
in a room, measure the wall height,
add together the lengths of all the
walls, then multiply the two figures.
Similarly, work out the area of
windows and doors in the room, then
subtract this from the overall area. To
work out how many litres of paint to
buy, divide this figure by the expected
coverage per litre. Measure the floor
to find the dimensions for the ceiling.

To save money, always buy paint in
the largest containers appropriate to
your needs. You can then decant paint
into a smaller paint kettle as you
work. This will also ensure that paint
colour is the same – even paint mixed
by computerized machines can be
slightly different in colour.

PROTECTING SURFACES

Unless you are confident that you have
a good eye and steady hand, it always
pays to mask off surfaces next to those
you'll be painting. This means sticking
lengths of masking tape to window
frames, door architraves and skirting
boards, as well as to wiring accessories
such as light switches and socket
outlets (unless you remove them, see
pp.18–19). The tape should stay in
place until the paint is touch dry.
Use only low-tack masking tape; any
other type will damage the surface to
which it is stuck.

Protect the flooring with a dust
sheet. If you have carpet in the room,
consider taking it up – it's the only
sure way to avoid getting paint on it.

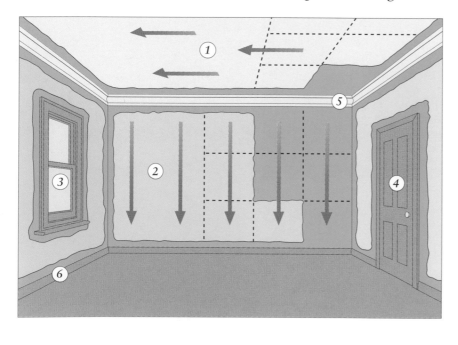

Helpful hints

It is never a good idea to use paint straight from the container it comes in, unless you plan to use the entire contents in one painting session. The main reason for this is that the paint may become contaminated by loose bristles from paint brushes and by dust, fluff and other particles picked up by the brush during the painting session.

In any case, if you have purchased your paint in economical 5 or 10 litre (5 or 10 qt) containers, they will be too heavy to hold comfortably. Instead, pour paint into a paint kettle or roller tray, depending on which implement you will be using.

LADDER SAFETY

Whether painting your ceiling or walls, you'll need a ladder for areas above your reach. Always make sure the feet of the ladder are steady on the floor and the braces are securely locked down before getting on a ladder.

When standing on a ladder, always lean toward it. Never extend beyond a comfortable reach, which could cause the ladder to tip over.

1 To protect adjacent surfaces such as wood trim, apply masking tape in short lengths, which are easier to handle and apply than longer ones. Firmly press down on the edge next to the surface you are painting to prevent paint from seeping underneath it.

2 Tape dust sheets to skirting boards to stop them from creeping and exposing floor coverings to splashes. Start with vertical strips to hold the sheet in place, then apply the tape horizontally so paint doesn't drip behind the sheet. Use fabric dust sheets that absorb paint splashes, rather than polythene ones, which do not.

3 If the tin of paint has already been partly used, strain the remaining paint through old nylon fabric such as a pair of tights stretched across the mouth of the kettle. If you are using a freshly opened tin of paint, simply pour the paint directly into your kettle.

4 Be prepared for pauses in your painting by having kitchen food wrap, a polythene bag or aluminium foil handy. Simply wrap the roller sleeves or brush bristles in the plastic or foil to stop the paint from drying out. A paint tray can be protected in the same way.

USING PAINT BRUSHES

Most people instinctively reach for a paint brush when they want to paint a wall or ceiling. It's a familiar tool that is easy to handle and control, and it gives excellent results with the minimum of skill. Choose a brush with plenty of long, thick bristles in a size to match the strength of your hands. A 100-mm- (4-in-) wide brush will suit most people, whereas a larger brush will be tiring to handle unless you do a lot of painting and have developed strong wrists.

You will also need a smaller brush – a 25 mm (1 in) size is ideal – for painting neatly into internal corners and angles and for painting around obstacles such as light fittings, switches and electrical points.

Depending on the smoothness and porosity of the surface, you'll normally need a litre (1¾ pt) of paint to cover 11 to 15 sq m (120 to 160 sq ft) of surface. Before you start the job, make sure you protect both any surfaces not to be painted and the contents of the room. The paint should be thoroughly mixed before pouring it into the kettle.

BRUSH CARE

To clean a brush after using it, first remove any excess paint by brushing it against newspaper, avoiding areas that become covered with paint in the process. Use hot water and washing-up liquid to clean emulsion paint from a brush; or use white spirit for oil-based paint, followed by soap and water. Once the brush is clean, shake out any excess water, wipe the brush against a clean, dry paper towel and store it wrapped in clean paper to help retain the shape of the bristles.

Helpful hints

Work the bristles of a new brush back and forth across the palm of your hand to dislodge loose bristles and dust. Wipe off the top of the paint container before opening it so that dust and other debris does not fall into the paint.

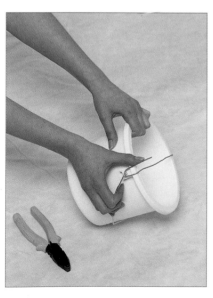

1 To scrape off excess paint after loading your brush – without drips running down the sides of the paint kettle – attach a length of wire across the neck of the kettle. Hook the ends around the handle and snip off the excess with wire cutters. Or use a piece of clean, lint-free string. You can also use the wire or string as a brush rest.

2 Load your brush by dipping the bristles into the paint to no more than half their length. Then draw it against the wire or string scraper to remove any excess paint, which will drip straight back into the paint kettle.

3 At internal angles, such as between the ceiling and a wall, use the small brush to create a neat edge, unless you are painting both areas the same colour. Either angle the bristles or hold the brush on edge, with the end of the bristles on the surface and the narrow edge leading the way. Alternatively, use masking tape.

4 Apply the paint to the surface in two or three parallel vertical strips, each slightly overlapping its neighbour. Brush across the strips at right angles to blend them together, and finish with gentle vertical brush strokes. Move to the next section, blending the work together.

5 To avoid a build-up of paint at external corners, brush the paint out toward the edge and let the brush run off the wall at right angles.

6 To reach into crevices and other hard-to-reach areas, use the end of the bristles to apply the paint by holding the brush perpendicular to the work and moving it in a dabbing, back and forth motion.

TEXTURED PAINTS

One way to create a three-dimensional effect on a surface is to use textured paint. After applying it to the surface with a wide brush or roller, you can give it a random or regular pattern. Among the tools for texturing are a sponge (left), a comb (right) and a moulded roller.

Before painting the walls, make sure you prepare them as you would for a traditional paint. The paint comes in white, but once it dries you can apply a colour by using emulsion paint.

To create a random stippled texture, use a large painter's sponge inside a plastic bag by dabbing it into the wet paint.

You can use a comb to create a variety of effects. To create these arches, start at the top and work your way down.

USING PAINT ROLLERS

The quickest way of painting walls and ceilings is with a paint roller. Most paint rollers for do-it-yourself use are 180 mm (7 in) or 230 mm (9 in) wide. As with brushes, the wider the roller the more effort you will need to push it – what you make up for in coverage for each pass of the larger roller, you lose in energy expended making the pass.

Select the sleeve to suit the surface you're decorating. You'll need a short-pile sleeve for smooth plaster and a longer pile for textured surfaces and relief wallcoverings. Sleeves are also available to create textured finishes.

Depending on the smoothness and porosity of the surface being covered, you'll need 1 litre (1¾ pt) of paint for 11 to 15 sq m (120 to 160 sq ft) of wall or ceiling. You are not limited to covering surfaces with one colour. You can use rollers (and paint brushes) to create stripes or blocks of colour next to each other (see box, facing page).

Before you begin painting, make sure you protect surfaces not to be painted, as well as the room's contents. You cannot apply paint in internal corners or near obstacles such as light switches with a roller, so you'll also need a small paint brush to tackle these areas.

CLEANING UP

Remove excess paint from a roller by running it over the ribs in the paint tray, then along newspaper (avoid areas on the paper as they are covered by paint). If possible, pull the sleeve off the cage. Wash it in hot water and soap for emulsion paint or white spirit for oil-based paint (wear rubber gloves if you use white spirit). Squeeze out any excess liquid and wrap the roller in aluminium foil or paper to store it.

> **Helpful hints**
>
> Before adding paint to the roller tray, you can line it with aluminium foil or plastic food wrap to make cleaning up quick and easy.

1 Pour enough paint into your roller tray to a depth of about 20 mm (¾ in). Run the roller down the slope of the tray and into the paint. Then roll it up and down the slope across the ribs a few times to load the sleeve and disperse the paint evenly through the pile.

2 To reach high walls or ceilings, you can use an extension pole fitted to the handle of many paint rollers. (First cut in at the edges; see step 3.) To avoid paint sprays, take care not to overload the roller, press it too hard or roll it too quickly. Consider wearing a hat to protect your hair, especially if you use an oil-based paint.

3 Because a roller cannot reach right into internal angles, use a paint brush about 50 mm (2 in) wide to paint a border around the wall (or ceiling) that you are working on. Also use the brush to paint around light switches, power points and other obstacles.

4 Start applying the paint by running the roller over a wall from top to bottom, letting each pass overlap the previous one. Cover an area of 1 sq m (10 sq ft) at a time, starting in a corner.

5 Without reloading the roller, run it over the paint just applied, this time rolling it at right angles to the original direction. This helps to spread the paint evenly and fill in any uncovered patches, especially on uneven or textured surfaces.

6 Reload the sleeve and paint the next area, blending it in with the previous one. Paint a whole length of a wall or ceiling at a time. Once you have a length completed, go over the work to smooth out the paint, gradually lifting the roller at the end of the pass. Reload and repeat the process to complete the surface.

PAINTING ALTERNATIVES

To make straight lines between areas of paint, align low-tack masking tape along a pencil line and paint up to it. After the paint dries, move the tape and paint the second colour.

You can use horizontal lines to create a mock dado rail or to frame a stencil applied around a room (see pp.128–129). Create stripes with vertical lines, either of equal widths or by mixing wider stripes with narrower ones. Use them on the full length of the wall or below a dado rail.

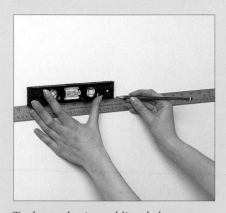

To draw a horizontal line, balance a torpedo spirit level on top of a metal straightedge or use a standard spirit level.

For vertical lines, hook one end of a chalk line on a nail tapped into the wall, hold the other end taut and snap the line.

USING PAINT PADS

YOU WILL NEED

Large paint pad
Small touching-in paint pad
Pad loading tray

MATERIALS

Emulsion paint

SEE ALSO

Painting basics pp.114–115

A nontraditional way of applying paint to walls and ceilings is by using paint pads. These consist of pieces of short-pile, mohair fabric mounted on foam plastic and stuck to metal or plastic handles. They are available in a range of sizes. You will need the biggest pad for fast coverage of large areas, plus a smaller one for painting clean edges and for touching in around obstacles such as lighting fittings, switches and electrical points. Some manufacturers offer speciality pads, including a wall/ceiling pad that has built-in edging wheels, which are designed to guide the pad precisely along the corners created where the walls meet the ceiling.

One benefit of using a paint pad is that paint coverage is generally a little higher than with brushes and rollers. This is because the pad applies a thinner film of paint to the wall. The disadvantage is that the adhesive holding the parts together can dissolve after prolonged use.

You can load the pad simply by dipping it into the paint, but it is easier to use a special tray with a roller. The design of this tray guarantees that the pad is evenly coated with paint every time.

1 If you are using an ordinary roller tray to load your pad, pour about 12 mm (½ in) of paint into the tray. Then dip the pile into the paint and remove excess paint by wiping the pad across the ribbed slope.

2 If you have a special tray for the pad, fill it with paint to the depth recommended by the manufacturer. Draw the pad across the roller, which transfers paint from the tray to the pad; then draw it along the back edge of the tray to scrape off any excess paint.

3 Start painting a room by creating a border around the perimeter of the walls by the ceiling. Use a pad with edging wheels or stick short lengths of masking tape on the adjoining surfaces and paint up to them. You can use a small pad to paint around obstacles.

4 Pull a large pad across 1 sq m (10 sq ft) of wall or ceiling in a series of parallel and slightly overlapping passes. Then run the pad across the painted area at right angles to the first passes. Finish off by making light passes, then move on to the next section.

USING A SPRAY GUN

YOU WILL NEED

Airless spray gun
Strainer
Safety goggles
Respirator

MATERIALS

Emulsion paint
Water **or** white spirit
(if required)

SEE ALSO

Painting basics pp.114–115

Small, electrically powered, airless spray guns are worth considering for painting walls if you have several completely empty rooms that require painting – for example, when moving house. However, they are not suitable for spraying ceilings. Although a spray gun can apply paint quickly, the fine overspray it produces means that you must completely mask all doors, windows, wood trim and floor coverings before using one. Spray guns are also difficult – as well as time-consuming – to clean, so you should carefully consider if using one is the right choice for you.

Runny types of paint generally work better in a spray gun than nondrip ones. In fact, the paint may require thinning before you can use it. Follow the manufacturer's recommendations. Make sure you strain the paint (see p.115), which will avoid blocking the nozzle on the gun.

You must wear a respirator and safety goggles to avoid inhaling the paint mist or getting it in your eyes while you work. You must also make sure that the room is well ventilated; however, avoid windy days when having windows open means that there are cross-draughts in the room.

1 Airless spray guns all have slightly different performance characteristics, so it is a good idea to first practise on an out-of-the-way surface to establish your gun's spray pattern and optimum spraying distance.

2 On flat surfaces, you must keep the gun nozzle the same distance from and at right angles to the wall as you move it from side to side. Do this by flexing your wrist as you complete each side-to-side pass. Make sure you do not spray in an arc.

3 At an external corner, spray the flanking wall to within about 150 mm (6 in) of the angle. Then stand in front of the end of the wall and paint across it, using short side-to-side passes of the gun as you work your way down. Repeat for the adjacent wall.

4 When painting an internal corner, spray each flanking wall first, again to within about 150 mm (6 in) of the angle. Then fill in the corner by pointing the gun into the angle and moving it from top to bottom in one pass.

PAINT EFFECTS: COLOURWASHING

YOU WILL NEED

Kettle for colourwash
Measuring jug
Small paint brush
100 mm- (4-in-) wide paint brush

MATERIALS

Vinyl silk emulsion paint for the base coat
Matt emulsion paint
Water-based glaze
Varnish (if required)

SEE ALSO

Painting basics
pp.114–115
Using paint brushes
pp.116–117
Using paint rollers
pp.118–119

Because colourwashing is easy to execute, the technique is an excellent introduction to the world of paint effects. Simply paint your wall or ceiling with a plain base coat, then apply a random broken wash of a second colour over it, allowing the colour of the base coat to occasionally show through.

Distemper or well-thinned oil-based paint was used as the wash coat in traditional colourwashing. Today, most people use ordinary emulsion paint mixed with a water-based glaze. You can protect your work with a final coat of varnish.

Pale colour combinations work best for all-over decorating, but darker shades can be used to create a dramatic effect on smaller self-contained panels.

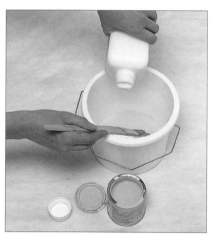

1 Apply the base coat and leave it to dry. Then make up the colourwash – one part matt emulsion paint to four parts glaze – and use a small brush to mix it thoroughly. A litre (1¾ pt) of colourwash is enough for two coats in an area about 3 sq m (30 sq ft).

2 Brush on the first coat of the colourwash mixture, using a series of random brush strokes to cover an area about 1 sq m (10 sq ft). Work all the paint out of the brush.

3 Break up the damp colourwash with the edge of the bristles, using a jabbing action. Move on to the next section. Repeat step 2, and, again, break up the wash with the edge of the bristles. Continue until the complete surface is covered with the wash.

4 After the coat of colourwash dries, repeat steps 2 and 3 to apply a second wash coat over it. This will build up the depth of colour. When the second wash is dry, you can apply a clear flat varnish to make the surface washable and more durable.

PAINT EFFECTS: DRAGGING

YOU WILL NEED

Kettle for glaze
100-mm- (4-in-) wide paint
brush
Small paint brush

MATERIALS

Eggshell paint for the
base coat
Proprietary oil glaze
White spirit
Universal stainers such as
artist's oil colours
White oil-based undercoat

SEE ALSO

Painting basics
pp.114–115
Using paint brushes
pp.116–117
Using paint rollers
pp.118–119

A thin translucent coat of paint, known as a coloured glaze, is applied over a lighter colour base coat to create dragging. Because you have to maintain even pressure throughout each continuous top-to-bottom brush stroke, it can be one of the more difficult paint effects to create. If you fail to apply pressure properly, you may leave tell-tale brush marks and denser colour at the start and finish of each stroke.

It is a good idea to work with a partner. The dragger should create each vertical strip in the glaze as soon as the painter has applied it.

The use of dragging on walls (it is rarely used on ceilings) creates a finely striped effect. It evolved from the technique of graining wood.

1 Apply the base coat and let it dry. For about ½ litre (1 pt) of the glaze, mix one part oil glaze, three parts white spirit, a tablespoonful of undercoat and stainer, if required – but first use a small brush to mix the glaze with the stainer on a white tile or saucer.

2 Brush a thin coat of the glaze onto the wall in overlapping vertical strokes, then horizontal ones; end in light, vertical strokes. From top to bottom, aim to cover an area about 460 mm (18 in) wide.

3 Drag a dry paint brush down the wall in one continuous stroke, using even pressure. It helps to start work alongside a vertical edge such as a corner or door frame. At regular intervals, use rags or paper towels to wipe off the build-up of paint on the brush.

4 Repeat the process to drag the next series of lines parallel with the first ones before the glaze dries, and continue until the surface is completely covered. The dried finish is durable, but you can give it a coat of clear varnish if you wish.

PAINT EFFECTS: SPONGING

YOU WILL NEED

Paint kettle
Paint tray
Natural sponge
100-mm- (4-in-) wide paint
brush for sponging off

MATERIALS

Emulsion paint (test pots
are ideal for second
colours) **or** vinyl silk paint
for base coat, proprietary oil
glaze and universal stainers
such as artist's oil colours
White spirit (if required)

SEE ALSO

Painting basics pp.114–115
Using paint brushes
pp.116–117
Using paint rollers
pp.118–119

You can create an almost infinite variety of looks by sponging. The final result will depend on the colour combinations you choose, the texture of the sponge you use and the actual painting method.

Sponging can be applied in two ways. The first is called sponging on, and it involves taking up paint or glaze on a sponge and dabbing it onto a wall or ceiling that has been given an overall base coat. The second method is called sponging off. Here the colour coat of glaze is brushed out over the base coat, then a clean damp sponge is used to dab some of the colour off.

You can add depth to a sponging finish by adding a second colour over the first one. For the best results, apply the darker colour first.

1 Apply the base coat and let it dry. Use emulsion paint if you intend to sponge on diluted emulsion colours, or vinyl silk paint if you'll be using tinted oil glaze (see p.126 for preparing the paint). To sponge on, load a little paint onto the sponge from a roller tray.

2 Dab the sponge on the wall, aiming to create an even, overall pattern. Vary the spacing of the dabs if you want a more random effect, and repeat the process with a second colour after the first layer has dried.

3 For sponging off (this technique doesn't work with emulsion paint), mix the tinted glaze (see p.126 for preparing the paint) and brush it on evenly but thinly over the base coat. Work on a 1 sq m (10 sq ft) section at a time so that the glaze stays workable.

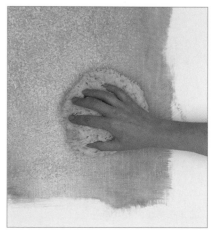

4 Soak the sponge in white spirit and wring it out. Then use it to dab the surface evenly, lifting off some of the glaze. When the sponge becomes saturated with glaze, wash it in white spirit and then washing-up liquid – it will then be ready for re-use.

PAINT EFFECTS: STIPPLING

One of the most delicate of paint effects, stippling is created by brushing a coloured glaze over a vinyl silk base coat, then dabbing the wet surface with a large flat, short-bristled stippling brush. This lifts off specks of the glaze, depending on how much pressure is applied.

This can be a difficult technique to execute well, and if using the stippling brush, it is easier if tackled by a two-person team – one applying the glaze and the other stippling the wet surface. On large areas, a quick alternative technique is to use a short-pile mohair paint roller to stipple the surface.

In stippling, tiny points of colour from the base coat appear through the top glaze, creating a subtle grainy or speckled effect.

1 Apply the base coat and leave it to dry. Then mix up and tint the glaze (see p.126), and brush it onto the wall in a thin even layer over an area of no more than 1 sq m (10 sq ft).

2 Use the stippling brush to dab the wet glaze firmly and evenly area by area, just letting successive dabs overlap. (If you are working with a partner, he or she can apply the glaze to the next section as you do the stippling.)

3 Periodically, you should remove the build-up of glaze from the bristles by wiping the brush on clean rags or paper towels.

4 To stipple with a short-pile roller, run it up and down in a series of parallel lines, then across them at right angles. Take care not to let the roller skid – this wipes off the colour instead of texturing it. Make light vertical passes over the glaze to remove any lines.

PAINT EFFECTS: RAGGING

YOU WILL NEED

Paint kettle for glaze
100-mm- (4-in) wide paint brush
Clean, lint-free fabric

MATERIALS

Water-based emulsion paint **or** eggshell paint for the base coat
Vinyl matt emulsion paint for the colour coat and water-based glaze **or** proprietary oil glaze and universal oil stainers such as artist's oil colours

SEE ALSO

Painting basics pp.114–115
Using paint brushes pp.116–117
Using paint rollers pp.118–119

One way to create a broken colour effect is ragging, which produces a coarser look than sponging. This simple technique involves brushing a coloured glaze onto the base coat, then lifting it off by pressing a crumpled ball of clean fabric against the surface in overlapping dabs.

The effect you achieve depends on how tightly the fabric is crumpled and on its absorbency. Natural fabrics absorb more paint then synthetic ones. It is easier to rag a wall or ceiling as a two-person team, with one person applying the glaze as the other one follows and rags it.

For the best results when ragging, use colours in tones that are close to each other, with the darker colour applied on top of the lighter one.

1 Apply the base coat: use emulsion paint as the base if you intend to use emulsion paint mixed with glaze for the top coat, or use eggshell paint if you're using a tinted oil glaze (see step 1, opposite). Let it dry, then brush the colour coat evenly over the base coat.

2 Crumple up a square of clean, lint-free fabric and gently press it against the wet colour to lift some of it off. Move to the next section of wall, carefully blending the two areas together.

3 Keep dabbing until the fabric becomes covered with glaze, then refold it to expose clean material. When the fabric becomes saturated with glaze, replace it with a new piece. Lay out the used fabric until it dries before throwing it away.

4 Continue to brush on the paint and dab it off until you reach the end of the wall. At a corner, apply the glaze by pulling the brush away from the edge to prevent a build-up of the glaze.

PAINT EFFECTS: RAG-ROLLING

YOU WILL NEED

Paint kettle for glaze
100-mm- (4-in-) wide paint brush
Small paint brush
Paint roller
Rags **or** paper towels
Clean, lint-free fabric

MATERIALS

Vinyl silk emulsion paint **or** eggshell paint for the base coat
Vinyl matt emulsion paint and water-based glaze **or** proprietary oil glaze and universal oil stainers such as artist's oil colours for the colour coat

SEE ALSO

Painting basics pp.114–115
Using paint rollers pp.118–119

A variation on ragging, rag-rolling uses additional – but still easy – techniques to create subtle differences in the final look. The glaze is stippled before the fabric is used to lift off the top colour and the crumpled fabric is rolled over the surface instead of simply being dabbed against it.

Because the glaze usually dries quickly, there is a case for assembling a team – one to apply the glaze and one to do the rag-rolling. When buying the materials make sure you purchase compatible products. You should never mix oil-based and water-based paints and glazes.

Create a random pattern by rolling the fabric across the surface in various directions or a blurry striped look by rolling the fabric down the wall.

1 Apply the base coat (see step 1, opposite). For a top coat, mix together the products using a small brush. Use four parts of emulsion paint for every one part of glaze. For an oil-based glaze, add the artist's oil colours a little at a time until the glaze is the desired colour.

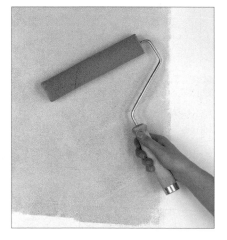

2 Stipple the surface using a paint roller with a short-pile mohair sleeve. Work in an area of no more than 3 sq m (30 sq ft) at a time. Remove paint build-up from the sleeve by wiping it on clean, absorbent rags or paper towels.

3 Crumple the fabric into a cylindrical shape. If you want to make vertical stripes, roll the fabric up the wall as if you were using a rolling pin. Try to keep the stripes parallel and slightly overlapping each other.

4 For a random effect, simply roll the rag cylinder in different directions, refolding it from time to time as it picks up glaze. When the fabric becomes saturated, replace it with fresh material. Let the old fabric dry out before discarding it.

PAINT EFFECTS: STENCILLING

YOU WILL NEED

Stencilling

Stencils (bought or home-made)
Masking tape **or** aerosol spray adhesive
Spirit level
Tape measure
Pencil
Stencil brush
Throwaway plastic **or** paper palettes
Paper towels

Using a stamp

Stamp **or** artificial sponge
Small paint roller
Scrap paper

MATERIALS

Artist's acrylic tube paint
Water

SEE ALSO

Painting basics pp.114–115
Painting and stencilling floorboards pp.184–185

Stencilling brings both colour and pattern to walls. An overall decorative effect can be created by making a border around a room at ceiling level. You can also use stencils in a grid pattern or randomly.

A template, or stencil, can be used to transfer a pattern to your walls. Simply place the stencil onto the surface, apply paint through it to create the first section of the pattern, then reposition it and repeat the operation. More complex patterns may require the use of two or more colours or separate stencil sheets. Take care to keep the colours in register. To help reposition them, most stencils have registration marks on them or parts of the pattern are repeated.

The best paint to use for stencilling is artist's acrylic paint, which is quick-drying and available in a huge range of colours. Vinyl silk paint is the best surface for stencilling on because it allows you to easily wipe off any mistakes. You can also stencil over paint effects such as colourwashing (see p.122) or ragging (see p.126).

1 For a horizontal design such as a frieze or border, use a spirit level to find a truly horizontal guide line, and make light pencil marks along the wall. If there is a dado or picture rail in place, you can use that as the guide. If the ceiling is uneven, lower the pattern so that the fault is less obvious.

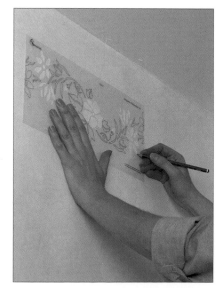

2 Measure the length of your pattern and plan its spacing from wall to wall. Start over a focal point of the room and work toward the corners. Some stencils can be turned around corners. Others are best planned to end at the corner by slightly adjusting the spacing between each repeat. Make light registration marks with a pencil.

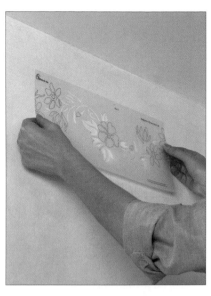

3 Position the stencil on the wall, carefully aligning it with the guide lines. To hold it in place, use low-tack masking tape or an aerosol adhesive sprayed on the back. When pressed in place with the spray, there is less chance of paint seeping under the stencil and you can simply peel off the stencil to reposition it.

4 Take a small amount of paint from your palette onto your stencilling brush, and dab the bristles onto clean paper until you get a smooth even colour; a little paint will go a long way. Start filling in each area of the stencil with a gentle stabbing motion. To create highlights, add a lighter colour.

5 Peel the stencil away from the wall and reposition it, carefully aligning it with the guidelines and any registration marks. Paint through it again to create the next pattern repeat. Wipe the stencil clean with paper towels whenever the paint builds up.

6 If you are using two or more colours, complete one colour application and allow it to dry before going back and repositioning the stencil to apply the second colour. To avoid getting one colour of paint into an area planned as another colour, use low-tack masking tape on the stencil to block out the area.

USING A STAMP

Instead of a stencil you can use a stamp to apply a random or regular pattern onto a wall. You can use a store-bought rubber stamp, or make your own to match patterns already in the room.

Use an artificial sponge to make a stamp with a simple pattern; cut out the shapes with a craft knife, leaving the area to be coloured raised. To make a more intricate pattern, you can purchase linoleum from an arts and crafts shop, along with a gouging tool to cut out the pattern.

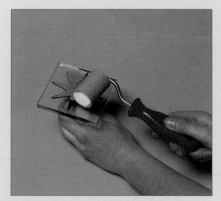

Use a small roller to spread the paint as evenly as possible, completely covering the raised area of the stamp.

Before applying the stamp to the wall, use it on scrap paper to get used to the amount of paint and pressure needed.

WALLCOVERING OPTIONS

POSSIBLE MATERIALS

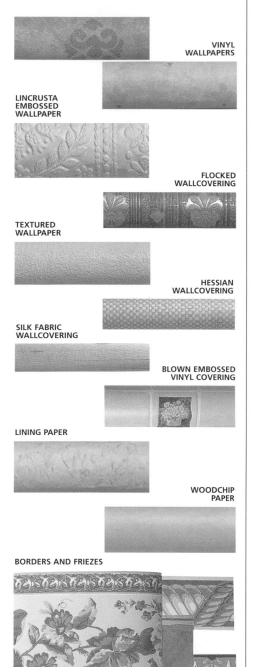

VINYL
WALLPAPERS

LINCRUSTA
EMBOSSED
WALLPAPER

FLOCKED
WALLCOVERING

TEXTURED
WALLPAPER

HESSIAN
WALLCOVERING

SILK FABRIC
WALLCOVERING

BLOWN EMBOSSED
VINYL COVERING

LINING PAPER

WOODCHIP
PAPER

BORDERS AND FRIEZES

Wallpapers, or more accurately wallcoverings – they are not all paper-based – have two advantages that paint can't provide: they can cover walls and ceilings in a regular pattern or design, and they can provide a surface texture. The finished effect may be purely decorative, but it can offer practical benefits too; for example, it may be hard-wearing and easy to clean. Decorating with wallpaper is not difficult once you have mastered the basic techniques, and it is a relatively quick decorating option. If you are a beginner, you should buy a ready-pasted wallpaper, and remember that some patterns are difficult to match and inexpensive paper has a tendency to tear.

▶ Floral wallpaper has a rustic and old-fashioned charm, which is completely in keeping with the style of this room. When restoring an old house, such wallpapers will help you recreate the look instantly.

▼ Borders and friezes are usually hung at dado rail or picture rail level, but they can also be used elsewhere to great effect. Here, a border makes a feature of an otherwise simple skirting board.

▶ In high-traffic areas such as a kitchen or hallway, use a hard-wearing, washable vinyl paper.

▲ Narrow areas are better in plain wallpapers, perhaps with small patterns – strong ones can be tiring on the eyes. You can limit the use of the paper to below a dado rail.

► You can use wallpaper to create an illusion of space. Stripes can provide a feeling of height and spaciousness in a small room.

► Wallpaper designs come in a range of patterns and textures, including paint effects. Paste up an instant rag-rolled effect or, as used here, a striped colourwash effect – without the work.

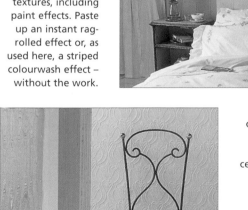

► Wallpaper will cover any multitude of cracks in poorly finished walls and ceilings, making it an invaluable resource for decorating older houses. Alternatively, you can hang lining paper and paint over it.

◄ There is a wide variety of wallpaper designs available, including plain colours (white is popular) with embossed patterns.

WALLPAPER BASICS

YOU WILL NEED

Tape measure
Bucket
Wooden stick (for mixing)
Dust cloth
Wallpaper brush
Pencil

MATERIALS

Size (if required)
Roll of wallpaper

SEE ALSO

Stripping old wallpaper
pp.26–27
Washing down and
preparing surfaces pp.30–31
Interior design tricks
pp.110–111
Painting basics pp.114–115
Wallcovering options
pp.130–131
Cutting, pasting and folding
wallpaper pp.134–135

There are preliminary stages you have to go through before you can start to paper a room. The first is to choose your wallpaper – a process that will be influenced by personal taste, but also by practical factors such as the need for a stain-resistant surface or a textured finish to disguise imperfections in the walls.

WALLPAPER PATTERNS

As well as looking for a pattern you like in the type of wallpaper you want, you should also consider how the pattern will line up between lengths; this may be important in estimating quantities. Unless the paper has a plain striped or randomly coloured design, there will be a motif that is printed over and over again across and down the roll. The vertical distance between successive motifs is called the pattern repeat. It may be as small as 50 mm (2 in) or as large as 300 mm (12 in), or even more if the motif is really big.

The horizontal distance between motifs affects the way edge-to-edge pattern matches between lengths of paper are made. Some patterns will line up straight across, but others will require the lowering, or dropping, of one of the lengths to line up the pattern. If the pattern repeat is large, this can waste paper – you may have to trim off more than a narrow strip.

PLANNING AHEAD

Measure your floor-to-ceiling height, and check that you'll get four lengths out of each standard 10 m (33 ft) roll of paper (see box). If in doubt as to the amount needed, order an extra roll.

Hang wallpaper on bare or painted plaster or plasterboard, never over old wallcovering. Unless there is a major feature in the room, start papering in the least obtrusive corner or next to the door; this will help to hide any problems with the pattern match when the last length hung meets the first.

PATTERN REPEATS
If a number of motifs repeats across a single width of wallpaper, there will be matching halves of the motif at opposite edges – these wallpapers have a straight pattern match. If a number of motifs repeats over two widths of the paper, the matching halves of the motif at opposite edges of each length will be offset by half the pattern repeat – such papers have an offset or drop pattern match.

ESTIMATING QUANTITIES

Measure the perimeter of the room; ignore the doors and windows unless they comprise more than 10 percent of the perimeter. A standard roll is just over half a metre (20 in) wide, so doubling the metric measurement of the perimeter tells you how many lengths of paper you need; divide that figure by 4 (or 3 for walls over 2.4 m/ 8 ft high or paper with a large pattern repeat) for the number of rolls to buy.

For ceilings, measure the length of one strip and count how many strips you need. Calculate how many strips you can cut from a 10 m (33 ft) roll to work out how many rolls you need.

Wall height		metres	9	10	11	12	13	14	15	16	17	18	19	20
		feet	30	33	36	39	43	46	49	52	56	59	62	66
2.0 m to 2.2 m (6 ft 6½ in to 7 ft 2 in)			4	4	5	5	5	6	6	6	6	7	7	8
2.2 m to 2.4 m (7 ft 2 in to 7 ft 10½ in)			4	4	5	5	6	6	6	7	7	8	8	9
2.4 m to 2.6 m (7 ft 10½ in to 8 ft 6 in)			4	5	5	6	6	7	7	8	8	9	9	10
2.6 m to 2.8 m (8 ft 6 in to 9 ft 2 in)			5	5	6	6	7	7	8	8	9	9	10	11
2.8 m to 3.0 m (9 ft 2 in to 9 ft 10 in)			5	5	6	7	7	8	8	9	9	10	11	12

Measurements around the room

The table above is a rough guide to the number of rolls required for wallpaper that has a straight pattern match. For Continental widths, see the pattern book.

1 Painted surfaces need no special preparation apart from washing down. The porous surface of bare plaster must be sealed with size; mix it according to the manufacturer's directions.

2 Apply a coat of size to the walls with a wallpaper brush. Without sizing, it will be difficult to slip the lengths of paper across the surface and match up the pattern as you hang them. Let the size dry before you start papering.

3 Mark where to start hanging the paper. If the room has a chimney breast or other prominent feature and the paper has a large motif, centre the first length on the feature, then work outward around the room in both directions. Otherwise, start in a corner or inconspicuous area.

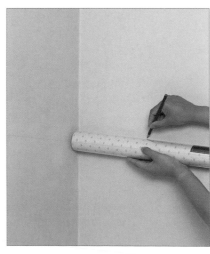

4 After deciding where to begin hanging, use a roll of wallpaper as a gauge to mark successive widths on the walls around the room. This will reveal any joins that will fall in awkward places – for example, near external corners. Alter your starting point slightly to avoid any problems.

HANGING AND TRIMMING WALLPAPER

The most important factor in getting a professional-looking result is the hanging technique. Wherever you have decided to hang the first length of wallpaper in a room, it is essential that you align it with a plumbed vertical line. Room corners are never perfectly vertical, and relying on one as a positioning guide can result in serious problems with your wallpaper pattern as you hang successive lengths. Stripes will not be truly vertical, and horizontal pattern motifs will begin to travel uphill, with very disconcerting effects at the ceiling and skirting boards.

BEFORE YOU START

Speed is of the essence for the best results, because the paste can dry out quite quickly and cause adhesion problems along seams and cuts. On painted walls, there will be an excess of paste that will need wiping away. Make sure you have all the tools you need to hand – ideally, in a decorator's apron around your waist.

Because you will have to be able to reach the ceiling, make sure you have a stepladder readily at hand. Clear the area around the walls of any obstructions to make moving the stepladder a less cumbersome task, and remember the rules of ladder safety (see pp.114–115).

It is usually easier to work clockwise around the room if you are right-handed, and anticlockwise if you are left-handed, so select your starting point accordingly.

Helpful hints

If the first length bubbles, increase the soaking time of further lengths. If you find a bubble after the paste has dried, make an incision in a X pattern, using a craft knife. Brush paste onto the underside of the paper and the wall surface, then press the paper in place and hold it for a few minutes. Wipe away any squeezed-out paste with a damp sponge and smooth the area with a seam roller.

1 If you are starting work in a corner, draw your first plumb line on the wall about 25 mm (1 in) less than the width of the wallpaper from the corner. This allows a small amount of paper to be turned into the internal angle. Hold the line and make two or three pencil marks down the wall to indicate the vertical.

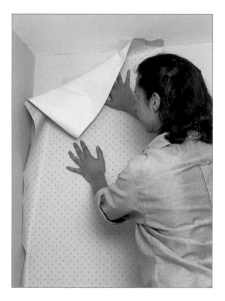

2 Carry your folded length of paper to the wall, climb onto your low steps and unfold the top end of the length so you can position it against the wall. First slide it upward and allow about 50 mm (2 in) of wallpaper to overlap onto the ceiling, then move it sideways so the edge of the paper lines up with your plumbed line.

3 Use your paperhanging brush to smooth the top half of the length onto the wall surface, working from the top downward and from the centre toward the edges to brush out any bubbles. Then allow the rest of the length to unfold down the wall and continue brushing it into place. Press the paper well into the corner.

4 Press the back of the blade of your paperhanging scissors between the wall and ceiling and draw them along to mark the paper. Peel the paper away from the wall and cut along the marked line. Discard the offcut and brush the trimmed end back into place. Repeat the process to trim the wallpaper at the skirting board.

5 Paste and fold the next length of paper, and bring it to the wall. Open the top fold as before, press it against the wall surface and align the pattern with that on the first length. Then brush the length into place and trim at the top and bottom as in steps 3 and 4. Wipe away any stray paste while it is still wet, using a damp cloth.

6 Unless you are hanging an embossed wallpaper, use a seam roller to ensure good adhesion of the edges to the wall. If a seam has dried out and is lifting, raise the seam and brush a little fresh paste behind the paper with an artist's paintbrush. Then roll the seam flat again and wipe off any excess adhesive.

HANGING LINING PAPER

Lining paper provides a smooth surface of even porosity when hanging wallpaper onto less-than-perfect wall surfaces. It can also be used on ceilings, and it can be covered with paint rather than wallpaper.

Hang the lining paper horizontally, with neat butt joints between lengths, using the same type of paste as for decorative wallpaper. Cut the lengths long enough to reach from one room corner to the next, and start hanging at the top edge of the walls.

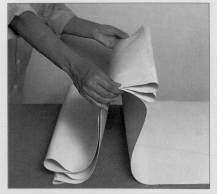

After cutting a length of lining paper and pasting it, fold it concertina fashion to make carrying and hanging it easier.

Brush the length out across the wall surface fold by fold. Repeat for each subsequent strip.

PAPERING AROUND CORNERS

I f you are hanging a wallcovering as a decorative feature on just one wall of a room, you won't have to tackle any corners. But most people paper an entire room, and so will have

A hallway is an ideal location for a washable wallpaper. It brings colour and pattern to a confined area, and it is easy to clean off smudgy fingerprints.

to take the wallpaper around internal corners, as well as around external corners in rooms containing chimney breasts or other projecting features.

Room corners are seldom truly square, so if you turn a length of paper from one wall onto the adjacent wall, the edge of the turned section will no longer be truly vertical. If this edge is used as a guide for hanging subsequent lengths of wallpaper, none of them will be true across the next wall. The solution is to draw a fresh plumbed line on each wall.

Helpful hints

If you're planning to hang a paper with vertical stripes or any other strong vertical design, hold a plumb bob and line to the wall at each internal and external angle to see if the wall corners are true. If any are not within 6 mm (¼ in) of being true, change your choice to a design without a vertical element.

1 After hanging the last full length before an internal corner, measure the distance from its edge to the internal angle at the top, centre and bottom of the wall. Add 25 mm (1 in) to the largest of the measurements, and cut a strip of paper to this width, making sure its machine-cut edge will butt the piece on the wall.

2 Paste the cut-to-size strip and hang it, butting its machine-cut edges of the two lengths snugly together. Use your paperhanging brush to tuck the hand-cut edge of the strip well into the internal angle. Save the leftover part of the length.

3 If the turned section of paper creases because the corner is not true, make release cuts in a vinyl paper or release tears in a standard wallpaper to allow the paper to lie flat.

4 Measure the width of the leftover length that was put aside, and mark a plumbed line on the next wall that distance from the internal angle. Paste and hang the strip with its machine-cut edge aligned with the plumbed line, and brush its hand-cut edge into the angle so it overlaps the turned section.

5 At an external corner, use a similar technique to steps 1 and 2 to turn about 25 mm (1 in) of paper around the angle and onto the adjacent wall. Again, make release cuts or tears, if necessary, to allow the turned section to lie flat.

6 Mark a plumbed line on the second wall, and hang the saved leftover length to the line so that its hand-cut edge overlaps the turned section, as in step 4. If you are hanging a vinyl paper, you'll need a special vinyl overlap adhesive to adhere the overlapping layers together at external and internal corners.

DOUBLE CORNERS

If you have a boxed-in pipe or a projecting buttress where a dividing wall was removed, you may have to turn the same length of wallpaper around both internal and external corners. This is best avoided; even if one corner is true the next one is unlikely to be. Approach the first internal angle as for a room corner, and treat the last one in the same way. "Feathering" (see far right) the edge of the bottom-layer paper makes it less noticeable through the top paper.

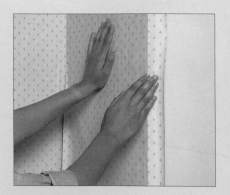

Cut a strip wide enough to cover the next section of wall leading to the first external corner, plus 25 mm (1 in) extra. Align the pattern at the external angle.

Let 25 mm (1 in) of the strip turn onto the next wall, and tear it along the edge. Hang additional strips in this way until you paper the whole projection.

PAPERING AROUND DOORS AND WINDOWS

Careful planning is the key to successful papering around doors and windows. It is difficult to match short lengths of paper both above and below a window to the next full length of paper. First paper above the window, where any misalignments would be more noticable, then hang the full-length strip next to it and, finally, hand the short lengths below the window.

Papering around a doorway poses new problems, and papering the recess around a window (known as the reveal) can be awkward. Adjust the starting point to avoid narrow strips alongside the door and to avoid edges falling at the corners of the window.

You'll be trimming your wallpaper to fit against the window frame or the architrave around a doorway, but gaps often open up along these angles. To get the best possible finish for your redecorating, take time to fill and paint these gaps before papering. Rake out any loose material and fill the joints with non-setting acrylic decorator's mastic, using a cartridge gun. Then paint the architrave or window frame, taking the paint over the mastic and onto the wall plaster.

1 If the door is in a corner, you can have a pattern misalignment in that corner without it being noticed. If it is away from a corner, the pattern should continue over and past it. Whichever the arrangement, hang the last full length before the door opening, then hang the next so it overlaps the architrave.

2 Press the paper against the architrave until you can see the corner of the moulding through the paper. Using your wallpaper scissors, make a diagonal cut to it from the edge of the length.

3 Use the scissors to press the paper into the angles between the wall and the architrave, and crease the cutting lines. Trim off the waste, then brush the wallpaper back into the angles.

4 Cut and hang a short piece of paper above the door, and fit the subsequent length as you did in steps 1–3. If it will go into a corner, cut the length to fit between the door and corner, with an additional 25 mm (1 in) so that you can turn it onto the flanking wall.

5 At a window reveal, hang a length so it overlaps the window reveal, and make horizontal cuts into the edge of the length to allow the flap of paper to be turned onto the side wall of the reveal. Trim its edge if it reaches the frame. Wait until you've fitted the underside of the reveal before fitting an infill strip on the side wall.

6 Cut and fit a patch for the underside of the reveal. Turn its front edge onto the above face wall by 25 mm (1 in), tucking it beneath the paper on the face wall and the side of the reveal.

7 Trim the back of the patch, then cut and fit an infill strip, if needed, at the side section of the reveal. Continue to hang short sections above the window, folding them onto the underside of the reveal, until you reach the next full-length strip. You may find small scissors easier to use for trimming.

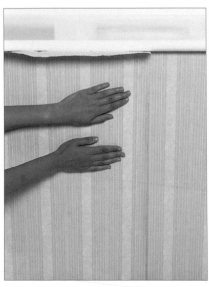

8 Plumb a line to hang the full-length strip at the far side of the window, and hang the length to that line. Trim the full-length piece as in step 5, and add the infill strip if needed. Complete the job by hanging short lengths below the window, adjusting them to match the full lengths on either side as best you can.

PAPERING AROUND OBSTACLES

YOU WILL NEED

Papering an arch
See *Hanging and trimming wallpaper* pp.136–137
Tape measure

Papering at a face plate
See *Hanging and trimming wallpaper* pp.136–137
Small screwdriver

Papering around fixed objects
See *Hanging and trimming wallpaper* pp.136–137
Small scissors (if required)
Sharp knife (if required)

MATERIALS

Papering an arch
Wallpaper
Paste (powder **or** ready-mixed)

Papering at a face plate
See above

Papering around fixed objects
See above

SEE ALSO

Wallpaper basics pp.132–133
Cutting, pasting and folding wallpaper pp.134–135
Hanging and trimming wallpaper pp.136–137
Papering around corners pp.138–139

Apart from major features such as doors and windows, every room contains its fair share of paperhanging problems – light switches, power points, mantelpieces, stair newel posts, even arches in alcoves and between rooms. These can all be awkward to cope with, but there is a solution in each case. The main thing that can go wrong is the paste drying out as you take the time necessary to trim and fit the wallpaper around the obstacle concerned. However, you can get around this problem by making sure you have some paste and a small brush to hand as you work.

Arches pose particular problems as far as pattern matching is concerned. It is impossible to get a direct match between the flat and curved surfaces. The best solution is to either use a plain or randomly patterned wallpaper or to paper the curve with a plain paper that complements what you are using on the walls.

BEFORE YOU START

Always remove as many wall-mounted obstacles as possible before you start papering. Shelves, display cabinets and the like will be fixed with screws driven into wallplugs (see pp.18–19).

If you have any wall lights, turn off their power supply at the consumer unit or fuse box. Then unscrew them from the wall, disconnect their supply cables and set them aside. Cover the bare cable cores with insulating tape before restoring the power supply. Whenever you work near a light switch, power point or light, always turn off the power first (see pp.18–19).

Helpful hints

If you want to paper behind a radiator, simply tuck about 150 mm (6 in) of wallpaper down behind the top edge of the radiator, and slide the paper behind the side edges as far as you can. A slim paint roller designed to fit behind radiators is ideal for pressing the paper into position. If there is a visible gap between the radiator and the skirting board, paper that too.

PAPERING AN ARCH

1 If you intend to paper an arch between two rooms, first tackle the walls on either side of the opening. Trim the lengths so that you can turn 25 mm (1 in) of paper onto the arch surface. Make small V-shaped cuts into the overlapping paper on the curved section so the tongues lie flat.

2 Cut two strips of paper to 3 mm (⅛ in) less than the thickness of the arch. Hang each one from the bottom up. You can match the pattern on the two vertical sections. Let the two lengths overlap at the head of the arch; cut through both pieces and discard the offcuts for a neat butt joint.

PAPERING AT A FACE PLATE

1 After turning off the power, loosen the screws holding the light switch or socket outlet to its backing box before you start papering. Paper over the face plate, then press the paper against it to mark the corners. Push your scissors through the paper over the centre of the face plate.

2 Make a cut to each corner of the plate, creating four triangular tongues. Then trim off all but about 6 mm (¼ in) of each of the tongues. You may find small scissors easier to manipulate here.

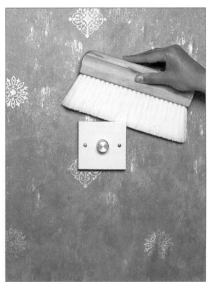

3 Tuck the four tongues carefully behind the loosened face plate, and use your paperhanging brush to ensure that the paper lies flat and bonds well to the wall. Then tighten the fixing screws to trap the tongues in place. Once the paper has been fitted around all the switches and sockets, you can turn the power back on.

PAPERING AROUND FIXED OBJECTS

1 To paper around a fixed obstacle such as a mantelpiece or stair newel post, start by allowing the paper to hang over the object and roughly cut it to shape.

2 At intricate corners, such as at the top corner of a mantelpiece or at tight curves, use small scissors to make a succession of small release cuts into the edge of the wallpaper; this allows it to lie flat against the wall. Trim off any protruding pieces to about 6 mm (¼ in) and continue to cut around the object.

3 You can now cut off each of the 6 mm (¼ in) strips, using a sharp knife for vinyl or small scissors for paper; then use a wallpaper brush to press the paper snugly into place. Remember to wipe away surplus paste as you go. It is much harder to remove when dry.

PAPERING A CEILING

People paper ceilings for one of two reasons. The first is that they prefer a pattern or texture rather than the flat effect that a coat of paint on smooth plaster creates. The second is that they want to conceal a less-than-perfect ceiling surface that may be suffering from unevenness and numerous hairline cracks.

You can, in theory, decorate a ceiling with any style of wallpaper; however, in practice, few people use wallpapers with patterns (especially strong ones) because they would need stripping and replacing at regular intervals to reflect changes in style or taste – and stripping old wallpaper off a ceiling is not an enjoyable job.

Papering a ceiling is not as difficult a task as it might at first appear. In fact, because ceilings have very few obstructions compared with walls, they are actually easier to decorate once you have mastered the knack of working above your head.

BEFORE YOU START

The most important consideration is to set up a proper work platform so you can reach the ceiling comfortably and move across the room on it as you work. Hire shops can offer a variety of options, of which staging on trestles is probably the best. Whatever you choose must be easy to reposition to allow you to hang successive lengths across the room.

Take down pendant lamps and light fixtures, making sure you first turn off the power at the consumer unit or fuse box (see pp.18–19). Finally, treat the ceiling with a coat of wallpaper size if it has not been painted.

Helpful hints

Holding wallpaper while you position it on the ceiling can be a clumsy task. You have two options: either enlist a helper to support the folds of paper as you position it on the ceiling or use a roll of wallpaper still protected by its wrapper to balance the pasted folds of paper above you as you work.

1 It is easier to hang paper across the width of the room rather than down the length. Use a pencil and tape measure or a chalked line to mark a guideline across the ceiling parallel with the wall and just less than the width of the roll away from it.

2 Paste your paper and fold it into a concertina fashion, and carry it to your starting point. Support the folds (or enlist a helper to do so) while you position the end of the length between the wall and ceiling and align it with the guideline. Push the paper into the corner, using your paperhanging brush.

3 Brush the rest of the length into place. Then peel back and trim the two ends and the long edge as you would with paper on the wall, and brush the trimmed edges back into place. Wipe away any surplus paste while it is wet, using a damp cloth.

4 Hang subsequent strips in the same way, butt-joining them and carefully matching any pattern or relief design. Except when hanging embossed papers, run a seam roller along the joins to ensure you acheive a good bond with the ceiling.

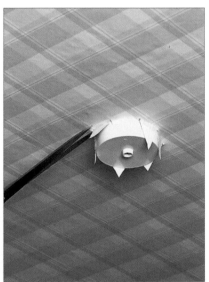

5 At a light fixture, with the power off, make a hole in the paper with the tip of your scissors, then make radial cuts out to the edge of the fixture (small scissors may be easier to use). Fit the tongues around the fixture, and trim them off so they fit flush against it. Wipe away any paste on the fixture, using a damp rag.

6 At a projection, let the paper hang down the wall and cut up to the ceiling. Cut off the excess, then brush and trim the paper into the angles between the ceiling and walls. To finish the ceiling, trim the final length in width before hanging it, but add 50 mm (2 in) extra to the width to allow for trimming at the wall.

PAPERING SLOPING CEILINGS

If you want to paper a loft room with a sloping ceiling, you have two choices. The first is to create an artificial break at waist or head level by putting up a decorative frieze, and to paper below it and paint above it. The second is to choose a paper with an unobtrusive and random pattern, and to paper the entire room with it. Draw a guideline along the centre of the ceiling and hang separate lengths from there down each roof slope.

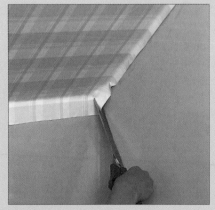

Start by papering the roof slope; make release cuts where it meets a corner.

After the ceiling is papered, hang the paper on the wall and trim it to fit.

USING FRIEZES

You can hang a frieze at ceiling level or in line with a horizontal feature such as a picture rail or dado rail (make sure it's the right way up). Apply it to a painted wall, or hang it over a complementary wallpaper. It comes in a range of widths in standard rolls 5 m (16 ft) or 10 m (33 ft) long.

You can hang a frieze (and a border, see opposite page) using ordinary wallpaper paste if you're putting it on a painted wall or over a standard printed wallpaper. However, ordinary wallpaper paste will not bond to a vinyl or washable wallpaper. If you want to apply a frieze on top of either

A band of pattern can be created by hanging a frieze around the perimeter of a room.

of these surfaces, use a suitable ready-mixed tub adhesive or select a self-adhesive product.

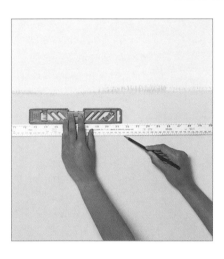

1 Unless you are aligning your frieze with a feature of the room such as the ceiling line or a picture rail, use a torpedo spirit level balanced on a metal straightedge, or use a standard spirit level, to draw a truly horizontal guideline around the room with a pencil.

2 Cut a section of frieze 100 mm (4 in) longer than the wall on which it will be placed, paste it, then fold it into a concertina and take it to the wall. Position it so that 50 mm (2 in) turns around a corner, and brush it into place. Wipe away any squeezed-out paste.

3 Prepare the piece for the next wall as before and hang it so it overlaps the turned end of the previous length. Match the pattern carefully and brush the length into place.

4 Using a utility knife and metal straightedge, cut through both lengths of frieze about 25 mm (1 in) from the corner. Peel back the strips and remove the offcuts, then brush the ends back into position to form a neat butt joint.

FRAMING WITH BORDERS

YOU WILL NEED

Torpedo spirit level **or** standard spirit level
Metal straightedge rule
Pencil
Pasting brush (unless product is self-adhesive)
Paperhanging brush
Paperhanging scissors
Utility knife
Seam roller

MATERIALS

Border
Paste (unless product is self-adhesive)

SEE ALSO

Wallpaper basics pp.132–133
Cutting, pasting and folding wallpaper pp.134–135

Narrower than friezes, borders are ideal for framing door and window openings, and for creating decorative display panels on a wall or ceiling surface within which a mirror or pictures can be displayed. As in the case of friezes (see opposite page), borders come in standard-size rolls.

It is a good idea to experiment with the positioning of borders (and friezes) before they are permanently in place. You can do this by sticking short pieces to the wall with low-tack masking tape or blobs of poster putty.

Decorative borders can enliven otherwise plain walls in a room – they are ideal for a nursery.

1 If you're using a border to frame a feature, draw pencil guidelines around it, using a metal straight-edge. To create a decorative panel away from a room feature, use a spirit level to draw true vertical and horizontal guidelines.

2 Position the first strip, letting its end overlap the adjacent guideline by about 25 mm (1 in). Brush the strip into place and wipe away any squeezed-out paste. Position an intersecting length, using a piece of paper to avoid paste getting on the bottom piece.

3 To create a neatly mitred corner, cut through both strips, using a sharp knife and a metal straightedge. (You can use the straightedge to align the mitre with a mitre in the door or window frame.)

4 Peel away and discard the waste pieces, and remove the piece of paper. Roll the mitred joint flat with a seam roller. For a self-adhesive product, peel off the appropriate amount of the backing paper and position the strips as indicated for paste.

PUTTING UP COVING

YOU WILL NEED

Tape measure and pencil
Shavehook
Fine-toothed saw plus mitre
box **or** mitre frame and saw
Adhesive spatula
Hammer
Putty knife

MATERIALS

Coving
Panel pins
Coving adhesive

SEE ALSO

Installing picture and dado
rails p.149

Coving, or cornice, is a decorative moulding fitted around a room between the walls and the ceiling. It may be a plain quadrant, or it may be elaborately detailed.

Plasterboard and moulded fibrous plaster are the traditional materials for coving; however, they are heavy and expensive, so they are used mainly for restoration work. Moulded foam plastic imitations are an excellent substitute – they are much lighter and easier to install. Some types of coving are put up with prefabricated corner joints, while others require cutting the corner joints during installation.

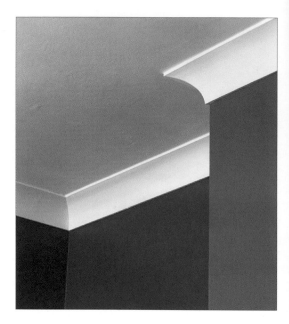

The coving frames the ceiling neatly, and it also conceals any gaps between the ceiling and the walls.

1 Pencil in guide-lines around the room on the walls and ceiling. Scratch the areas between the guidelines with a shavehook to provide a key for the adhesive to grip. For a plaster-type coving, you must remove any wallpaper in the area.

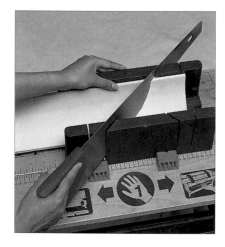

2 Start at the left-hand end of the longest wall in the room. Cut the correct mitre: the one here is for the left-hand end of an internal corner (or right-hand end of an external corner). Use the opposite angle for a right-hand internal corner (or left-hand external corner).

3 Apply adhesive to its rear face and stick the length into place. Use panel pins to support it temporarily. Mitre and fit a matching length at the opposite end of this wall. Then fit plain lengths as required between the two end sections, the last one cut to size.

4 Start the next wall, butting the mitred ends together and filling the joint with adhesive. For a chimney breast, cut mitres on both ends and fit the coving for the back walls of the alcoves; then fit the coving along the sides of the chimney breast and, finally, the front.

INSTALLING PICTURE AND DADO RAILS

YOU WILL NEED

Spirit level and pencil
Tape measure
Tenon saw
Power drill plus twist,
countersink and masonry
drill bits
Screwdriver
Coping saw
Mitre box
Putty knife

MATERIALS

Picture **or** dado rail
Countersink-head screws
Wallplugs (if required)
Panel pins
PVA adhesive
Wood filler

SEE ALSO

Putting up coving p.148

Picture and dado rails are wooden mouldings that are fixed to walls, the former above head height and the latter at waist height. Picture rails allow pictures to be hung without marking the walls with picture hooks, and they provide a visual break in rooms with high ceilings. Dado rails protect the wall from damage by carelessly moved furniture, especially from chairs. The area below a dado rail is often panelled or finished with a lincrusta-type wallcovering; the wall above is painted or papered.

Both picture and dado rails became fashionable in Victorian times, and they are, once again, popular.

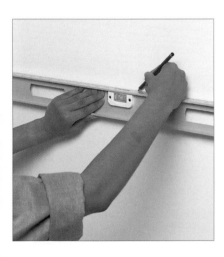

1 Picture and dado rails are installed in the same way, using screws and wallplugs or just screws for plasterboard walls (see p.229). Start by drawing a horizontal pencil guideline around the room at the level you want to fit the rail.

2 Drill clearance and countersink holes in the rails at 600 mm (24 in) intervals. Hold a length up with one end in an internal corner, mark the screw positions on the wall and drill and plug the holes, if needed. Screw the length to the wall, with the screw heads recessed.

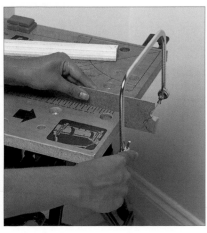

3 Butt joint further lengths together until you reach the next internal corner. Trace the rail profile onto the end of the next length; cut it to shape with a coping saw. Repeat the stages in step 2 to fit it, and continue fitting the rail around the room.

4 At an external corner, cut mitres at a 45° angle on the rails, using a tenon saw and mitre box. Glue and pin the joint once the lengths have been fixed to the wall; this prevents them from opening up in the future. Finally, cover the screw heads with a wood filler.

TILING OPTIONS

POSSIBLE MATERIALS

HAND-MADE TILES

TERRACOTTA TILE

RELIEF BORDER TILES

RELIEF PATTERN TILE

STANDARD FIELD TILE

DADO-STYLE BORDER TILE

ROPE TWIST BORDER TILE

BORDER TILE

PICTORIAL TILE

ROUND-EDGE TILES

MOSAIC TILES

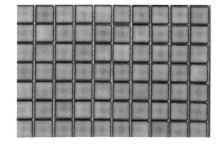

Ceramic tiles are used as a wall covering in two main areas of the home – the kitchen and the bathroom. In each case they are chosen mainly because they offer a hard-wearing and completely waterproof surface that is easy to clean. They are stuck in place with a special tile adhesive, and they can be fixed to plaster, plasterboard, waterproof plywood and even old tiles. Tiles come in a wide range of plain colours and decorative patterns, and are made in several standard sizes. Tiling a wall is an easy task (but perhaps a little time-consuming), once the tile layout has been properly planned. However, as a wall decorating option, it is relatively expensive.

► Small mosaic tiles are perfect for tiling over large areas – the lines of grout help break up the colour. Avoid using dark tiles for a shower recess if you live in a hard water area; otherwise, the tiles will always appear to be covered in a white film of limescale.

◄ Half tiling – up to a height of about 1220 mm (4 ft) – is an economical and stylish option for the bathroom. White tiles are usually the most economical. Finish off the upper edge of the tiled area with a row of border or edge tiles (you can use these to add some colour); plastic edge trims or wood beading are other alternatives.

◀ The variety of designs and patterns available on ceramic tiles is extensive, enabling you to create your own decorative effects. Some tiles fit together to create a larger motif.

▲ Patterned tiles can be used as borders or friezes. Here, the lower, narrow border breaks up the strong colour of the tiles. At the top edge, the dado-style border tiles complement the patterned border tiles between them.

▲ The total area of a kitchen splashback is relatively small, so you can use strong colours that could be overpowering on a larger scale.

▼ You can tile more than just the walls in a bathroom: tile the floor, as well as the bath panel, for a more unified look.

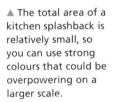

◀ In kitchens, tiles are used to create a splashback, providing a hard-wearing, easy-to-clean wall surface between the worktops and cupboards. You can combine colours to create a simple geometric pattern with the tiles. Alternatively, you can scatter patterned tiles at random across a field of plain tiles.

TILING BASICS

YOU WILL NEED

50 mm x 25 mm
(2 in x 1 in) softwood batten
Pencil
Tile spacers (if required)

MATERIALS

Tiles

SEE ALSO

Dealing with cracks, dents
and stains pp.20–21
Patching holes in walls
pp.22–23
Stripping old wallpaper
pp.26–27
Removing other wall
decorations pp.28–29
Washing down and
preparing surfaces pp.30–31
Tiling a wall pp.154–155

PLOTTING THE TILES
*A plain wall without any
obstructions should have
cut tiles – shown below in
orange – of equal width
(left). When planning a
partially tiled wall, use
whole tiles at the top edge,
perhaps finished with a
row of dado-profile tiles
(centre). If you tile around
a window, it is best to
centre the tiles around it –
this may mean that you
have to cut tiles of uneven
sizes at the ends of the
rows and columns (right).*

Tiling a wall may appear to be a straightforward job. Wall tiles are relatively small and easy to handle, and modern tile adhesives are strong enough to stick them to almost any surface. You can even buy small plastic spacers to ensure that the tiles line up accurately with each other. However, in practice, things can be a little more difficult.

PLANNING THE LAYOUT

Because ceramic tiles are a fixed size, you'll have to cut a number of tiles to complete the job. To achieve a professional look, centre the whole tiles across the wall. Cut tiles of equal size to fit at each end of any horizontal row of tiles, as well as at the top and bottom of the wall-to-ceiling columns. These pieces should be between one-quarter and three-quarters of the width of the tile; anything narrower or wider is difficult to cut accurately. Because rooms are not truly square, you'll have to place all the whole tiles before you can

measure and fit each of the cut pieces. This makes planning the tile layout the most important part of the job.

Centring the tiles is relatively easy on a wall with no major obstacles such as door or window openings. Introduce these obstacles, however, and things get more complex, especially at windows. Because a window is such a major feature on the wall, you'll have to centre the tiles on this instead.

PREPARING THE WALLS

To allow the tile adhesive to adhere to the wall, remove any wallpaper or sand down any paint, using coarse paper with a sanding block. You may need to strip the paint (see *Helpful hints*). Wash down the prepared wall with sugar soap or detergent. Fill any large cracks and holes; the adhesive will fill minor ones. Seal new plaster or bare plasterboard with a plaster primer or emulsion paint. If existing tiles are sound and flat, you can tile over them after washing down the surface to remove dirt and grease.

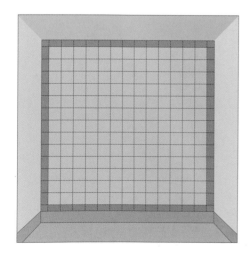

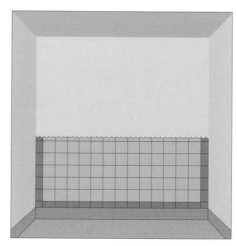

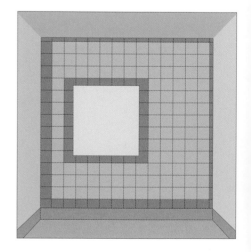

1 To plan the layout of the tiles, make a tile gauge. Use a 1 m (3 ft) length of 50 mm x 25 mm (2 in x 1 in) softwood that has been planed to a true straight edge. Use several tiles – plus tile spacers to allow for the grout joints if the tiles do not have lugs (see step 4, p.155) – to mark their widths along the gauge.

2 Hold the gauge horizontally against the bottom of the wall to work out where the whole tiles will fall. Adjust it so that the pieces at the ends will be of equal size. However, if there is a window, centre the tile layout on the window opening, with cut pieces of equal size fitting at each side of the window.

3 If you centre the gauge and find that you will be faced with cutting narrow pieces of tile (less than one-quarter of its width), move the gauge along by half a tile's width to increase the width of the cut tile.

4 Repeat the process in the vertical plane. This process will tell you how many tiles will be needed for each row (count cut tiles as whole tiles) and how many in each column.

ESTIMATING QUANTITIES

Once you have determined where the whole and cut tiles will be positioned, it is a simple matter to multiply the number of tiles in one column by the number of tiles in one row to find the quantity of tiles required. This total counts cut pieces as whole tiles, but you should add some extra tiles to allow for breakages. How many depends on the scale of the job and how good you are at cutting tiles, but 5–10 percent of the total is a reasonable number. Finally, find out how many tiles come in a pack and calculate how many packs you will require for the job.

You will also need tile adhesive (check the tubs for the wall area each will cover), plus grout to fill the gaps between the tiles, unless you are using a combined adhesive/grout.

Helpful hints

It is always wise to save a dozen or so extra tiles after the job is completed. They will be useful for replacing tiles that may have to be removed to make repairs, such as to pipes or wiring hidden in the wall behind them, or for replacing any tiles that have been drilled to install fixtures or have become damaged. (To remove a damaged tile, see p.28.)

Not all painted walls can be tiled. The best way to test the surface is to stick adhesive tape on an area and leave it overnight. Pull off the tape. If the paint comes off with it, the paint must be stripped (see pp.28–29) – otherwise the tiles will fall off the wall.

TILING A WALL

YOU WILL NEED

Softwood battens
Masonry nails
Spirit level
Hammer
Notched adhesive spreader
Tile spacers (if required)
Tape measure and wax pencil
Platform atile cutter

Mosaic tiles

Battens and masonry nails
Spirit level
Hammer
Notched adhesive spreader
Wooden mallet and carpet-covered board
Utility knife **or** scissors

MATERIALS

Adhesive **or** combined adhesive/grout
Tiles

Mosaic tiles

Adhesive **or** combined adhesive/grout
Sheets of mosaic tiles

SEE ALSO

Tiling basics pp.152–153
Tiling at corners, windows and doors pp.156–157
Tiling in bathrooms and kitchens pp.158–159
Grouting and sealing pp.160–161

When you are tiling a whole wall or room, the most important thing to remember is that walls are seldom square to each other. Even apparent horizontals, such as skirting boards, may not be true, so do not use them as tile guides. Instead, fix horizontal and vertical guide battens to each wall, positioned in accordance with the starting points you planned earlier with your tile gauge. However,

if you are tiling above a bath or kitchen worktop that you know to be level, there is no need for guide battens. The first row of tiles can be fixed so they rest immediately on top of the bath or worktop.

For more details on tiling at corners and around doors and windows, see pp.156–157. Tiling in bathrooms and kitchens may demand using a special adhesive (see pp.158–159).

MOSAIC TILES

Sheets of small tiles stuck to a net backing or paper facing are available – these are known as mosaic tiles. The sheets allow you to apply over 100 tiles at a time, without having to space each individual tile.

Mosaic tiles use the same adhesive and grout as their larger cousins. Press the sheet into the bed of adhesive, allowing grouting space between sheets. Tap the tiles in place, using a wooden mallet against a carpet-covered board. Trim the facing or backing if you need to fill areas with strips or single tiles. If there is a paper facing, wait for the adhesive to dry before soaking off the paper with a wet sponge.

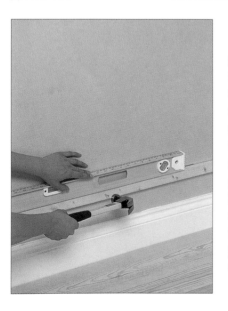

1 Pre-drill holes in your horizontal guide batten to take masonry nails. Hold the batten in place, following the marks made previously with the tile gauge, and use a spirit level to get the batten truly horizontal. Drive the nails in partly, leaving the heads proud so you can prise them out later.

2 Fit a second batten at one edge of the area to be tiled, at right angles to the horizontal batten, to act as a vertical guide to the edge column of tiles. Attach horizontal and vertical battens to other walls being tiled.

3 Scoop out some tile adhesive and spread a band of it on the wall, a little wider than the height of the first row of tiles, starting at the lower corner created by the battens. Press the teeth of the spreader firmly against the wall to leave ridges of adhesive that are of equal height.

4 Rest the edge of the first tile on the horizontal batten, align it with the vertical one and press it into the adhesive. Working horizontally, press the next tile into place. Butt together tiles that have spacing lugs; use plastic tile spacers for square-edged tiles. Continue the process until all the whole tiles are in place.

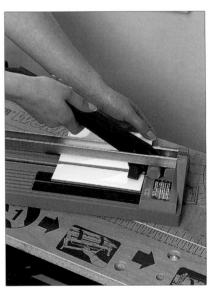

5 Leave the adhesive to harden for at least four hours, then prise off the vertical battens. Measure each edge tile individually for cutting, using a wax pencil to make your markings. You will get the best results (and the fewest breakages) if you use a platform tile cutter rather than a pencil-point tile cutter.

6 After cutting a tile, set it into place by spreading the adhesive on the back of the tile instead of on the wall. Continue cutting and setting each edge tile, one at a time.

7 After completing the edge tiles up the sides of the wall, remove the horizontal battens and tile along the bottom edge. To fit a tile into a corner, you may have to cut it both horizontally and vertically. Once the adhesive on the edge tiles has set, you can finish off with grout and any sealant (see pp.160–161).

Helpful hints

Notched adhesive spreaders apply an even coat of adhesive. However, if a section of the wall is slightly undulating, the tiles may not lie flat. As you work, use a spirit level laid across the faces of several tiles to make sure they are flush with each other. If one is protruding, gently push against it until it is flush.

Wipe off any adhesive that gets onto the face of the tile while it is still wet – the adhesive will be difficult to remove once it has dried.

TILING AT CORNERS, WINDOWS AND DOORS

If you are tiling adjacent walls or a whole room, you will have to tile at internal and, possibly, external corners. Because corners are seldom straight or true, tile each wall in isolation, working from the horizontal guide battens. Take particular care in setting the levels of the horizontal guide battens on adjacent walls so that they are levelled with each other. If they are fractionally out of alignment, the tile columns will run out of true as you work, and if you are tiling to ceiling level, the tile rows will not align where they meet above the door.

When tiling around a window recess, tile the face of the wall with whole tiles first, then the cut tiles, the sides of the recess and the sill. If the door to the room is in the centre of a wall and you are tiling to ceiling level, centre the tile layout on the wall as best you can to avoid narrow cut pieces beside the door and at the room corners. If the door is in the corner of the room,

Finishing a window recess with tiles will help it blend in with a wall tiled from ceiling to floor.

set out the two walls as usual, then cut tiles in the area above the door to complete floor-to-ceiling tiling. A window is shown being tiled here, but the principles also apply to a door.

1 If you are tiling to ceiling level, place all the whole tiles up to the window, but not over the window. Fit a batten to the wall, with its top edge aligned with the bottom edge of the lowest row of whole tiles above the height of the window. The batten supports the whole tiles applied above the window.

2 Fill in the cut tiles around the window. Start near the sill, where you may have to make an L-shaped cut (see step 3) or use tile nippers (see step 5) to fit the tile around the sill. Make sure you plan the tile layout ahead of time to avoid making difficult cuts (see pp.152–153).

3 If you have to cut an L-shaped tile, mark cutting lines on the tile face with a wax pencil. Clamp the tile between scrap wood (or the wooden jaws of a work station) to cut the first line with a tile saw. Score and snap the second cut; smooth the edges with a tile file. If the tile is thin, clamp it horizontally to help prevent it breaking.

4 Wait for the adhesive to set before removing the batten at the top of the window and fitting the remaining tiles on the wall. You may have to cut L-shaped tiles to fit at the corners. Make sure you plan ahead to avoid thin strips that can easily break as you make the cuts.

5 If you have to trim off only a thin strip, make a score mark with a tile cutter, then nibble away the waste area with tile nippers. Finish off by using a tile file to smooth the cut. (You can also use tile nippers to make a curved edge if you score the tile with a hand-held tile cutter.)

6 Place all the whole tiles inside the window recess. If the tiles do not have spacing lugs, make sure you use tile spacers between the bottom tiles and window sill to allow for a grouting gap.

7 Finally, measure and cut each individual tile to fill in the back of the window recess. Once the adhesive dries, after about 4 hours, you can finish off by grouting (see pp.160–161).

Helpful hints

For an internal corner, cut and fit each of the tiles in the last column on one wall so that they run to the corner. Then fit the last column of tiles for the second wall, using tile spacers to leave a grouting gap in the angle between the two columns.

At an external corner, place whole tiles on each side of the angle. If the tiles you are using have fully glazed edges, let the tiles on the most prominent wall overlap the others; otherwise, use a plastic corner trim embedded in tile adhesive.

TILING IN BATHROOMS AND KITCHENS

A small area of tiles makes an ideal waterproof splashback around a washbasin, even if the rest of the room is decorated in another finish.

Ceramic tiles are perfect for areas in the bathroom and kitchen that require protection from water. You can use them to create a splashback at a washbasin, bath or kitchen worktop. They provide a waterproof finish for the solid walls of a shower cubicle, but all corners and joints with other materials must be completely waterproof. You can also tile the panelling around the bath.

Tiling a splashback for a worktop or bath is simple. It should be at least 600 mm (24 in) high to protect the wall from moisture. For a bath, place whole tiles at the outer edges of the splashback, aligned with the edge of the bath, and fit cut tiles in the internal angles. To tile a shower cubicle, apply the adhesive to the walls and set the bottom row of tiles so they overlap the edges of the shower tray.

Treat a bath panel as you would any tiled area, centring the tiles if you are fitting only the panel along the side of the bath. Fit the tiles so their top edges are beneath the rim of the bath. To fit both a side and an end panel, place whole tiles on each side of the external angle and fit cut tiles in the internal angles where the panels meet the walls.

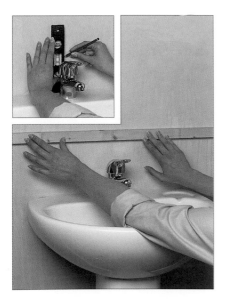

1 A splashback around a basin can be as narrow as the basin itself or can extend by one or two tiles at each side of the basin. Centre the tiles behind the basin, using a tiling gauge to determine the layout of the tiles. Use a torpedo spirit level to mark the centre of the layout and a standard spirit level to find a true horizontal line.

2 If the tiles extend beyond the basin, attach a batten so that its top edge is flush with the top of the basin. If the tile will be close to the edges of the tiled area, put the adhesive on the back of the tile to avoid getting it onto untiled areas; use the notched spreader to spread the adhesive evenly. In larger areas, apply the adhesive to the wall.

3 Begin by applying the first row of tiles above the basin, starting from the centre and working toward the edges. Depending on the size of the tiles, you should have at least one or two rows to make a splashback roughly 300 mm (12 in) high.

4 To fit tiles around the curve of the basin, use a profile gauge to transfer the shape to the tiles. Clamp the tile flat on a work surface and use a tile saw to make the cut; then use a tile file to smooth the cut edge. Continue applying the tiles, using a batten to keep them vertically aligned at the edges.

5 To add border tiles around the splashback, centre them along the top. After applying the last whole tile, measure and mark a tile to make a mitre corner. Make sure you mark the measurement at the bottom of the tile; the top of the mitre will extend beyond the tiled area. Clamp the tile to a work surface; cut it with a tile saw.

6 Test fit the second mitred tile before applying the adhesive to the back of the tile. You may have to use a tile file to help the fit of the joint. Finish applying the last of the border tiles, and wait for the adhesive to dry before adding the grout and sealant (see pp.160–161).

Helpful hints

To tile a bath panel, replace the standard plastic panel with exterior-grade plywood, supported on a strong wood framework. Start by clamping a batten below the bath rim. Then fix a batten to the floor, directly below the top batten. Cut vertical posts to fit between the two battens, set them in place at 460 mm (18 in) intervals and drive screws through them into the horizontal battens. Cut plywood panels to size and tile them. Attach them to the frame using dome-head screws (to drill a hole in a tile for a screw, see right) – you can unscrew a panel if you need to reach the plumbing.

MAKING HOLES IN TILES

To tile around the water supply pipes for a bath or shower, turn off the water valves and remove the handles. Centre the tiles at the pipes; use tile nippers to cut away semicircles to fit around them.

To drill a hole in a tile (for example, to install a towel rack), use a masonry bit. Mark the position for the hole with a wax pencil, then cover it with clear tape to prevent the bit from slipping.

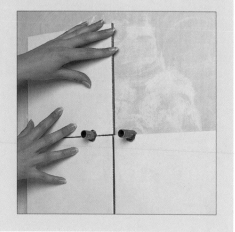

GROUTING AND SEALING

An area of ceramic tiles is not waterproof until the gaps between the tiles have been filled – a process known as grouting. You can buy grout in powder form or as a ready-mixed product, or you can use your tile adhesive as grout if the manufacturer says it is suitable for that purpose. Most people choose white grout, but coloured grout is also available and can look striking set against white or mainly white tiles.

SEALANTS

Where an area of tiles meets another surface, such as a bath, shower tray or kitchen worktop, there is always a risk of water penetration should the two surfaces move apart. To eliminate this hazard, seal the gap with silicone sealant – a waterproof compound that bonds to both surfaces, yet remains elastic enough to cope with any movement without cracking or splitting. This sealant is available in

A shower cubicle requires grouting between tiles, as well as sealant between the bottom row of the tiles and the shower tray, to become truly waterproof.

white, as well as in several popular colours. It comes in cartridges that fit into a special gun fitted with a trigger, and more recently, in a squeezable tube with a nozzle.

1 Use your grout spreader to press some grout into the gaps between the tiles, drawing the blade across the tiles at right angles to each grout line. Scrape away any excess grout from the face of the tiles as you work.

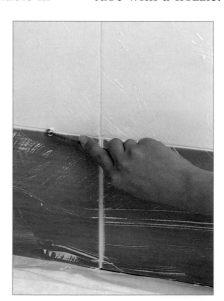

2 Draw a grout finisher along the grout lines to give them a neat concave finish. Alternatively, you can use a piece of dowel or other rounded object, such as a ball-point pen top, to create the same effect.

3 Leave the grout to harden, then wipe the tile surface with a clean damp sponge to remove any excess grout. If a combined adhesive-grout is used, it should be wiped off while it is wet – it's difficult to remove once it has dried.

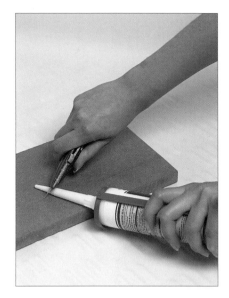

4 Cut the sealant cartridge nozzle at a 45° angle along a point that will give an extruded bead wide enough to bridge the gap between the two surfaces. Place the cartridge into the gun holder.

5 Following the manufacturer's directions, squeeze the trigger and push or pull the nozzle along the gap as you hold it at a 45° angle to both surfaces. On cartridges that are pushed, the edge of the nozzle helps to shape the sealant bead into a neat concave shape as it is extruded. If your cartridge doesn't state what to do, push it.

6 When you have finished applying the sealant, release the trigger and set the gun aside. You can draw a moistened finger (or wet lint-free cloth) along the bead of sealant to smooth it if necessary.

7 Finally, finish off by using a dry cloth to wipe away any remaining traces of grout – there is often a fine white residue left over from the previous sponging.

Helpful hints

Getting a smooth straight bead of silicone sealant between a tiled area and another surface can be more difficult than it looks. To get a feel for using the gun, practise on a piece of scrap material such as cardboard or hardboard.

Before starting to seal the gap, you can place strips of masking tape on each surface, leaving a space a little wider than the gap you need to fill. Peel off the strips of masking tape once the sealant is touch dry.

CLADDING OPTIONS

POSSIBLE MATERIALS

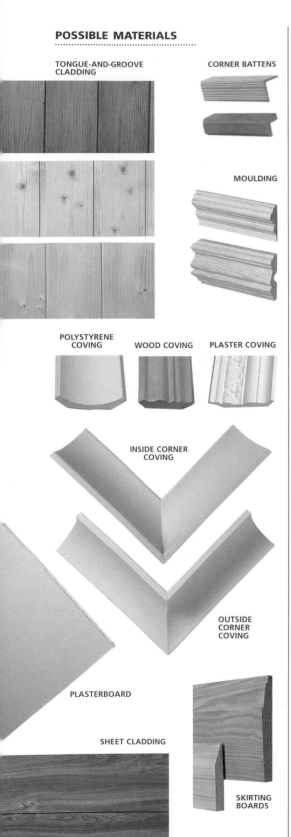

TONGUE-AND-GROOVE CLADDING

CORNER BATTENS

MOULDING

POLYSTYRENE COVING   WOOD COVING   PLASTER COVING

INSIDE CORNER COVING

OUTSIDE CORNER COVING

PLASTERBOARD

SHEET CLADDING

SKIRTING BOARDS

Lining interior wall surfaces with wood in the form of panelling or cladding has been popular for centuries. The surface created is hard-wearing, warm to the touch and an excellent cover-up for less-than-perfect masonry or plasterwork. It can be crafted and finished in a number of different ways, depending on how the cladding is used.

Cladding has practical applications, too. Fitting insulation behind cladding on exterior walls dramatically reduces heat loss – this is useful in homes with solid walls, which are otherwise difficult to insulate effectively. Cladding can also help reduce noise transmission between rooms when it is used on interior walls.

▲ A less expensive alternative to wood cladding are man-made sheets known as wallboards. These are available with a range of surface finishes, including wood veneer, and many are finished with a protective coating. Because of the size of the sheets, wallboards are best used on unobstructed walls.

◄ You can finish natural wood cladding with paint, varnish or wood stain. If you're using varnish, you can choose either clear or coloured varnish. The latter will give the wood a moderate depth of colour; use a wood stain and clear varnish if you want a dark shade.

◄ You can install the cladding vertically or horizontally. Conceal any joints, such as those at a window, with lengths of beading. You can use coving at ceiling level and skirting boards at floor level.

▶ Boarded ceilings were popular in Victorian times as an alternative to lath and plaster. The wood boards were always painted.

◄ There is no need for a supporting framework when cladding a ceiling. The boards are fixed in place by driving nails through the existing ceiling surface and into the joists above. Light fixtures are the only obstructions that you'll have to work around.

▲ Cladding up a wall to waist level and topping the area with a dado rail can be used to good effect in the bathroom or hallway. You can use cladding to panel around the bath, too.

▶ Prepare wood-clad walls for painting like any other wood surface. The boards can look particularly attractive if treated with a paint effect such as stencilling, dragging or colourwashing.

▶ To preserve the look of natural wood, protect the cladding with a clear matt varnish (see pp.182–183). For a paler finish, try liming wax.

PREPARING WALLS FOR CLADDING

YOU WILL NEED

Fixing the battens
Tape measure and pencil
Spirit level
Tenon saw **or** power jigsaw
Power drill plus twist bit **or**
power drill on hammer
action plus masonry bit (for
plaster walls)

Insulating a wall
Work gloves
Dust mask
Staple gun (if fixing a
vapour barrier)

MATERIALS

Fixing the battens
50 mm x 25 mm
(2 in x 1 in) wood battens
(sawn softwood is less
expensive than planed)
Masonry nails **or** screws and
wallplugs

Insulating a wall
Insulation batts (for an
exterior wall or sound-
proofing) and polythene
vapour barrier (for an
exterior wall) **or** rigid
expanded polystyrene
insulation board

SEE ALSO
Fixing tongue-and-groove
cladding pp.166–167
Fixing sheet cladding
pp.168–169

If you are installing floor-to-ceiling wood cladding or sheet cladding, you will probably be fitting it to just one wall of the room as a decorative feature. Waist-high cladding, typically finished with a dado rail on top, is likely to run around the room in which it is being installed.

You'll need horizontal battens running across the wall surface to which the boards will be fixed. Wall-to-ceiling cladding requires battens at floor and ceiling level and at 760 mm (30 in) intervals in between. For waist-high cladding, three equally spaced battens are ideal. The top one should be at 860 mm (34 in). If you want to run tongue-and-groove cladding horizontally, put up the battens vertically. For more details on sheet cladding, including using an adhesive instead of battens, see pp.168–169.

You can use the existing skirting board as the lowest batten if it is thick enough. Removing skirting boards

without damaging them is difficult (see pp.36–37), so it is usually best to leave them in place and to finish the wall with new boards that closely match the existing ones (see pp.38–39).

Insulation is not necessary on an interior wall, unless you want to soundproof it. You should always insulate an exterior wall and use a vapour barrier before cladding it.

Helpful hints

When you are estimating the quantity of tongue-and-groove cladding you'll need for the job, remember that the actual face width of each board is noticeably less than the nominal width, thanks to the presence of the tongue and groove. For example, a board that is nominally 100 mm (4 in) wide will have an exposed face width of about 90 mm (3½ in) once it is interlocked with its neighbours.

It is also important to find out in what lengths your timber merchant stocks cladding, so that you can minimize wastage. Buying wood in 1.8 m (6 ft) lengths for use as waist-high cladding 860 mm (34 in) high would waste far less than cutting pieces from wood that is 2 m (6 ft 6 in) long.

FIXING THE BATTENS

1 For waist-high cladding, measure up from the floor 860 mm (34 in) and mark the wall for the first batten, using a spirit level. Draw a line for the middle batten 430 mm (17 in) up from the floor in the same way. For full-height cladding, start by fixing lengths of batten at ceiling level.

2 To install a batten, cut it to size. Drill equally spaced pilot holes along its length or to match the wall studs (see p.229) in a plasterboard wall. For a plaster wall, position the batten on the wall and mark the holes; drill holes into the wall and insert wallplugs. Screw the batten to either type of wall.

3 When cladding more than one wall, butt together the battens at external corners. At internal corners, with one batten fixed, position the adjacent batten and hold a tongue-and-groove offcut between them to leave a gap for the cladding. Install the batten as in step 2. (Fit the cladding running to the corner first.)

4 Use a small piece of cardboard, folded over to the required thickness, to fill any gaps between the batten and the wall before screwing the batten on.

INSULATING A WALL

1 Wearing gloves and a mask, cut off small lengths off insulation and push them between the battens. If you plan to install sheet cladding, first secure vertical battens between the horizontal ones, centred where the ends of the sheets will meet (see p.168).

2 A vapour barrier is only neccessary on external walls. Cut a length of polythene and staple one end to the top batten. Get a helper to pull the length down taut. Starting from the top, staple the taut polythene onto the other battens. Trim off the excess at the floor.

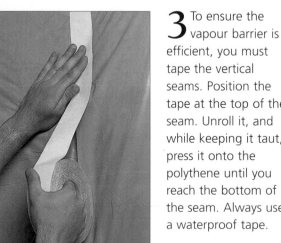
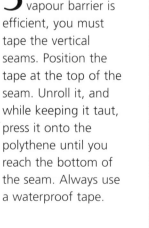

3 To ensure the vapour barrier is efficient, you must tape the vertical seams. Position the tape at the top of the seam. Unroll it, and while keeping it taut, press it onto the polythene until you reach the bottom of the seam. Always use a waterproof tape.

EXPANDED POLYSTYRENE BOARDS

You can use rigid expanded polystyrene boards rather than insulation batts. Cut pieces to size with a fine-tooth saw and wedge them between the battens. These boards are waterproof, so there is no need for a vapour barrier when installing them.

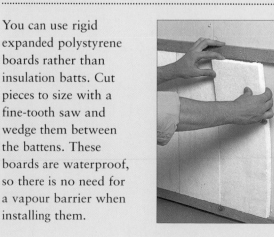

FIXING TONGUE-AND-GROOVE CLADDING

YOU WILL NEED

Tape measure
Spirit level
Scribing block and pencil
Tenon saw **or** jigsaw
Work surface
Clamp
Hammer
Fine nails **or** panel pins **or** fixing clips
Nail punch
Power drill plus twist bit
Padsaw
Plane
Putty knife

MATERIALS

Cladding
Dado rail
Skirting board
Wood filler

SEE ALSO

Replacing skirting boards
pp.38–39
Preparing walls for cladding
pp.164–165
Fixing sheet cladding
pp.168–169

Tongue-and-groove cladding that has been finished with a dado rail and skirting board is one attractive way to break up a large expanse of wall.

With the wall battens installed (see pp.164–165), it is time to cut and fix the cladding in place. Cladding at waist height is typically fixed around a room. However, the steps below describe how to fit the end boards in case you don't wish to do a complete room (especially when using the cladding at floor-to-ceiling height).

You can nail through the face of the boards, then punch in and fill over the nail heads. However, you will get a neater finish if you nail through the tongue of each board or use fixing clips that grip the grooved edge of the board. In each case the fixing is concealed by the adjacent board.

Stack the cladding in the room a few days before installation to allow it to acclimatize to the temperature and humidity of the room. This minimizes the risk of the wood shrinking or splitting after the cladding is installed.

Helpful hints

A light switch or socket outlet on the wall that you are cladding may have to be repositioned if it is flush mounted. After turning the power off at the mains, disconnect it and remove the mounting box. Insert packing in the recess and reposition the box so its edge will be flush with the finished surface. If it is surface mounted, fit the boards around the box to leave it flush mounted. In either case, fix short lengths of batten around the wiring accessory to support the cut ends of the boards (see p.168).

1 If you are cladding just one wall, the first board (and the last one) needs to fit snugly against the adjacent wall. Cut the board to length. With its grooved edge against the flanking wall, use a spirit level to check that it is vertical; temporarily fix the board to the top and bottom battens, using panel pins.

2 Position a scribing block (a small block of wood) and a pencil at the top of the board. With the block touching the flanking wall, bring the block and pencil down the board, transferring the profile of the wall onto the board. Remove the panel pins; clamp the board to a work surface and cut along the line with a jigsaw.

3 Nail the first board onto the battens by fixing nails through its tongue at a 45° angle. Use a nail punch to drive the nails below the surface so the groove of the next board can fit over the tongue. Push the next board in place, with the tops level, and nail as before. Drill fine holes for nails if the tongues are brittle and split.

4 Continue to the last board for the wall, which may need trimming with a saw or plane to fit, or scribing if you are not cladding the next wall. When cladding internal corners for more than one wall, butt the first board of the second row snugly into the flanking cladding and nail it in place.

5 Where cladding meets at an external corner, temporarily fit the last board with its end protruding beyond the corner. Use the cladded wall as a guide to draw a pencil line on the protruding board. Remove and clamp the last board to a work surface, and plane or saw off the wastage indicated by the pencil line.

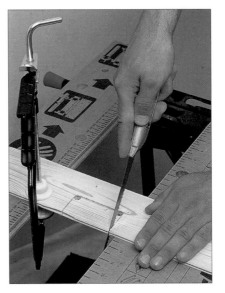

6 To cut out the profile of a switch plate or power point, mark out its position on the board. Clamp the board to a work surface and drill a hole in each corner. Insert a padsaw into a hole and cut along the marks. (To fit battens around an electrical box, see step 2 on page 168.)

7 When fixing battens up to window or door reveals or to end at an external corner, they should stop short by the thickness of a board. Finish the end of the cladding by cutting a piece of cladding lengthways the same width as the end of the run of cladding. Then nail it in place onto the ends of the battens.

8 To finish the top of the cladding, cut lengths of board to the width from the front of the cladding to the wall. At corners, cut mitres at the ends (see p.148). Nail the lengths on top of the cladding. Cut the dado rail and nail it to the face of the cladding; use a nail punch to sink the nails below the surface and cover with a wood filler.

FIXING SHEET CLADDING

YOU WILL NEED

Tape measure and pencil
Panel saw and padsaw **or** jigsaw
Hammer
Screwdriver (if required)
Utility knife
Scribing block
Work surface
Profile gauge
Cartridge gun (if required)

MATERIALS

Softwood battens
Masonry nails **or** screws and wall plugs
Fine fixing nails **or** screws **or** panel adhesive
Wallboards
Skirting board (if required)
Coving (if required)

SEE ALSO

Replacing skirting boards pp.38–39
Adding coving p.148
Preparing walls for cladding pp.164–165
Fixing tongue-and-groove cladding pp.166–167

The wallboards for sheet cladding have either a natural wood veneer finish or a printed and laminated decorative surface layer. The base of the board may be hardboard or thin plywood, and these come in standard 2440 mm × 1220 mm (8 ft × 4 ft) sheets. Because of the large size of individual sheets, it is important to plan how the joints will fall on the wall. Door or window openings provide obvious sites for joints.

You can nail or screw the boards to a framework of wall battens, in much the same way as natural wood cladding is installed. Modern panel adhesives are capable of securing full-height boards with ease, although nailing or screwing them in place does at least mean that the boards can be removed more easily if you wanted a change of decor in the future.

Smaller obstacles such as light switches and power points may need repositioning (see pp.166–167) if the

If you want to give one or more of your walls the appearance of wood cladding or ceramic tiling, without the expense or the intricate fixing methods, then a man-made wallboard could be the solution.

boards are being fixed over battens. Once the wall has been cladded, seal the vertical seams between the sheets with a sealant the same colour as the vertical grooves in the laminate.

1 If you're installing the sheets over battens, position both horizontal and vertical battens to support all the sheet edges, and add intermediate battens at 610 mm (2 ft) intervals. Cut and install the battens in the same way as for those on pp.164–165.

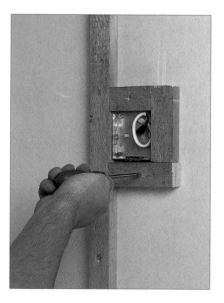

2 Fit battens around light switches and power point boxes. Cut the battens to fit snugly against the box, then drill equally spaced pilot holes in them. Mark the positions of the pilot holes on the wall, drill and insert wall plugs (avoid the cables, see p.229), then screw the battens in place. (For plasterboard walls, use panel adhesive.)

3 To cut the sheet to the height of the wall, it must be well supported. Measure and mark the required length with a pencil line; then score along this line with a utility knife to prevent the laminate from splitting while sawing. Have a helper hold the sheet steady while you saw along the waste side of the scored line.

4 You may have to scribe and cut the first sheet to fit tightly against the adjacent wall (see p.166). Once cut, hold the sheet firmly against the battens. Starting at the top, drive nails or screws through the sheet into the vertical and horizontal battens until you reach the bottom. Butt the next sheet against this and continue the process.

5 To make a cut-out around a light switch or power point, lay the sheet on a work surface. Mark the position of the light switch on the sheet and drill a hole into the waste area at each corner. Insert a padsaw into the holes and cut along the drawn lines.

6 When a sheet is butted up to an internal corner, the profile of the skirting board must be cut out. You can use a profile gauge to transfer the shape of the skirting board to the bottom of the sheet. Cut along the pencil line with a jigsaw. Once the cladding is installed, add skirting board and coving if you wish.

USING ADHESIVES

Instead of nails or screws, you can use a panel adhesive on the battens to secure the sheets to the walls; follow the manufacturer's directions. If the walls are smooth and without any imperfections, you can dispense with the battens and glue the sheets directly onto the walls.

To fit around a flush switch or power point, with the power off at the mains, remove the faceplate. Make a cut-out for the box (see step 5), then refit the faceplate using longer screws.

Apply glue to the back of the sheet in a zig-zag line around the edges, across the middle and diagonally from corners.

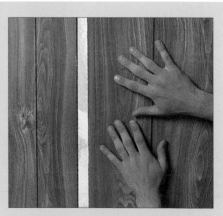

Position one end against the bottom of the wall. Slide it up to the adjacent sheet, then press it firmly into place.

BUILDING A PARTITION WALL

YOU WILL NEED

Tape measure and pencil
Chalk line
Panel saw **or** jigsaw
Spirit level
Power drill plus twist bit and masonry drill bit (for masonry walls)
Claw hammer
Screwdriver
Wide filler knife

MATERIALS

100 mm x 50 mm
(4 in x 2 in) sawn softwood
100-mm- (4-in-) long round wire nails for assembling framework
Screws and frame plugs
Plasterboard
Plasterboard nails
Joint tape
Joint filler

SEE ALSO

Replacing skirting boards pp.38–39
Repairing door frames pp.78–79
A new door: measuring up and fitting hinges pp.82–83
A new door: hanging it and fitting handles pp.84–85
Painting basics pp.114–115
Putting up coving p.148

Few homes make the best use of the room space available, and family needs often change as time goes by. One way of altering the way you use the space you have is to subdivide existing rooms – for example, to create two separate bedrooms out of one larger room, to form an en suite bathroom or to partition off a dining area in a large living room.

The actual erection and cladding of the wall framework is a straight-forward, two-person job. However, the job requires careful planning to get optimum results. If the wall runs parallel with the existing floor joists, you should position it directly over a joist if possible. Make sure new doors will have room to open without any obstruction. Lastly, plan to run any extension to the house wiring, plumbing or heating within the framework of the new wall. You will also have to alter the existing room lighting arrangement.

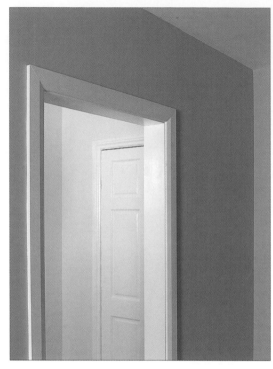

A partition wall can allow you to reorganize the space in your home to suit your own needs.

Helpful hints

Seek advice from your local authority to make sure your new partition wall meets the Building Regulations. For example, a bedroom must have a window and a bathroom must have some type of ventilation such as an extractor fan.

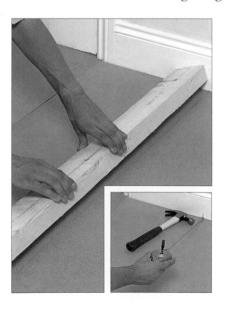

1 Mark the position of the wall on the floor with a chalk line. Position the sole plate along the chalk line, leaving a gap for a door, if necessary, and secure it to the joists below with wire nails (or screws if upstairs). Mark positions for the stud on the sole plate at 600 mm (24 in) centres; use intervals of 400 mm (16 in) for extra support.

2 Measure and cut vertical end studs to fit between the head and sole plates, making notches to fit over skirting boards. Prop the head plate in place; tap the studs into position, using a spirit level to keep them vertically aligned above the sole plate. Drill clearance holes in them and the walls, tap in frame plugs and drive in the screws.

3 Measure, cut and fit the remaining studs one by one. Cut a piece of wood to a length that matches the stud separation, and use it between the studs as a nailing support. Check that the stud is vertical by using a spirit level, then fix it to the sole and head plates by skew-nailing, with the nails at a 45° angle.

4 After you fix a stud, make sure that the frame is truly vertical, using a spirit level. If it starts to wander out of alignment, use a hammer to tap the head plate into the correct position. Drive a screw through the head plate, between fixed studs. (Nailing can crack the ceiling.)

5 After you have fixed in place all the studs (leaving space for a door, if necessary) add horizontal braces, known as noggings, halfway up the wall. Stagger them as shown so that you can nail through the studs into the ends of the noggings. Skew-nail the noggings at the end studs.

6 To frame a door opening, measure and cut a stud, or door head, to fit horizontally between the two studs that form the sides of the door. Nail through the studs into the ends of the door head. Then fix a short vertical stud between the door head and the head plate, skew-nailing it at the head plate.

7 If you have no plumbing or wiring experience, hire someone to run any necessary additions in the wall frame. Use a utility knife to trim the plasterboard to fit horizontally or vertically, and nail it to both sides of the wall frame. Use notches above each side of the door frame to accept a piece of plasterboard above the door.

8 Run joint tape down each joint, then cover it with joint filler. Use the filler to cover any nail heads. Then add coving, skirting boards and architraves, and hang the door. Of course, you'll also want to paint your new walls. Make sure you use a primer to seal the plasterboard before applying the first coat of paint.

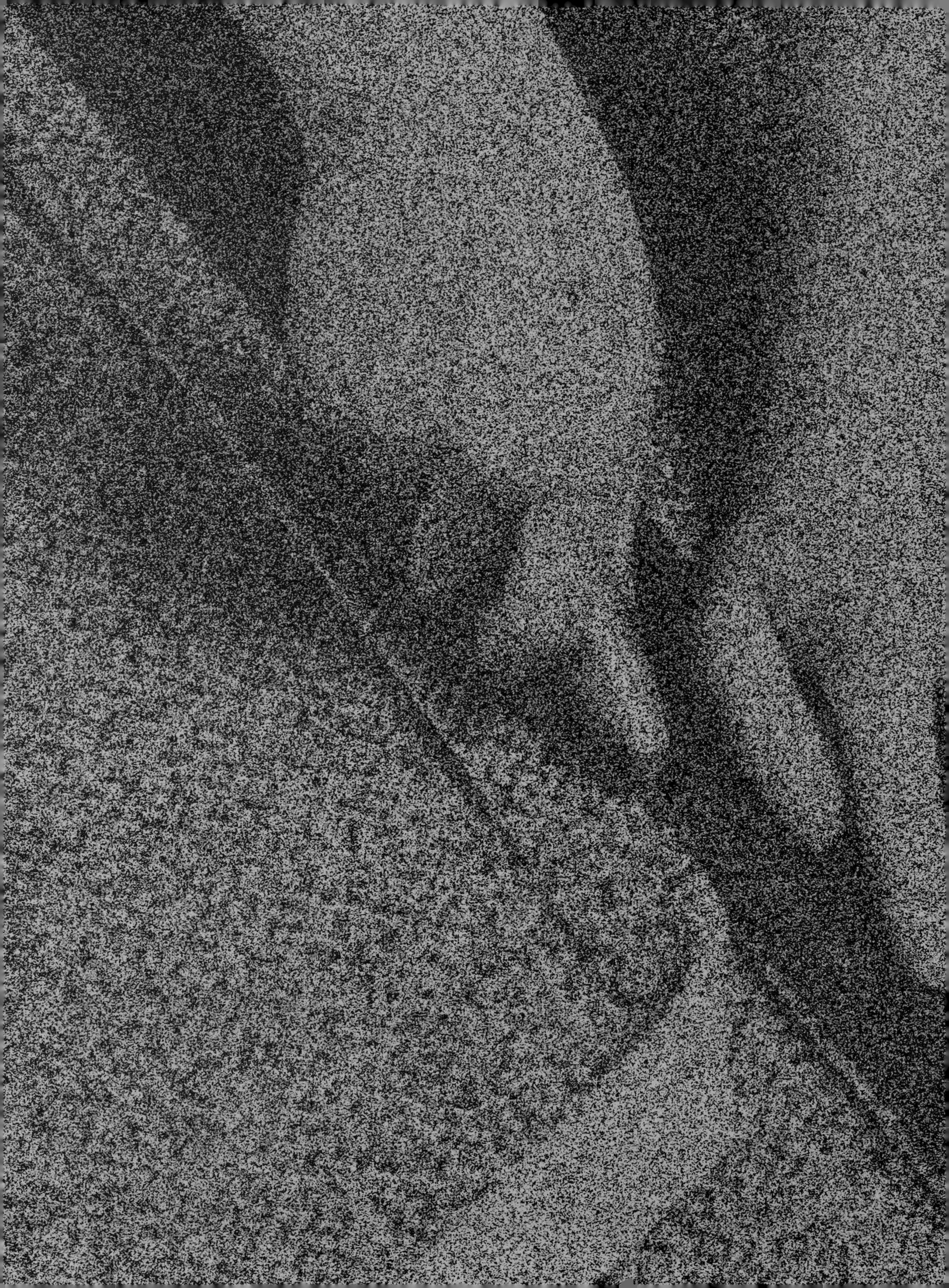

4

FLOORS

FLOORS DIRECTORY

WOOD FLOOR OPTIONS

SEE PAGES 178–179

For the basic floor itself, you should use either softwood floorboards or sheets of chipboard. As a decorative wood floor covering, you can choose from solid hardwood strip flooring laid as a "floating" floor, thicker "laminate" flooring (hardwood veneer on a softwood base) nailed on top of or to replace an existing floor, mosaic floor coverings (small strips laid in a pattern such as "basketweave") or solid woodblock flooring (which is appropriate for solid concrete floors).

Wood floorboards should be sealed with varnish; you may want to stain or paint the wood first, or create a special decorative effect with the paint by using liming wax or stencilling.

SANDING FLOORBOARDS

SKILL LEVEL High
TIME FRAME 1 day
SPECIAL TOOLS Floor sander (hired), edging sander (hired) or belt sander, dust mask, safety glasses, protective ear muffs, hand scraper
SEE PAGES 180–181

Sanding can revive the appearance of old floorboards that have become grimy with years of use. Don't worry if you have a newer board that seems to be a lighter hue – sanding will restore all the boards to their original colour. They should then be protected with a varnish (see below).

Another reason for sanding floorboards is to provide a flat surface before laying a decorative floor covering on top of them. Never sand laminated floorboards.

You'll have to learn how to use an industrial floor sander, which is readily available for hire – ask for a demonstration from the shop.

STAINING AND VARNISHING FLOORBOARDS

SKILL LEVEL Low
TIME FRAME 1 to 2 days
SPECIAL TOOLS Paint brushes, rubber gloves, wire brush
SEE PAGES 182–183

Instructions on how to enhance new floorboards or existing older ones that have been sanded and otherwise repaired. Stains give the wood a deeper colour; varnishes protect it from future damage. The time necessary depends on the number of coats applied and on the types of products that are used.

Also included are details for liming floorboards, which enhances the natural grain of open-grain woods such as oak and ash.

PAINTING AND STENCILLING FLOORBOARDS

SKILL LEVEL Low to medium
TIME FRAME 1 to 2 days
SPECIAL TOOLS Paint brushes, stencil brush
SEE PAGES 184–185

Methods of achieving a decorative paint effect on either new floorboards or existing older ones that have been sanded. Details are given on how to stencil in a diamond- or square-shaped overall repeat (to stencil a border around the perimeter of a room, follow instructions on pp.128–129), as well as on how to "age" paint, where small areas of floorboard (or a base coat) are exposed through a top coat.

The time necessary depends on the number of coats applied and on the type of products used.

LAYING NEW FLOORBOARDS

SKILL LEVEL High
TIME FRAME 2 days
SPECIAL TOOLS Floorboard clamps (hired), panel saw or jigsaw, crowbar, plane
SEE PAGES 186–187

If the old floorboards in a room are beyond repair, or you want exposed floorboards but the existing ones include mismatched replacement boards, the solution is to replace them with new softwood floorboards. This means cutting them to length and using floorboard clamps to make sure they are laid with no gaps. For "secret nailing" tongue-and-groove floorboards, see pp.194–195.

BELT SANDER

DUST MASKS

CIRCULAR SAW

BLACK&DECKER
KS 855N   1200W

SAFETY GLASSES

LAYING A CHIPBOARD FLOOR

SKILL LEVEL High
TIME FRAME 2 days
SPECIAL TOOLS Power drill plus screw-driving bits, circular saw, jigsaw
SEE PAGES 188–189

A less expensive – and easier – method of replacing old floorboards is to use sheets of chipboard, either squared edged or tongued and grooved. The same techniques can also be used for laying a new floor in an extension or loft conversion. Smaller sheets will be easier to handle.

Chipboard is not a material that you would want to leave exposed as finished floor covering; however, it provides an ideal surface for covering with decorative floor coverings such as carpet, a sheet of vinyl flooring or vinyl tiles.

LAYING A FLOATING FLOOR

SKILL LEVEL High
TIME FRAME 2 days or more
SPECIAL TOOLS Panel saw, circular saw or plane, crowbar, tenon saw
SEE PAGES 190–191

By laying woodstrip flooring over an existing wood floor with mismatched boards or a solid concrete floor, you can provide an atractive decorative finish. With the exception of the two end rows, the floorboards are attached to each other with adhesive or special clips that are provided by the manufacturer – not to the floor below – hence the term "floating".

Time must be allowed for the flooring to acclimatize before it is laid and for preparing the existing floor surface. The total time depends on the size and complexity of the room.

MOSAIC FLOORING

SKILL LEVEL Medium to high
TIME FRAME 2 days or more
SPECIAL TOOLS Notched adhesive spreader, tenon saw
SEE PAGES 192–193

An alternative to woodstrip flooring, this material, which is usually hardwood, comes as four "tiles" in which strips of wood – known as fingers – are held together on a backing. The fingers are set in a variety of patterns, including basket-weave and herringbone.

Mosaic flooring is fixed to the floor with an adhesive.

The total time necessary depends on the size and complexity of the room.

LAYING LAMINATE WOODSTRIP FLOORING

SKILL LEVEL High
TIME FRAME 2 days or more
SPECIAL TOOLS Tenon saw, nail punch, circular saw or plane, profile gauge
SEE PAGES 194–195

These thicker strips of wood can either be laid in place of existing floorboards or laid on top of them. However, unlike solid woodstrip flooring, the surface hardwood veneer cannot be sanded down if it becomes damaged.

The technique described is known as secret nailing, in which nails are driven through the tongue of one strip before being covered with the groove of the next. It isn't difficult if you have a hammer and a nail punch. The total time necessary depends on the size and complexity of the room.

ROLL FLOOR COVERINGS OPTIONS

SEE PAGES 196–197

The choices available in sheets of "soft" floor coverings – which come in rolls – include carpet, natural floor coverings (such as sisal and jute), vinyl and linoleum. All are quiet and soft underfoot and are good choices for bedrooms and living rooms. They come in a variety of colours and patterns, and some of the coverings, such as carpets, have different textures. Some types, such as vinyl and linoleum, are easy to clean, making them a good choice in bathrooms, kitchens and children's rooms. Linoleum is best laid by a professional.

LAYING A VINYL FLOOR COVERING

SKILL LEVEL Low
TIME FRAME 1 day
SPECIAL TOOLS Adhesive spreader
SEE PAGES 198–199

Probably the most popular of all "roll" floor coverings, vinyl sheet has the combined advantages of being soft and quiet underfoot and of being easy to clean – as well as being inexpensive and relatively easy to lay.

This section describes how to lay a slightly oversized

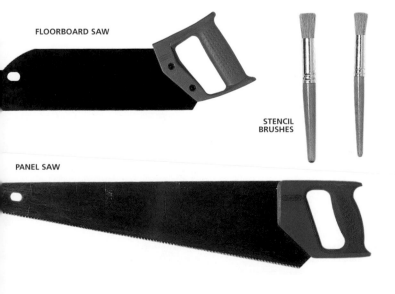

FLOORBOARD SAW

PANEL SAW

STENCIL BRUSHES

FLOOR SCRAPER

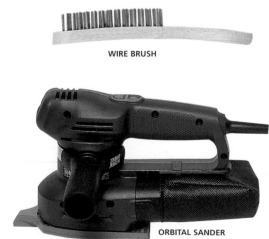

WIRE BRUSH

ORBITAL SANDER

sheet of vinyl in one go, cutting it to fit within a room that has no obstacles such as a toilet or kitchen island.

If you have a large room that requires two sheets of vinyl, details are given for joining them – make sure the seam is placed where there will be the least amount of foot traffic.

USING A TEMPLATE FOR VINYL FLOORING

SKILL LEVEL Low to medium
TIME FRAME 1 day
SPECIAL TOOLS Adhesive spreader, weights, wax pencil
SEE PAGES 200–201

The best way to lay vinyl flooring in a room with permanently attached obstacles – particularly a bathroom with basin and toilet pedestals or a kitchen with an island – involves making a paper pattern, or template, of the shape of the room. This allows you to cut the vinyl sheeting roughly to shape in a larger room before laying it as described on pp.198–199.

To make the template so it follows the contours of the room precisely, you must use a wood block and pencil in a procedure known as scribing. The only difficult part of the job is to take care that you always hold the pencil at the same angle.

LAYING FOAM-BACKED CARPET

SKILL LEVEL Low to medium
TIME FRAME ½ to 1 day
SPECIAL TOOLS Staple gun, bolster chisel, hacksaw, utility knife plus carpet trimming blades
SEE PAGES 202–203

This type of carpet is the easiest to lay, even for the inexperienced do-it-yourselfer, and it can be laid virtually anywhere within the house – apart from stairs. Basic floor preparation is likely to be the main part of the job.

The actual laying of the carpet is not difficult: it simply requires stapling a paper underlay in place, applying double-sided tape around the perimeter of the room and trimming the carpet after you position it. To stop the carpet from fraying and to prevent people from tripping, you'll have to fit a threshold strip at any doorways in the room, using screws or masonry nails.

LAYING HESSIAN-BACKED CARPET

SKILL LEVEL Medium to high
TIME FRAME 1 to 2 days
SPECIAL TOOLS Staple gun, tenon saw, utility knife plus carpet trimming blades, kneekicker (hired), bolster chisel, hacksaw
SEE PAGES 204–205

While this type of carpet is much more luxurious than foam-backed carpet – both visually and to the touch – hessian carpet is also more difficult to lay. It requires laying down a separate rubber or felt underlay, as well as fitting gripper strips around the perimeter of the room, and the carpet itself must be stretched to the walls with a kneekicker in order to prevent it from eventaully creasing after use.

The total time necessary depends on the size and complexity of the room and how quickly you adapt to using a kneekicker.

LAYING STAIR CARPET

SKILL LEVEL Medium to high
TIME FRAME ½ to 1 day
SPECIAL TOOLS Tenon saw or hacksaw, utility knife with carpet

trimming blades, staple gun, bolster chisel, rubber mallet
SEE PAGES 206–207

Hessian-backed carpet can be used for staircases, either as "fitted" carpet, with the material running to the two edges of the stairs, or as a stair "runner", with a 50 mm (2 in) gap on either side. Before laying the carpet, gripper strips must be fitted on each step at the angle between the riser and tread, and rubber or felt underlay must be fitted on the treads. If you have a lot of steps, you may find pounding the carpet into the angles a tiring job.

The complexity of the job depends on the type of staircase – straight flights are much easier to carpet than stairs with landings, and carpeting a curved staircase will require a high skill level and much more time.

FLOOR TILE OPTIONS

SEE PAGES 208–209

The choice of tiles falls into two categories: "hard" materials, such as ceramic, terracotta and quarry, and "soft" materials, including cork, vinyl, carpet, linoleum

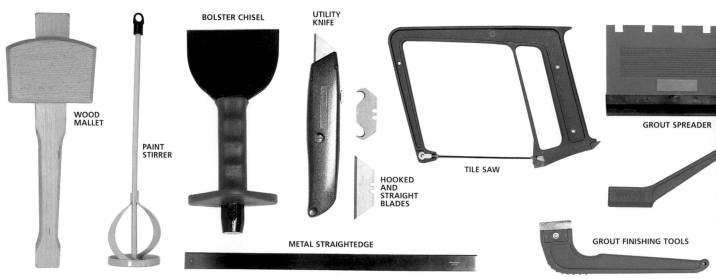

WOOD MALLET

PAINT STIRRER

BOLSTER CHISEL

UTILITY KNIFE

HOOKED AND STRAIGHT BLADES

METAL STRAIGHTEDGE

TILE SAW

GROUT SPREADER

GROUT FINISHING TOOLS

and rubber. Hard tiles are more durable, but they can be cold to walk on with bare foot and noisy if wearing shoes. Soft tiles are not only quiet and warm, but they are generally much easier to lay. Another advantage is that it is easier to replace a damaged tile than a section of a larger flooring material.

Tiles are available in a huge range of colours, and ceramic, vinyl and linoleum tiles come in a variety of patterns. Ceramic tiles also come in a range of sizes. Tiles allow you to create your own patterns by mixing ones of different colours, using soft tiles cut on a diagonal or by adding "inset" tiles at the corners.

LAYING SOFT FLOOR TILES

SKILL LEVEL Medium
TIME FRAME 1 day
SPECIAL TOOLS Notched adhesive spreader
SEE PAGES 210–211

One of the easiest of all flooring jobs is laying soft tiles – they are lightweight, small and easy to cut, using only a utility knife and metal straightedge. The instructions given are for vinyl tiles, but

you can follow them for laying other types of soft tiles, including carpet, cork and rubber.

Most of the work will be in preparing a flat smooth surface on which to lay the tiles, planning how to lay them from the centre of the room and cutting the tiles to fit around the edges and any obstacles within the room. Each edge tile should be measured and cut individually, following the three-tile cutting method. The tiles may be laid using an adhesive, but they may be self-adhesive (such as some vinyl tiles) – you simply peel off a paper backing before pressing them in place.

LAYING CERAMIC FLOOR TILES

SKILL LEVEL Medium to high
TIME FRAME 2 days
SPECIAL TOOLS Platform tile cutter, tile file, notched adhesive spreader, angle grinder, rubber grout squeegee
SEE PAGES 212–213

Although similar to ceramic wall tiles, ceramic floor tiles stand up to more abuse, so they are thicker, stronger and generally bigger – which makes them harder to cut.

As with all floor coverings, the basic floor must be smooth and dry. Tiling starts by laying whole tiles from the middle of a room, working outward to the edges. You should let them set before fitting the edge tiles, and you'll need to wait again before filling the gaps between tiles with grout.

Border tiles for framing the perimeter of the room are available. These require more complicated planning before starting the job.

LAYING QUARRY TILES

SKILL LEVEL High
TIME FRAME 3 days
SPECIAL TOOLS Notched adhesive spreader, spirit level, mallet, platform tile cutter, tile-cutting saw, grout spreader
SEE PAGES 214–215

Quarry tiles are more durable than ceramic tiles, have a non-glazed surface and are more porous. Because they are not glazed, they are less slippery, making them a suitable flooring material for an entryway. Handmade tiles will be more difficult to lay than machine-made tiles, which are more readily available. Terracotta tiles are similar to

quarry tiles, but they are warmer and quieter; you can lay them in the same way as quarry tiles.

Quarry tiles are laid in a cement-based adhesive, and a cement-based grout is used to fill the gaps, which are larger than those left between ceramic tiles. These tiles are difficult to cut successfully, and are best restricted to areas that won't require a large amount of cutting.

PAINTING A CONCRETE FLOOR

SKILL LEVEL Low
TIME FRAME 1 day
SPECIAL TOOLS Flexible filler knife, paint brush, paint roller with extension pole
SEE PAGES 216–217

One of the best methods for treating a solid concrete floor is to paint it. Paint makes it look more attractive and easier to clean, and it prevents dust from collecting. This treatment is appropriate for workshops, garages and utility rooms.

The job itself is not difficult once you have removed all the furniture and equipment in the room and prepared the floor surface.

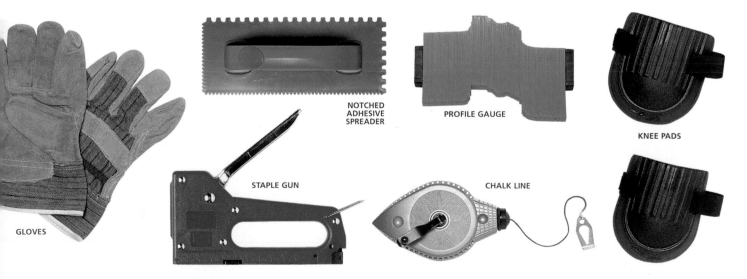

GLOVES

NOTCHED ADHESIVE SPREADER

PROFILE GAUGE

KNEE PADS

STAPLE GUN

CHALK LINE

WOOD FLOOR OPTIONS

POSSIBLE MATERIALS

FLOOR VARNISH

WOOD STAIN

LIMING WAX

GLOSS FLOOR PAINT

FLOOR WAX

FLOOR STAIN COLOURS

WOOD MOSAIC PANELS

LAMINATED BOARD

TONGUE-AND-GROOVE-SOFTWOOD BOARD

SQUARE-EDGED PINE BOARD

The natural beauty of wood has made it a popular choice as a flooring material. The main structure of the floor, consisting of planks of wood – the floorboards – nailed down to floor joists, may be left uncovered (but protected with a varnish) if the floorboards are in good shape. A wood floor covering is a decorative feature and may be laid over existing floorboards, chipboard sheeting or concrete floors. There are many options to choose from, depending on whether you are replacing or renovating an existing floor or putting in a wood floor covering over an existing floor.

▶ The clean simple lines of a warm and practical wood floor makes it one of the few flooring materials that look great in any room of the house. Wood ages gracefully, increasing in character as the years go by.

◀ Footsteps and chairs being moved across a wood floor may create noise in a room below it – a problem experienced by many people who live in flats. Laying an underlay of a sound-insulating material, such as cork or a special sound-proofing foam, increases the sound insulation between floors.

▲ Larger widths of natural wood flooring are usually more expensive than narrow widths because they require higher-quality wood.

▶ All wood floorboards (except laminated veneer strips) can be stained with a colourwash or tinted varnish.

▶ Wood floors can be treated with a number of special painted finishes, including liming and stencilling.

▲ Laminated wood floors are relatively inexpensive because only the top layer of each panel is expensive hardwood. Unlike solid wood floors, laminate flooring cannot be rejuvenated by sanding it down at a later date.

◀ Mosaic wood flooring is often incorrectly known as parquetry. These square tiles consist of small strips of wood arranged in a basketweave, herringbone or similar pattern.

▶ Paint can be applied to the floorboards in a variety of ways – for example, as a solid colour or in a chequerboard pattern. You should apply top coats of varnish to protect it.

SANDING FLOORBOARDS

In time, natural wooden floorboards will begin to show signs of age as the wood warps, splits, and builds up a residue of wax and other finishes. Salvation is at hand in the form of sanding down. Sanding floorboards is a three-stage process: sanding the main floor area with coarse or medium-grade sanding belt; repeating with a fine-grade belt; then finishing off the edges. You have to hire an industrial floor sander, as well as an edging sander (unless you own a belt sander) for finishing off the edges.

BEFORE YOU START

You must first of all strip the floor of any covering if there is one (see pp.40–41) and repair any damage to the floorboards (see pp.42–45). The one thing that is particularly important to do before you sand is to make sure there are no nails or staples (which are widely used for anchoring underlay to the floor)

protruding above the floor surface – these will rip the sanding belt and possibly damage the sander. Nail heads may appear during the sanding process and will need driving down with a nail punch.

You must remove all the furniture from the room to give a clear area to work. The whole sanding process creates a lot of dust, so you might want to remove items such as pictures hanging on the wall; completely seal other items, such as built-in bookcases with books, with plastic sheets and tape. It is also a good idea to tape over the door edges to prevent dust getting into the rest of the house and to open all the windows in the room.

Before using the sanding machine, make sure you clearly understand the instructions for using it and for fitting the sanding belts securely. Once the floorboards are sanded, stain them if you wish and protect them with a varnish (see pp.182–183).

1 Before starting a sanding machine, tilt it backward. Make sure the machine's flex is well out of the way (preferably over your shoulder). Turn the power on and lower the machine; you'll have to hold on firmly to stop it running away from you.

2 If you are dealing with "curled" floorboards, fit a coarse belt to the machine and sand diagonally across the room, starting in one corner. Go over each area several times, then sand across the other diagonal. A dustbag will collect most, but not all, of the dust produced.

3 Give the room a quick vacuum to remove dust, and fit a medium-grade belt to the machine (with floorboards that are not curled, you can start with this belt). Re-sand the floor, this time working along the line of the floorboards; if you're sanding a herringbone block floor, follow the diagonal lines.

4 As you work, keep an eye open for any nailheads that may be exposed by the sanding. If you come across one, use a nail punch to drive it below the surface of the wood. Switch to a fine-grade belt on the machine and, once more, sand along the line of the floorboards.

5 Go around the edges of the room, using an edging sander or belt sander. Turn the power on before you lower the sander to the floor. Move the sander in a circular motion and allow it to overlap the area sanded by the industrial floor sander. Start with a medium-grade paper, then finish with a fine-grade paper.

6 Most power sanders won't reach into corners or under obstructions such as radiators. Use a hook-blade scraper or abrasive paper wrapped around a sanding block (but don't use the block at the skirting boards) to reach into these areas. To blend in scraped areas with those sanded by machine, use the abrasive paper.

7 Sweep up all the dust and go over the whole floor with a vacuum cleaner, then use a tacky rag or cloth to remove any leftover dust particles, which could ruin any finish you then apply.

Helpful hints

There are a few points that an inexperienced user of an industrial sanding machine should know before operating one. Sanding is a noisy process – make sure you wear ear muffs to protect your hearing. To avoid upsetting your neighbours, do the sanding when it will be least likely to disturb them. Once the sanding belt makes contact with the floor – you'll know it has from the increased noise – never let it sit in one place or try to hold it back; otherwise, it will gouge the floor.

One of the best methods for removing fine dust is to use a "tacky" rag – it has been impregnated with a resin that will pick up dust.

STAINING AND VARNISHING FLOORBOARDS

YOU WILL NEED

Staining and varnishing
Steel wool
Lint-free clean cloth
100-mm- (4-in-) wide
paint brush
Fine abrasive paper
Sanding block
Paint kettle (if required)
Dust cloth **or** newspapers
Small brush (if required)
Rubber gloves

Liming floorboards
Wire brush
Small brush
Steel wool
Rubber gloves
(See above for varnishing)

MATERIALS

Staining and varnishing
Water-based stain **or** oil-based stain
Water-based varnish **or** oil-based varnish
White spirit (if required)

Liming floorboards
Liming wax **or** liming paste
Water-based varnish **or** oil-based varnish

SEE ALSO

Removing floor coverings
pp.40–41
Sanding floorboards
pp.180–181

The natural grain and texture of a wood floor are highlighted by a stain and protective varnish finish.

Natural wood floors can be transformed and protected by using stains and varnishes. The best effects will be achieved on new floorboards, but you can stain and varnish existing ones that are in good condition. You'll have to remove any old floor covering to inspect the boards, and they will require sanding before you can apply a new finish.

THE STAINS AND VARNISHES

A stain penetrates into the wood itself, giving it a new colour; a varnish treats the surface of the wood, enhancing and protecting it. Varnishes are available in matt, semi-gloss and gloss finishes. You can use the varnish alone or after you apply a stain, or you can use a coloured varnish (which may simulate various types of wood).

Stains and varnishes are available in environmentally friendly, water-based versions, as well as the traditional oil-based products. These should never be used together. Stains can be mixed to create a new colour. A water-based stain raises the wood grain, which requires a light sanding after it dries.

1 Before applying a stain, first clean the floorboards with steel wool and white spirit to make sure that there is no wax or grease on the floorboard surface – otherwise, the stain may not be absorbed evenly, which can cause patches.

2 Unless you are happy with one particular stain colour, mix together different stains to achieve the colour you want. Use a folded drop cloth or newspaper to prevent spills on the floor. A small brush is the best mixing tool. You can also mix coloured varnishes. In both cases, use compatible products from the same manufacturer.

3 Apply the stain using a clean, lint-free cloth, such as cheesecloth or a section of an old sheet, or use a paint brush. Work quickly along the length of a few boards at a time so that the stain does not dry out in the middle of a length. If the colour is not deep enough after one application, apply a second coat.

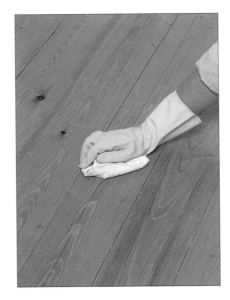

4 Allow the stain to dry thoroughly before applying the varnish. Thin the first coat – which acts as a primer – by 10 percent with white spirit for an oil-based varnish or water if water-based. (Never shake a tin of varnish; this creates bubbles that leave marks in the finish.) Use a clean, lint-free cloth to rub the coat into the wood.

5 After the varnish dries, lightly rub the surface with fine abrasive paper wrapped around a sanding block; work with the grain to avoid scratches. This creates a "key" for the next coat and smooths the surface. Before applying a new coat of varnish, use a clean dry cloth to remove the dust created by the sanding.

6 Apply up to six coats of varnish to achieve the necessary protection, sanding between coats. Use a 100-mm- (4-in-) wide paint brush to apply the varnish quickly. If using a coloured varnish, use clear varnish for the final coat – or coats if the colour is dark enough. Each new coat of coloured varnish will make the floor darker.

LIMING FLOORBOARDS

Wood can be limed with a wax or paste before being varnished. The wax is easier to apply, but it will eventually wear away. The wood should be unvarnished and clean, although it can be stained. Before applying the wax or paste, use a wire brush in the direction of the grain; this opens the grain, helping it to take the wax or paste. Apply the paste with a hessian cloth or extra-fine steel wool, first in one direction, then the other; remove the dried paste with a rag or a hessian cloth.

Rub liming wax into the wood with extra-fine steel wool. Allow it to dry before removing the excess with a cloth.

Liming enhances the natural grain of open-grain wood, such as oak and ash, either of which can be stained first.

PAINTING AND STENCILLING FLOORBOARDS

YOU WILL NEED

Stencilling floorboards
String, nails and pencil
Straightedge metal rule
Stencil
Spray mount adhesive **or**
low-tack masking tape
Stencil brushes
Large paint brush

Ageing paint
Small paint brush
Large paint brush
Paint roller and tray
Lint-free cloth
Fine abrasive paper
Scraper (if required)

MATERIALS

Stencilling floorboards
Water- or oil-based paint
Floor-grade varnish

Ageing paint
Beeswax **or** petroleum jelly
Water-based paint
Floor-grade varnish

SEE ALSO

Making minor repairs to a
wood floor pp.42–43
Replacing a damaged
floorboard pp.44–45
Sanding floorboards
pp.180–181
Staining and varnishing
floorboards pp.182–183

The most straightforward way of painting new or refurbished floorboards is to paint the whole floor the same colour, using a paint brush around the perimeter of the room and a roller for the centre. You can use any type of paint (water- or oil-based), as long as it is covered with three coats of floor-grade varnish. You can also cover the floor with a special paint effect, perhaps "ageing" the paint to evoke an old-fashioned kitchen or decorating with a repeat pattern, using a stencil. Before painting floorboards, repair any surface damage, sand them down and use steel wool with white spirit to remove any wax or grease.

MAKING A STENCIL

You can buy ready-made stencils or make your own. A transparent acetate sheet is the best material to use: lay it over a pattern for tracing, then cut out the design, leaving "bridges" so parts of the design don't fall out of the

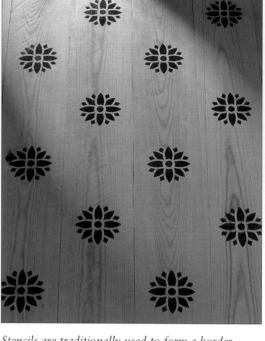

Stencils are traditionally used to form a border (see pp.128–129), but you can use them to create your own design, including a diamond pattern.

stencil. The best tool for cutting the stencil is a craft knife with a sharp blade. A continuous pattern requires a registration mark to align the stencil: use an element in the design or draw a line on the stencil.

1 Plan out your pattern on a scale drawing of the floor, starting at the centre of the room and using small squares to indicate how often the pattern is repeated. On the floor itself, find the centre (see p.192 and p.210), but instead of using chalk lines, use two lengths of string tied to small nails tapped partway into the floorboards.

2 Measure and mark the positions for several of the surrounding patterns. By marking the patterns as you go, you can make slight adjustments if you start to go off course. With each new group of marks, double check for overall appearance before you commit yourself by applying the paint.

3 The easiest way to secure the stencil to the floor is to spray the back with a spray mount adhesive. This will hold the stencil in place while you paint, but allow you to peel it off and reposition it afterward. Or you can use masking tape.

4 Load a stencil brush with some of the paint and dab it on a sheet of white paper to find the right amount to use (a little stencil paint goes a long way). Apply the paint to the floor, using a short dabbing motion to prevent the paint from going under the edges of the stencil.

5 If you want to use a second colour, allow the first one to dry completely (water-based paints will dry quickly). If using more than one stencil sheet (some ready-made stencil kits have a separate sheet for each colour), make sure the stencil is correctly aligned over the previous image before applying the new colour.

6 Remove and reposition the stencil, continuing until you finish the room. When the paint has completely dried, cover the final result with three coats of floor-grade varnish, painting the full length of a few planks at a time.

AGEING PAINT

It is easy to make painted floorboards look older than their true age. Before painting, apply a barrier in random patches onto clean floorboards to prevent paint from seeping into the wood. Once the paint is dry, simply remove the barrier (use a scraper on difficult lumps) and blend in the painted and unpainted areas. Seal the work with a few coats of protective varnish. For a unique look, give the floorboards a coat of a contrasting base colour before applying the barrier.

Randomly apply lumps of a barrier, such as beeswax or petroleum jelly, to the floorboards before painting them.

After the paint dries, use a cloth to remove the wax and lightly sand the edges to blend in with the painted areas.

LAYING NEW FLOORBOARDS

YOU WILL NEED

Panel saw **or** jigsaw
Plane
Try square
Tape measure
Hammer
Nail punch
Flooring clamps (hired) **or** wood wedges and batten

MATERIALS

Floorboards
Floorboard nails

SEE ALSO

When you replace individual damaged floorboards, the new ones won't blend in completely – they often are a slightly different size, look flatter and smoother, and they will be a different colour whatever you do to the floor. If your old floorboards are damaged in several places, it might be better to replace all of them with new ones. These can either be square edged or tongued and grooved; the laying technique varies only slightly. If tongue-and-groove floorboards will be left exposed, you can "secret" nail them to the joists in the same way as woodstrip flooring (see pp.194–195), and they won't need clamping.

Floorboards come in different widths and thicknesses. The correct thickness depends on the joist spacing; the width affects the appearance. Use the size of the old boards as a guide. The starting point, after you remove all the old floorboards (and the skirting boards), will be the bare joists. Carefully check the joists for damage and make sure they are level. Have any damaged sections replaced and weakened sections strengthened before you start.

INSPECTION HATCHES

Suspended ground floors invariably conceal pipes and electrical wiring. Wherever there is a joint or connection box, leave an inspection hatch – a short length of floorboard screwed down – for future access. With tongue-and-groove floorboards, cut the bottom half of the groove away so that the section will lift easily.

Helpful hints

When laying new floorboards, you have an ideal opportunity to insulate suspended ground floors. The easiest way to do this is to staple netting over the joists, letting it drop into a U shape between them, to support rolls of loft insulation material pushed down between the joists. The material should already be the correct size to fit between the joists – if not, cut it to size with a panel saw while in the roll.

1 Start by removing the first floorboard (see pp.44–45). Once it is up, use a crowbar to lever up the other boards where they are nailed to the joists below. Inspect the joists; if they are weak or damaged, seek professional help. Save a few boards to use as a work platform; lay them at a right angle to the joists where you plan to work.

2 Fit the first board along a wall at a right angle to the joists; leave a 10 mm (³⁄₈ in) gap between the board and the wall (fit tongue-and-groove boards with the groove facing the wall). Bang two nails in at each joist, avoiding any pipes lying in notches cut into the joist; punch the nail heads just below the surface.

3 Ideally, a board should fit the whole length of the room, less 20 mm (¾ in) for expansion gaps. Where the boards are less than the length of the room, cut them so that the joints between boards will be exactly centred on a joist, but stagger the joints across the room.

4 Lay the next five or six rows of boards without nails for the moment (unless you're secret nailing), leaving the same 10 mm (⅜ in) gap at each end of the rows and making sure that any joints are centred on joists and are staggered from one board to the next.

5 Push the boards tightly together as you go. For tongue-and-groove boards, make sure the groove fits snugly over the tongue of the previous board by using an offcut with a groove (to protect the tongue) and hammering the boards together. (If you're secret nailing tongue-and-groove boards, proceed to step 8.)

6 Wedge the group of floorboards together with two floorboard clamps spaced 180 cm (6 ft) apart (use an offcut to protect the edge of the board). Starting in the centre and working toward the ends, nail down each of the floorboards.

7 Instead of using floorboard clamps, you can cut wood wedges (use offcuts of the flooring material), then hammer in pairs of wedges opposed to one another in the gap between the last floorboard and a wood batten temporarily nailed to the joists a short distance away – again use offcuts to protect the boards.

8 Continue until you have less than one floorboard's width left. Saw or plane the last row of boards down so that they will fit with a 10 mm (⅜ in) gap to the wall, and slot them into place. Take off the bottom of the groove from tongue-and-groove floorboards if they do not fit easily into place. Replace the skirting boards.

LAYING A CHIPBOARD FLOOR

You will probably think of a chipboard floor for a new extension or, perhaps, for covering the floor of the loft, but you could also use it to replace existing damaged floorboards if you cover it with a floor covering; chipboard on its own is not particularly attractive.

Flooring-grade chipboard comes in two thicknesses – 19 mm (¾in) and 22 mm (⅞ in); use the thinner grade only where the spacing between joists is less than 45 cm (18 in). Chipboard usually has tongue-and-groove edges on four sides and should be laid with the long sides at right angles to the joists. Square-edged chipboard is laid the other way around, with the long edges meeting along the centre of a joist (you may have to cut down the boards) and the joint between short edges supported by a 75 mm × 50 mm (3 in × 2 in) wood "nogging" nailed in place between the joists. These have to be nailed at an angle.

As with laying new floorboards (see pp.186–187), start by checking and repairing the floor joists.

INSPECTION HATCHES

Creating an "inspection hatch" is vital with chipboard flooring that is being nailed down, because it is virtually impossible to get up once it has been laid. Determine the position of the inspection hatch over a cable junction box or joint in a pipe. Once the sheet has been installed, cut a hole for the hatch and screw down the cover to wood noggings. The hatch can then be removed easily in the future.

Helpful hints

Many carpenters use 50 mm (2 in) ring-shank nails to secure sheets of chipboard (they go in easier if you pre-drill the holes). However, you'll get a more secure fixing with screws, and the boards will be easier to lift in the future. Because there are a lot of screws to be driven home, using a power screwdriver will make the task a lot easier.

1 After removing the floorboards and skirting boards, if necessary, lay a sheet in one corner of the room, with its two grooved faces facing the walls and with a gap of 10 mm (⅜ in) between the sheet and each wall. Mark the position of the joists at either side of the sheet and join the marks up with pencil lines.

2 Move the sheet until the pencil lines are no longer over the joists. Drill and countersink clearance holes for the screws – 5 mm (³⁄₁₆ in) holes for No. 10 screws – on the pencil lines 30 cm (12 in) apart. For nails, don't move the board, but drill pilot holes right through the sheet and a short way into the joists (or noggings).

3 Reposition the sheet and use a smaller drill to make pilot holes into the joists – 2.5 mm (^{3}/$_{32}$ in) for No. 10 screws – before putting the screws into place; the countersink should be just deep enough so that the screw head is flush with the surface.

4 Position the next sheet alongside the first, and mark and drill it in the same way. Before fixing it, apply adhesive to tongue-and-groove joints; use a large hammer or a mallet to force the sheet tightly into place, protecting the edge of the sheet with an offcut of the material. Continue in the same way for the other sheets.

5 To cut a sheet of chipboard to fit at the edge of the room, clamp the sheet to a work surface, using a straightedge batten to guide a circular saw fitted with a TCT (tungsten-carbide tipped) blade. You'll also have to cut the underside of the groove off the last row to be fitted (set the circular saw blade to a narrow depth).

6 The edges of the sheets must be supported by a joist or a supporting "nogging". Where necessary, cut pieces of 75 mm x 50 mm (3 in x 2 in) wood battens to fit between two joists. Skew nail them in place by driving the nails in at a 45° angle.

7 To create an inspection hatch large enough to fit a hand in, determine its position and mark it on the sheet. Using a jigsaw with a fine-tooth blade, make a plunge cut into the sheet: angle the saw so the blade's teeth cut through the face of the sheet; slowly lower it (or drill a hole and insert the blade). Cut out the hatch.

8 Clamp and screw noggings to the sides of the opening, with half their width protruding into the opening. These will support the cover – the piece of chipboard cut out to make the opening. Screw the cover in place. Finally, fit skirting boards (see pp.38–39) to cover the expansion gaps around the edge of the room.

LAYING A FLOATING FLOOR

The thinner types of woodstrip flooring are not attached to the floor below; instead, the individual strips are secured together. Because this flooring is relatively thin, it must be laid on a flat smooth surface. Before laying the boards, make sure existing wood floor surfaces are in good condition, and level a solid floor with floor-levelling compound if necessary. Cover wood floorboards with sheets of hardboard, or, if the floorboards are uneven, with sheets of plywood to provide a flat level surface. Some woodstrip manufacturers recommend an additional underlay to reduce noise; on solid floors, a damp-proof membrane must be used.

Decide on the direction in which to lay the flooring – normally with the length of the boards running the length of the room – and check how many widths are required. To avoid cutting a narrow width for the last strip to be laid, you may need to cut

"Floating" floorboards are not connected to the floor, so they can expand and contract as the temperature in the room changes.

the first length down; use a circular saw or plane on the tongue side of the strip. The floorboards may require sealing after being laid; follow the manufacturer's recommendations.

1 If needed, remove the skirting boards (see pp.36–37). Lay the underlay, following the manufacturer's instructions – in this case, the felt side should be face down. Overlap the lengths and seal the joints with waterproof tape. Run the underlay up the wall, just above skirting board height; use low-tack tape to hold it in place.

2 Place cork expansion strips along the side walls. To allow an expansion gap, use spacer blocks between the strip and wall and set the first length of floorboard with its grooved edge 10 mm (⅜ in) from the wall. Cut the next length to reach the other side wall (the leftover piece can start the next row), allowing for the cork strip.

3 Where clips are used to secure strips together, these are fitted before each strip is laid. For all methods, apply PVA adhesive to the groove end of the board before pushing the tongue at the end of the other board into it. Wipe off any squeezed out adhesive, using a damp cloth.

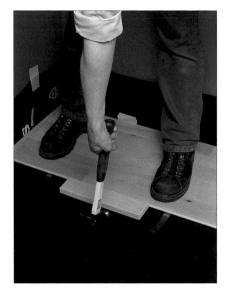

4 To fit an adjacent row, align each strip (with the joints staggered) and engage the clips with a hammer. If you're not using clips, apply adhesive to the long grooves, then push them over the tongues of the first row. For either method, force the strips together by tapping with a hammer against a protective block.

5 When you come to the end of each row, force together the strips using a small crowbar or a special tool that comes with the boards. Continue across the room until you reach the opposite wall, where the last strip will have to be sawn or planed down to fit, leaving room for a 10 mm (⅜ in) expansion gap.

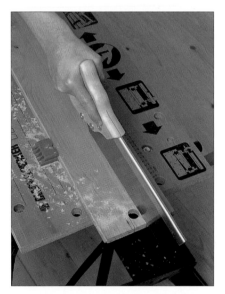

6 To fit a board around a pipe, mark its position on the relevant piece of flooring. Drill a hole to fit the pipe, using a hole saw bit, then cut a wedge from the hole to the wall edge of the strip, which can be glued in place after the floorboard has been laid.

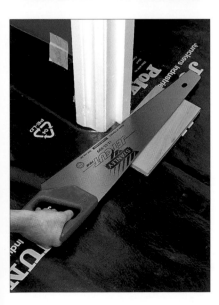

7 To fit the flooring around the door architrave, use a saw resting on an offcut of floorboard (it gives the correct height for the cut). Trim it halfway if the flooring will end in the room – install a reduction or threshold strip – or trim all the way around if the flooring will continue into the next room. To trim the door to fit, see pp.76–77.

8 Replace the skirting boards if necessary. If the skirting boards were not removed, cover the expansion gaps by pinning hardwood quadrant or scotia moulding onto the skirting boards – not the floor. Trim off the overlay, using a utility knife. Finish off by applying sealant to the floor surface.

MOSAIC FLOORING

YOU WILL NEED

Square
Chalk line
Tape measure
Pencil
Notched adhesive spreader
Clean rag
Felt-tip pen **or** wax pencil
Tenon saw
Utility knife
Hammer
Nail punch

MATERIALS

Mosaic flooring
Adhesive (unless flooring is
self-adhesive)
Cork expansion strips
Finishing sealant
Hardwood quadrant **or**
scotia moulding (if required)
Panel pins (if required)

SEE ALSO

Removing skirting boards
and mouldings pp.36–37
Replacing skirting boards
pp.38–39
Making minor repairs to a
wood floor pp.55–45
Replacing a damaged
floorboard pp.46–47
Laying a hardboard overlay
pp.46–47
Levelling a concrete floor
pp.50–51

The advantages of mosaic flooring include it being easy to lay and its ability to cope with a slightly uneven surface. In fact, mosaics have a degree of flexibility unmatched in any other type of wood floor. Mosaic flooring should be laid on as flat and smooth a surface as you can manage, which means laying hardboard sheeting, rough side up, over repaired existing wood floors or levelling a solid floor with floor levelling compound.

Before you start, check each of the panels. They should be exactly square and all the same size; an irregular panel in the middle of the floor leaves unsightly gaps. However, you can put aside any mosaics that are a different size and cut them down as edge pieces for the perimeter of the room.

Leave the mosaics in the room where they will be laid for a few days to allow their moisture content to adjust to the humidity. When laying the mosaics, leave a gap around the room

Wood flooring gives a warm feeling to any room. It also provides an unsuitable environment for house dust mites (which trigger asthma in some people).

to allow them to expand. Mosaic tiles are held in place with adhesive, which is normally supplied separately. Some tiles are self-adhesive and require only the removal of a backing paper.

1 This type of wood flooring is laid starting at the centre of the room, so start by "snapping" a chalk line from the midpoints of opposite walls to find the centre point. Use this as a reference point for setting out the tiles. For a room without true square walls, see p.210.

2 Starting at the centre, lay a dry run of tiles along the length of the room and across the width to work out any gaps at the walls (but allow for the expansion gaps). Divide the gaps equally between the edge tiles, adjusting the centre tile as necessary to avoid making cuts along the length of a "finger", or strip.

3 The centre tiles are laid first. Draw lines on the floor parallel to the centre marking lines and extending well beyond the position of the first tiles. Spread the adhesive (use one suggested by the manufacturer of the tiles) on the floor, using a notched adhesive spreader.

4 Lay the central tiles in place, firmly pressing them into the adhesive. Working outward from the centre in a quarter of the room at a time, position the remaining whole tiles. Use a clean rag to wipe off any excess adhesive that squeezes through the joints while it is still wet.

5 To cut the edge tiles to size, lay a whole tile over the last full tile to be laid and lay a third tile on top of this, with its edge the correct distance from the wall (use pieces of cork strip to allow for the expansion gap). Draw a cutting line onto the middle tile.

6 To trim tiles to fit around the edge, you can break off a whole "finger" by cutting through the hessian backing with a utility knife. Use a tenon saw to cut across a "finger". For easier handling of the mosaic, remove a section at a time. Fit the edge tiles in place.

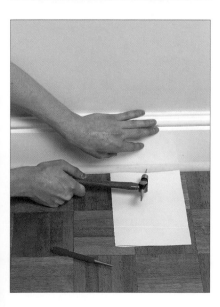

7 Fill the expansion gaps between the tiles and walls with cork strips. Refit the skirting boards, or nail hardwood quadrant or scotia moulding to the skirting boards, using panel pins and a small hammer (protect the mosaics with paper). Sink the pins with a nail punch (see p.38) and fill the nail holes (see p.195). Apply any recommended finish.

Helpful hints

As with other types of wood flooring laid on top of an existing suspended wood floor, you should make an inspection hatch for access to pipes and electrical house wiring. It will allow you to make repairs without damaging the flooring. If you are unfamiliar with plumbing, heating and electricity, call in an expert to determine where to place any hatches.

The easiest method for creating an inspection hatch in mosaic flooring is to make it exactly one tile wide and lined up with a similar-sized panel cut into the hardboard underlay below. At the same position, cut out a section of a suspended floorboard to the same length, preferably with one end of the board resting over a joist. Secure a piece of wood to the underside of the neighbouring floorboards to support the free end of the removable board (see p.189).

LAYING A LAMINATE WOODSTRIP FLOORING

YOU WILL NEED

Hammer
Nail punch
Tenon saw
Circular saw **or** plane
Work surface
Small crowbar
Profile gauge
Jigsaw
Flexible filler knife

MATERIALS

Laminate woodstrip flooring
Lost head nails
PVA adhesive
Hardwood quadrant **or**
scotia moulding
Floor sealant
Wood filler

SEE ALSO

Removing skirting boards
and mouldings pp.36–37
Replacing skirting boards
pp.38–39
Making minor repairs to a
wood floor pp.42–43
Replacing a damaged
floorboard pp.44–45
Staining and varnishing
floorboards pp.182–183
Laying a floating floor
pp.190–191

This flooring simulates traditional floorboards and is available in a wide choice of attractive woods.

Unlike thinner woodstrip flooring (see pp.190–191), most thicker laminate flooring is nailed down to the existing floorboards. A special technique known as "secret nailing" is used, where each strip is secured to the surface below with nails passing through the inside corner of the tongue before being covered by the groove of the adjacent board. It is essential that the nail doesn't interfere with the joint between the tongue and the groove, and that the correct type of nails are used – lost-head nails, which can be punched below the surface.

Make any repairs to the floor before laying the new strips. Measure the room, allowing for the expansion gaps, to see how many strips you will need; normally, the strips are laid with their length parallel with the longest walls of the room. If the last strip will be too narrow, cut both the first and the last strips to equal size with a circular saw, cutting the groove off the first piece and the tongue off the last.

The flooring usually comes with a sealed finish, but it may require further coats of sealant once it is laid. For the type of sealant to use, follow the manufacturer's recommendation.

1 Lay the first strip parallel with the wall (the long grooved side facing the wall), allowing for an expansion gap (follow the manufacturer's recommendations). Place nails through the face close to the wall edge, 400 mm (16 in) apart, and force them below the surface with a nail punch. Then secret nail the tongue (see step 3).

2 Continue the row, applying PVA adhesive to the short grooved ends to join adjacent strips. Using a tenon saw, cut the last length for the first row to size, allowing for the expansion gap. Place the cut edge near the wall.

3 Use the offcut from the previous row to start the next one, making sure the joints are staggered. Use a hammer against a block of wood to fit the groove tightly into the tongue. Secret nail by fixing the nail just above the tongue, at a 45° angle to the board, and punch it below the surface. Continue to apply glue to the short ends.

4 Continue in the same way across the room until you reach the opposite side. For the last row, use a small crowbar against a small piece of offcut to force the boards together. This last row cannot be secret nailed, but will have to be nailed through the face. Punch the nails below the surface and fill the holes.

5 To trim around a door architrave, use a profile gauge to transfer the shape to the strip. This device is simply pressed into the architrave to capture its shape. You can also use compasses: with the strip placed near the architrave, use the steel leg to follow the architrave's contour – the pencil will trace it onto the strip.

6 With the strip securely clamped in place, use a jigsaw to cut out the contour. Alternatively, you can trim the architrave and slide the flooring underneath (see step 7, p.191). To fit a strip around a pipe, see pp.190–191.

7 Replace the skirting boards if you've removed them. Or fit quadrant or scotia moulding to cover the gaps, nailing them to the skirting board or using an adhesive. Fill the nail holes in the flooring with a wood filler, as well as any holes in the moulding. Apply the recommended finish to the flooring; paint the moulding.

Helpful hints

Laminate woodstrip flooring laid on top of existing floorboards can raise the floor level considerably. You can choose to leave the skirting boards in place and trim the boards around the door architrave, as shown here. Alternatively, you can remove the skirting boards and replace them once the flooring has been laid, and cut through the bottom of the architrave so that the flooring fits underneath, as shown in *Laying a floating floor* (see pp.190–191). Whichever method you choose, the door itself will have to be trimmed so that you can open it over the new floor covering (see pp.76–77).

ROLL FLOOR COVERING OPTIONS

POSSIBLE MATERIALS

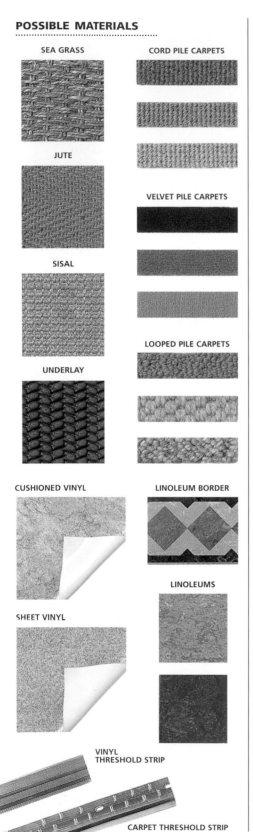

SEA GRASS

CORD PILE CARPETS

JUTE

VELVET PILE CARPETS

SISAL

UNDERLAY

LOOPED PILE CARPETS

CUSHIONED VINYL

LINOLEUM BORDER

LINOLEUMS

SHEET VINYL

VINYL
THRESHOLD STRIP

CARPET THRESHOLD STRIP

The two main types of flooring that come in a roll are carpet, (including natural floor coverings) and "sheet" flooring – mainly vinyl and linoleum. Carpets are generally described by the type of backing they have (foam or hessian) and the way in which the fibres are connected to it, known as the pile. The fibres may be natural wool, man-made or a combination of the two.

Natural floor coverings are becoming increasingly popular; these include coir (coconut fibre), sisal and sea grass. Out of these, sisal is the most hardwearing. Sheet vinyl and linoleum are also hard-wearing. Laying sheet vinyl is an easy job; however, putting down linoleum is best left to a professional.

▲ Sheet vinyl is available in a huge range of colours and patterns, including this chequerboard pattern (which imitates a common tile pattern). There are two main types of vinyl: plain vinyl and backed vinyl (also known as cushioned vinyl), which has an additional resilient underlayer, making it softer, warmer and quieter to walk on.

◄ Sheet vinyl and linoleum are particularly useful in the kitchen because food and grime cannot become trapped as they can do between tiles, and cleaning the floor is much easier. However, some vinyls can become slippery when wet.

◄ All carpets have a rating that indicates their suitability for use in different rooms in the home. A carpet with a rating of "Medium Domestic" is suitable for a regularly used bedroom. "Light Domestic" carpet is a good choice for an occasionally used, spare bedroom.

◄ The fibres in natural floor coverings are derived from plants and woven together to form a mat. Sometimes the fibres are woven with wool, to create a softer texture without losing the character of the natural fibres.

► Carpet in a neutral colour provides a suitable backdrop for many decorating schemes. Protect pale carpet from spillages by treating the carpet with a stain inhibitor.

▲ Striped or patterned carpet, or carpet with borders, can bring life to an otherwise plain flight of stairs. Carpet also helps deaden noise – an ideal choice for a wood staircase.

◄ The price of carpet increases in relation to the amount of wool used, which is the most expensive fibre in roll-floor coverings. Within each price range there will be different piles to choose from. Here, the velvet pile is very short, giving the feel and look of velvet.

◄ For areas where dirt is likely to be brought in from outside, particularly in a hallway, the best choice is a carpet in a dark colour.

LAYING A VINYL FLOOR COVERING

Where a room is not too large – 4 m (13 ft) wide or less – you can lay a single sheet of vinyl floor covering. This has the advantage that there will be no seam, but the laying is slightly more difficult. Shorter widths are lighter and easier to move about.

Before you start, repair any damage to wood floorboards and lay down hardboard sheets; if necessary, level a concrete floor. Measure the room carefully: include features such as alcoves and bay windows and add on half the depth of any door thresholds. A pattern should lead away from the main entrance into the room. If more than one sheet is needed, allow extra to match up any pattern repeats.

To allow it to acclimatize, leave the roll unwrapped and loosely unrolled in the room where it is to be used for two days. Some vinyl flooring will not require all-over adhesive – follow the manufacturer's instructions. To fit it around odd shapes, see pp.200–201.

Vinyl flooring offers an extensive choice of patterns, colours and textures for dressing up an otherwise drab room or utilitarian hallway.

Helpful hints

Instead of adhesive, use double-sided carpet tape around the perimeter of a room if it isn't subjected to heavy foot traffic. The flooring will be easier to remove at a later stage.

1 Unroll the vinyl sheet onto the prepared floor, making sure any pattern is the right way around. Brush it down with a broom to remove any air bubbles, pushing from the centre of the room toward the edges. Use a utility knife or scissors to cut the vinyl roughly to size; allow 5 cm (2 in) overlap at each edge for final trimming.

2 At an external corner, roll the vinyl back and insert a protective material such as hardboard between the layers. Using a utility knife, make a cut to the end of the sheet, starting 5 cm (2 in) from the corner. Slightly angle the cut toward the waste side (to the left in the situation shown here).

3 At an internal corner, pull down the "V" and make a cut down the centre with the utility knife. Overlap the two flaps (see inset), then cut up along the corner. Remove the offcuts and push the ends in place.

4 To apply adhesive, peel back half of the sheet (start away from the door). Spread the adhesive with a notched tool: follow the manufacturer's instructions. In some cases the adhesive may be applied only around the edges of the room. Reposition the vinyl and, once again, brush it down flat. Repeat for the other half of the floor.

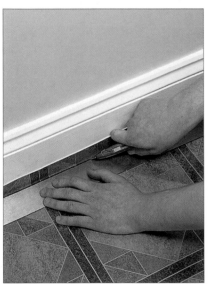

5 To trim the sheet to size, use a metal straightedge to push the vinyl firmly into the corner made by the floor and the skirting board. Cut the vinyl by running a sharp utility knife at a 45° angle along the straightedge.

6 At a doorway, make a series of vertical cuts, following the shape of the architrave moulding, then cut out the shape carefully. Trim the end of the sheet so that it lies under the middle of the door.

7 Finish off by fitting a threshold strip at the doorway. These come in various styles, depending on the type of floor covering in the next room, and are screwed down to the floor. On a solid floor, drill holes (using a masonry drill bit) to take plastic plugs for the screws.

TRIMMING TWO SHEETS

If using two sheets of vinyl, work from each side of the room. Before cutting the edges to fit, overlap the sheets and match the pattern where the seam will be (avoid high foot-traffic areas such as by a door). Cut through the overlap so the two sheets join exactly. Unless you are using adhesive, secure the join with double-sided tape.

USING A TEMPLATE FOR VINYL FLOORING

YOU WILL NEED

Weights
Soft broom
Scissors (if required)
Utility knife
Small wood block
Pencil
Wax pencil (for vinyl with a shiny surface)
Notched adhesive spreader (if required)

MATERIALS

Paper underlay
Adhesive tape
Sheet vinyl
Adhesive (if required)
Threshold strips and screws

SEE ALSO

Making minor repairs to a wood floor pp.42–43
Replacing a damaged floorboard pp.44–45
Laying a hardboard overlay pp.46–47
Levelling a concrete floor pp.50–51
Laying a vinyl floor covering pp.198–199

A paper pattern, or template, of a room with an unusual shape or several obstructions can be used as a guide to cut a sheet of vinyl flooring. The technique to create the paper template is known as "scribing", a process in which you transfer the exact profile of the room walls and other shapes onto the paper. You can use the paper normally sold for laying under carpets; alternatively, tape together several lengths of brown paper.

Measure from the longest points of the room, and consider that any pattern should run from the door. Before you start, repair any damage to wood floorboards and lay hardboard sheets to provide a smooth surface; level a concrete floor if necessary.

It is generally best to use adhesive to secure the vinyl in a bathroom (or other rooms where water gets splashed about such as a kitchen) as this will avoid any possibility of water getting under the edge of the sheet.

Trimming sheet vinyl for a room containing a number of obstacles, such as a toilet and basin in a bathroom, is made easier by using a template.

Helpful hints

While cutting the template to fit the room, you may accidentally move the paper. One way to avoid this is to weigh down the paper, using books or other heavy items, until you have trimmed it and taped it in place for scribing.

1 Cut the paper roughly to the shape of the room, allowing about 50 mm (2 in) on each edge for trimming. If you need to use two pieces of paper, tape them together using strong adhesive tape on both sides. Make pencil marks across the seams to use as a guide in case the sheets are separated.

2 Use scissors or a utility knife to cut the paper to about 12 mm (½ in) less than the size of the room, and make a cut the same distance around shapes. The exact distance is not crucial, but it must be less than the thickness of the wood "scribing" block (see step 3). Tape the paper to the floor to keep it from moving about.

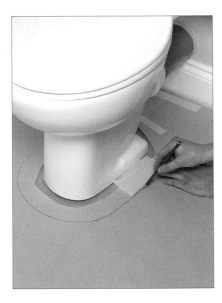

3 Starting in a corner, hold a wood block 25 mm to 50 mm (1 in to 2 in) wide firmly against the wall, with a pencil placed against the other end. Draw a line on the paper, sliding the block along the wall. Use it around any shapes, taking care that the block doesn't tilt. Keep the block the same way around all the time.

4 At a water pipe, use the block as a guide to draw a box the width of the pipe. Draw the lines perpedicular to the wall, then mark the distance away from the wall, using the short side of the block to measure from the front and back of the pipe. Use compasses to draw a circle in the box.

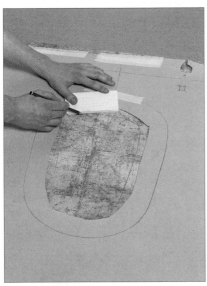

5 In another (larger) room, lay the vinyl flat on the floor, right side face up, and secure the paper template to it, using adhesive tape. Now use the wood block (positioned the same way around) to draw a line onto the vinyl, working outward from the line on the paper. Copy any shapes, including those for water pipes.

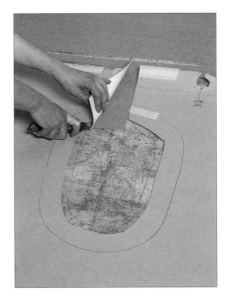

6 Trim the vinyl with a utility knife. To cut the hole for the pipe, use a short length of pipe of the same size (use a file to sharpen the inside of the end of the pipe, but do not reduce the diameter). Cut slits from any holes to the edge of the vinyl so that the sheet can be slipped around the obstacles.

7 Position the vinyl in the room. Turn back half of the vinyl and spread the adhesive, following the manufacturer's instructions. Now reposition the vinyl and use a broom to brush out any bubbles (see pp.198–199). Repeat on the other half. If you don't use adhesive, use double-sided carpet tape at any slits.

8 Finish off at the pedestals by squeezing a bead of waterproof sealant around them, holding the gun at a 45° angle. As well as sealing the edges, the sealant will hide any rough cuts. To install a threshold strip, see pp.198–199.

LAYING FOAM-BACKED CARPET

Foam-backed carpet can be laid almost anywhere in the house, except for on stairs.

One of the advantages of foam-backed carpet is that it's easy to lay: it doesn't require an underlay or stretching. It comes in rolls of different widths and in different wear qualities.

The basic floor must be dry, free from dust and level before the carpet is laid. Repair floorboards (see pp.42–45) and fit sheets of hardboard, unless the existing flooring is flat; level a concrete floor, and damp-proof it, if necessary (see pp.48–49). You should carry out all decorating (especially painting) before laying a new carpet.

A paper felt underlay on wood floors prevents staining of the carpet from dust below the floorboards – it may be all you need on chipboard floors or smooth floorboards. Before you start, remove all furniture from the room and take the door off its hinges (it may need trimming later on, see pp.76–77).

1 After clearing the room of furniture and preparing the floor, put down paper felt underlay. Cut the underlay to fit around the room, then use a staple gun to hold it in place; make sure that the staple heads do not tear the paper. If in a little used room, lay the underlay to the walls; where there will be heavy use, leave a border for the tape.

2 Stick double-sided tape around the perimeter of the room, leaving the backing paper in place. In large rooms, put down additional double-sided adhesive tape across the width of the room to secure the carpet. If the room will be heavily used, make sure the tape is laid directly onto the floor – and not the paper underlay.

3 Measure the room; in a larger room (or in the garden if it is a nice day) cut the carpet roughly to shape, adding 50 mm (2 in) to each edge for trimming. If using more than one length, check that the piles are going the same way (facing away from the main window). With the carpet laid in the room, trim it to 25 mm (1 in).

4 For an internal corner, make a diagonal cut across the corner of the carpet so that it can be pushed into its final position. For an external corner, make a cut parallel with (but slightly outside) the sides of the alcove, using a plank of wood underneath the folded carpet to avoid cutting through the carpet underneath.

5 Smooth the carpet down all over the room; then, working along one wall at a time, remove the backing from the double-sided adhesive tape and firmly press the carpet into place.

6 Use the back of the knife to push the carpet into the floor-wall angle; then cut it to size with the trimming knife held at a 45° angle and guided along the skirting board. Replace the blades on the knife often; they dull very quickly. Use a wide electrician's bolster chisel to push any loose fibres down at the edges.

7 To join two pieces of carpet, overlap the edges; then cut through both of them with a utility knife guided along a metal straightedge. Remove the offcuts and butt the edges together. Lift them up, lay down a strip of double-sided tape, then apply latex adhesive to the edges to stop them from fraying. Push the edges down in place.

Helpful hints

Use a hacksaw to cut threshold strips for any doors to length, then screw these down to the floor after cutting the carpet neatly to fit underneath. On solid floors you will need an power drill with a masonry bit to drill holes for wallplugs to take the screws. Alternatively, use an epoxy-based adhesive.

To fit carpet around plumbing or heating pipes, make a cut from the edge of the room to the position of the pipe, then use your utility knife to carefully cut neatly around the pipe until the carpet lies flat.

Use a vacuum cleaner to remove loose bits of carpet fibres before replacing the furniture.

LAYING HESSIAN-BACKED CARPET

YOU WILL NEED

Staple gun
Tape measure
Tenon saw
Utility knife plus carpet trimming blades
Hammer
Kneekicker (hired)
Electrician's bolster chisel
Screwdriver
Hacksaw
Power drill plus masonry bits (if required)

MATERIALS

Paper felt underlay (if required)
Gripper strips
Epoxy-based adhesive (if required)
Rubber **or** felt underlay
Hessian-backed carpet
Double-sided adhesive tape
Carpet seaming tape and latex adhesive (if required)
Threshold strip

SEE ALSO

Making minor repairs to a wood floor pp.42–43
Replacing a damaged floorboard pp.44–45
Laying a hardboard overlay pp.46–47
Laying foam-backed carpet pp.202–203

A carpet stretched from wall to wall creates a luxurious floor covering that is comfortable for relaxing on and against bare feet.

Hessian-backed carpet must be stretched as it is laid to prevent it from creasing later on. Given the right tools (such as a kneekicker) and the proper laying technique, you should achieve a reasonable result.

You must first prepare the floor (see pp.42–47 for a wood floor and pp.48–51 for a concrete floor); you'll also need to put down a felt or foam rubber underlay before laying the carpet itself.

GRIPPER STRIPS OR TACKS

Professional carpet layers use "gripper strips" – thin strips of wood with tacks set at an angle – to hold hessian-backed carpet in place. They are nailed down around the edges of the room (or glued down on concrete floors); the carpet is forced down over them. The tack points are sharp, so handle them with care. The strips are fairly costly, but they give an excellent result.

You can use carpet tacks on wood floors, with the carpet folded under itself and the tacks driven through both thicknesses. The only advantage is cheapness; tacks don't give as good a grip and the final result is not smooth.

1 Fit pre-nailed gripper strips around the room. Use a tenon saw to cut the strips to length (use short lengths around door mouldings and for bay windows); then nail them down to the floor – the gripper teeth should face toward the wall. On a concrete floor, you'll have to use an epoxy-based adhesive instead of nails.

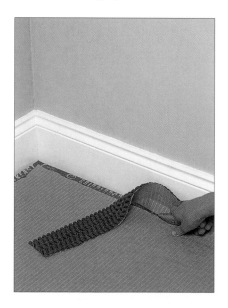

2 On a wood floor, staple down a paper underlay to prevent dirt blowing through floorboards. Lay down a felt or rubber underlay, cut it to fit inside the gripper strips and staple it in place; use double-sided adhesive carpet tape between lengths. On a concrete floor, use the double-sided tape for the whole underlay.

3 In a larger room (or in the garden if a nice day), cut the carpet roughly to size; allow 100 mm (4 in) for trimming at each edge. Lay it out in the room, adjusting it if necessary to square up any pattern. Walk out any large wrinkles in the carpet, moving from the centre of the room toward the walls.

4 Make diagonal cuts at both internal and external corners and make cut-outs to allow for any alcoves in the room (see step 4, p.203). Before you make the cut at an internal corner, trim off some of the excess to help the carpet lay in place.

5 Use the utility knife to trim the carpet along the skirting board, holding it at a 45° angle. (If you're not confident with the knife, leave a 10 mm (⅜ in) allowance and finish off after stretching the carpet in step 6.) Hook the carpet to the gripper strips at one corner, then along the two adjoining walls to the far corners.

6 Stretch the carpet with a kneekicker first across, then along the room, hooking it onto the gripper strips at the two remaining walls. As you secure the carpet to the strips, push the carpet down behind them, using an electrician's bolster chisel. (Or finish the trimming after stretching the carpet, then push the carpet down with the chisel.)

7 At a door, use a special threshold strip that contains gripper tacks. Screw it down on a wood floor; for a concrete floor, glue it down or screw it to wall plugs fitted into holes made with a power drill fitted with a masonry drill bit. Fit the carpet over the teeth, then bang down the top of the strip, protecting it with a piece of carpet.

Helpful hints

You may have to join two lengths of carpet in a large room. The traditional method is to sew them together, but because this is not easy, use carpet seaming tape instead. Place it below the joint between the two pieces of carpet and give it a generous coating of latex adhesive; use more adhesive on the back of the two pieces of carpet and on the edges up to the bottom of the pile (to prevent fraying). Allow the adhesive to become touch dry before pressing the two pieces of carpet together along the tape – a wallpaper seam roller is ideal for pressing down the joint. You can use the adhesive and carpet tape to repair any cuts.

LAYING STAIR CARPET

Laying carpet on stairs requires working on each step in turn while in a confined space – however, the final result will make the effort well worthwhile.

There are two methods of carpeting a staircase – fitting the carpet to cover the stairs completely or laying a "runner" with a gap along each side. A stair runner is easier to lay, and you can easily move it to distribute wear evenly at the front edge, or nosing, of the steps. A fitted carpet will always look better, but is more difficult to lay.

To find the length needed for straight stairs, add together the depth of one tread (front to back) and the height of one riser; multiply by the number of steps. If the stairs turn a corner, measure from the deepest part of the tread. Carpets are sold by the metre (or yard); order the next highest metre (or yard) above your measurement.

1 After doing repairs and painting, nail down gripper strips at the angles between the treads and risers. Use L-shaped stair gripper strips or two normal strips, with the tacks pointing toward the angles. Fix the riser strip 12 mm (½ in) from the angle, then the tread strip 12 mm (½ in) from the angle (use a spacer between the strip and the wall).

2 At a landing, cut the gripper strips to length with a tenon saw, and fit them as you would fit gripper strips around a room (see pp.204–205). Fit all the gripper strips for the complete staircase before going on to the next step.

3 Cut the underlay to the width of the carpet and into short lengths the width of a tread plus 25 mm (1 in). Position a length on the top tread, letting it overhang the nosing. Use carpet tacks or staples to secure the length in place, fixing it along the back and side edges. Continue until all the treads are covered.

4 Take the carpet from the landing above and cut it so that it covers the top riser, using a utility knife fitted with a carpet trimming blade. Push the carpet firmly into the gripper strip (see step 6), then trim off the excess.

5 While balancing the runner on the step below, position the top of the runner so that it's centred on the tread. Push the end down into the gripper strip and secure it in place with a chisel and mallet (see step 6). Allow the roll to move down, one step at a time, as you secure the carpet to the gripper strips.

6 For each step, check that the carpet is properly aligned, and repostion the roll if necessary. Use an electrician's bolster chisel to push the carpet into the gripper strips, working along the angle from end to end; then secure the carpet by hitting the chisel with a rubber mallet as you, once again, work along the angle.

7 At the end of each flight, trim off the excess carpet, using the utility knife; then return to the top of the steps to trim off any excess at the top of the run. Fit the carpet at the landing in the same way that you would fit hessian-backed carpet in a room (see pp.204–205).

Helpful hints

To move the carpet when it wears at the nosing, don't fit a gripper strip on the top tread. Instead, fold a wearing allowance (the depth of the tread) underneath, and use carpet tacks through both layers of carpet. Lay the carpet as described. Whenever the carpet begins to wear, pull it up and reposition it, with the allowance gradually shifting to the last riser.

To cope with fitting carpet on winding stairs, cut a fitted carpet for each step (tread and riser below) just slightly over size; then fit it to the gripper strips before cutting it to size. Where a stair runner is being used on a curved staircase, instead of cutting the carpet, make angled folds on each riser, then use carpet tacks through the layers of carpet.

FLOOR TILE OPTIONS

POSSIBLE MATERIALS

QUARRY TILE

CERAMIC TILE

TERRACOTTA TILE

QUARRY TILES

ENCAUSTIC BORDER TILE

BORDER TILES

INSET TILE

VINYL TILE

RUBBER TILE

CORK TILE

CARPET TILE

VINYL TILES

The advantage of using floor tiles is that you can mix and match colours and use patterns in a greater diversity than other floor coverings. Tiles can be easier to lay, especially in awkwardly shaped rooms, because you don't have to handle large sheets of material. However, they can take more time to lay because a lot of cutting may be needed, and the planning of where to start laying the tiles is vital.

Tiles for floors break down neatly into two groups: soft tiles, which include carpet, cork, linoleum, rubber and vinyl, and hard tiles, including ceramic, quarry and terracotta. Each is used in a different situation for a different purpose, and laying methods vary.

► A large room can handle the strong effect created by mixing black and while ceramic tiles in a chequerboard pattern. These and other hard tiles are characterized by their durability and natural beauty – and also by the fact that they are cold and noisy underfoot.

◄ Quarry and terracotta tiles are durable, and they come in a range of earth colours and a variety of shapes and sizes, with a smooth or textured surface. If they are machine made (they'll be a regular size), they can be as easy to lay as standard ceramic tiles – but cutting them is considerably more difficult.

▶ Vinyl tiles are the most popular of the soft floor tiles and come in a variety of patterns, including simulated brick, marble and stone.

▼ Plain white ceramic tiles are made more interesting by using ones octagonal in shape and adding coloured inset tiles.

▲ Carpet tiles have the appearance of carpet, but have the advantage that if a single tile is damaged, it can be easily replaced (always buy spare tiles). You can use them in bedrooms, kitchens, bathrooms and home offices.

▶ Carpet tiles are often set in a chequerboard pattern, but you can achieve interesting effects by cutting tiles diagonally in half or into even smaller sections.

◀ Pattern has been created when laying these vinyl tiles by combining solid colour tiles of a variety of colours. Like all soft floor tiles, vinyl tiles are soft and warm underfoot, quiet and easy to keep clean. However, remember they can be slippery when wet.

▶ Ceramic floor tiles are one of the easiest surfaces to keep clean, making them ideal for bathrooms and kitchens. The dark colour of these tiles is less likely to show dirt and footprints.

LAYING SOFT FLOOR TILES

One of the most effortless of all flooring jobs is laying soft floor tiles, which are easy to cut and handle. All types – vinyl, linoleum, carpet, rubber and cork – are laid in the same way, except the adhesive used may be different. The manufacturer will recommend the correct adhesive. Some carpet tiles can be laid with adhesive at only the perimeter of the room, and some vinyl and cork tiles are self-adhesive: simply remove the backing paper before positioning them.

The tiles are thin and the adhesive layer is not thick enough to cover any irregularities, so a smooth and flat, dry floor surface is the necessary starting point. Hardboard sheeting is the ideal way of preparing existing wood floors; solid concrete floors should also be in good condition and level.

Solvent-based adhesives dry more quickly than water-based ones but may be flammable – always follow the manufacturer's safety precautions.

You can create a dramatic effect by mixing plain coloured tiles to form a chequerboard pattern and using complementary tile insets.

Helpful hints

To lay tiles on a diagonal, use chalk lines snapped from the corners of the room as guidelines. If you use lines snapped from the midpoints of the walls, establish the diagonals by using the procedures in steps 1 and 2.

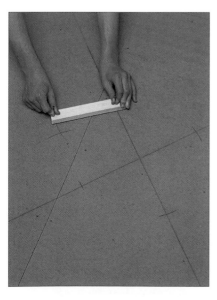

1 To find the centre of a room, snap chalk lines from the midpoints of the walls (see p.192). If the room is not square, snap the lines from the corners of the room. Hammer a nail through the ends of a batten. With one nail at the centre of the chalk lines, scribe arcs on the lines; then scribe bisecting arcs from the first ones.

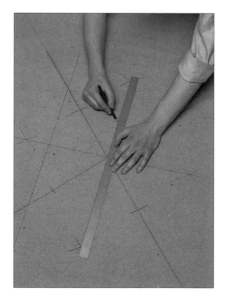

2 The bisecting arcs should be centred between the chalk lines. Draw a line through the centre of two opposing bisecting arcs, using a metal straightedge as a guide. Repeat with the other two bisecting arcs. Extend these lines to the edge of the room – these are the centre lines.

3 Dry lay tiles from the centre point down the centre lines to establish how the tiles should be laid. Try to minimize cutting at the edges. Ideally, no edge tile should be cut less than half a tile's width, but you might want to have whole (or nearly whole) tiles where they are more visible, with thinner strips against a less visible wall.

4 Mark any changes in the position of the centre, extending beyond the position of the central tiles. If required, spread adhesive on the floor, covering about 1 sq m (10 sq ft) at a time, starting in one quarter. With rubber tiles, spread adhesive on the tiles too; for carpet tiles, hold the first one down with double-sided adhesive tape.

5 Start positioning the tiles on the adhesive (or, one at a time, remove the backing paper, then position the tile). Some tiles have arrows on the back, indicating the pattern (or pile) direction. Make sure adjacent tiles butt together. Continue laying the tiles to the edges of the room, adding any inset tiles as you go.

6 To trim a tile to fit the edge, lay a whole tile exactly on top of the last whole tile laid. Lay a third tile on top of that, with an edge against the wall, and run a utility knife along its opposite edge to cut the central tile. (To mark a carpet tile, nick the edges with a utility knife and draw a cutting line on the back of the tile.)

7 To cut a corner tile to fit, follow the procedure in step 6 for one width, then repeat against the adjacent wall for the other. If you're not confident about your cutting abilities, use a pencil to draw cutting lines on the central tile; then remove it to do the cutting on a work surface, using a metal straightedge as a guide for the knife.

8 To mark gentle curves, you can use a template (see pp.200–201), but for intricate shapes (such as door architrave) use a profile gauge (see p.195) to transfer the shape to the tile. Trim the tile with a utility knife. To cut a hole for a water pipe, see p.201. To install a threshold strip at a door, see p.199. Cork tiles may need sealing.

LAYING CERAMIC FLOOR TILES

YOU WILL NEED

Chalk line
Floor tile spacers
Wood batten
Notched adhesive spreader
Spirit level
Hammer and wood block
Felt-tip pen **or** wax pencil
Platform tile-cutter
Angle grinder with ceramic tile-cutting blade (if required), plus protective goggles and heavy-duty work gloves
Rubber squeegee
Damp sponge **or** cloth

MATERIALS

Ceramic floor tiles
Adhesive
Grout

SEE ALSO

Making minor repairs to a wood floor pp.42–43
Replacing a damaged floorboard pp.44–45
Laying a hardboard overlay pp.46–47
Levelling a concrete floor pp.50–51

Ceramic floor tiles are ideal in a bathroom, but they can also be used in a kitchen, utility room, conservatory or hallway.

Although a floor laid with ceramic tiles can be cold and noisy, it will be durable and easy to keep clean. The technique for laying ceramic floor tiles is similar to that required for putting ceramic tiles on a wall (see pp.152–155); the differences are that the tiles are thicker – so they are more difficult to cut – and that you start

in the middle of the tiled area rather than in one corner.

A normal (waterproof) ceramic tile adhesive will allow the necessary degree of flexibility if you're tiling onto a wood floor; on a concrete floor, use a cement-based adhesive. In either case, the underlying floor surface must be both smooth and level: lay thick hardboard or plywood sheets on a wood floor or using floor-levelling compound on a solid floor.

CHOOSING THE CENTRE

Once you have found the centre of the room (by snapping chalk lines; see p.192 and p.210), choose one of these starting points for the central tiles: a single tile centred on the centre point; two tiles meeting at the centre; or four tiles meeting at the centre. You may want to adjust the centre point to align the tiles with a room feature, such as a chimney breast, or to set the tiles on a diagonal (see p.210).

1 Working from the centre, dry lay a row of tiles (allowing for the recommended grouting gap) along and across the room. You may need to adjust the centre lines so that the edge tiles are equal in size and no less than one half a tile's width.

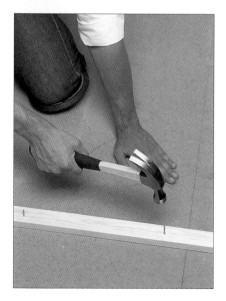

2 Divide the room in two and nail a batten to the floor along the chalk line (or the adjusted chalk line). Sink the nails only enough to hold the batten in place, which will have to be removed at a later stage. On solid floors, use masonry nails.

3 Starting in the half of the room farthest from the door, spread adhesive on an area 1 m (3 ft) long and just wider than the tiles. Lay the tiles against the batten (starting at the centre), using tile spacers to create a grouting gap between the tiles. Some manufacturers recommend applying adhesive to the tile as well as to the floor.

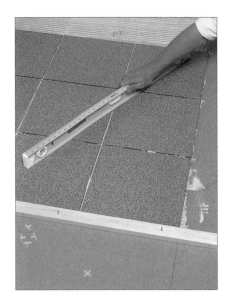

4 Use a spirit level to ensure that the tiles are flush. If not, tap a tile in place with a hammer against a wood block. Lay all the full tiles for one half of the room; then, after the adhesive sets, carefully remove the batten and repeat for the other half, finishing at the door. Allow the adhesive to set before fitting edge tiles.

5 Mark the edge tiles by using the three-tile technique: that is, lay a whole tile exactly on top of the last full tile laid, lay a third tile on top of that (using spacers at the wall to allow for grouting gaps); then draw a line on the middle tile of the sandwich, using the top one as a guide.

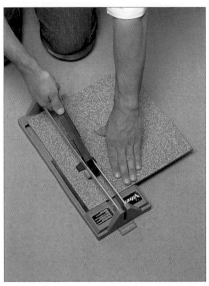

6 A platform tile-cutter is the best tool for cutting ceramic floor tiles. Make a single, deliberate score on the tile, then use the handle to snap the tile along the score by pressing it down at the end of the tile. Apply adhesive to the back of the edge tiles before inserting them in place.

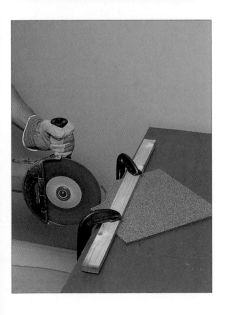

7 If you have to make a curved cut (see p.211 for marking it), securely clamp the tile to a work surface with the section to be cut hanging off the end. Wearing protective goggles and work gloves, use an angle grinder with a ceramic tile-cutting blade (which can be hired) to cut the curve. You can smooth the cut with a tile file.

8 Leave the tiles for the adhesive to dry for 24 hours. Use the recommended grouting medium for the tiles (this must be a flexible type if used on wood sub-floors). Work the grout into the spaces between the tiles with a rubber squeegee, then wipe off any grout from the surface of the tiles with a damp sponge or cloth.

LAYING QUARRY TILES

YOU WILL NEED

Chalk line
Wood batten
Notched adhesive spreader
Spirit level
Mallet and wood block
Platform tile-cutter **or** tile-cutting saw, with protective goggles and heavy-duty work gloves
Grout spreader
Hosepipe (if required)

MATERIALS

Quarry tiles
6 mm (¼ in) dowels
Cement-based adhesive
Cement-based grout
Silicone-rubber compound **or** caulking
Sealant and floor wax (if required)

SEE ALSO

Making minor repairs to a wood floor pp.42–43
Replacing a damaged floorboard pp.44–45
Laying a hardboard overlay pp.46–47
Levelling a concrete floor pp.50–51

A traditional flooring material, quarry tiles provide an earthy coloured hard-wearing floor.

Although qarry tiles are less likely to crack than ceramic tiles, they are more difficult to cut, and handmade ones (machine-made versions are more common) are more difficult to lay. Terracotta tiles are similar to quarry tiles, but are warmer and quieter.

The floor surface must be smooth and level. A solid floor surface is the best substrate. Wood floors must be covered with exterior-grade plywood (which is laid in the same way as hardboard, but screwed down). Doors may require trimming to accommodate the extra height (see pp.76–77). Quarry tiles are always laid with a cement-based adhesive and a cement-based grout is used to fill the gaps.

You cannot cut quarry tiles using a hand-held tile cutter. Because some platform tile-cutters have difficulty coping with quarry tiles, use one that specifically claims to be able to cut them, or hire a tile-cutting saw. Before you start, soak the tiles in water to reduce their absorbency; otherwise, the adhesive may be weakened.

Helpful hints

To fit a tile around a pipe, mark the exact position of the pipe on the tile. Drill a hole the size of the pipe, using a hole saw with a ceramic cutting blade; then cut the tile in two so that the halves fit on either side of the pipe.

1 If you have skirting tiles, do a dry run – with the dowels – to establish the grouting gap and corner tiles. Adjust the tiles to avoid cuts, keeping whole tiles in more visible areas. Use a tile-cutting saw (see step 6) if you must cut a tile, starting at the thick end. Apply adhesive to the back of the tiles and set them in place.

2 Snap chalk lines (see p.192 and p.210) to find the centre of the room. Set a dry run of two rows of tiles (with dowels to allow for the grouting gap) and reposition them to align with the skirting tiles and to avoid making cuts; re-snap the chalk line. If you must cut tiles, adjust the lines to avoid cutting narrow strips.

3 Nail a batten down across the centre of the room (leave the nail heads raised to remove later on) and spread about 1 sq m (10 sq ft) of adhesive on the floor, using a notched adhesive spreader to create good-sized ridges. The adhesive should be at least 6 mm (¼ in) thick, especially if the tiles vary in thickness.

4 Lay the first whole tiles right up against the batten, using short lengths of 6 mm (¼ in) dowelling rod to create the grouting gaps. Press the tiles down firmly into the adhesive, using a spirit level to check that they are flush, and sliding the tiles, if necessary, to ensure the gaps for the grout are straight and uniform.

5 If the tiles are not level, tap a mallet against a piece of wood laid across them. Continue with all the whole tiles until half of the room is covered. Remove the central batten and finish off the other half of the room. Leave for 24 hours before fitting the edge tiles. Measure and mark each edge tile (see p.213).

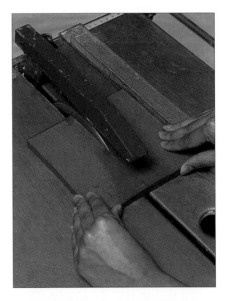

6 Cut and set each edge tile, with the adhesive on the back of the tile. For a clean cut without cracking the tile, use a tile-cutting saw: it has a water-cooled diamond cutting wheel. It will only cut straight lines (including L-shapes). To make a convex cut, use an angle grinder fitted with a masonry cutting disc (see p.213).

7 After 24 hours, use a squeegee to apply a cement-based grout (one part sand to one part cement) to fill the bottom of the joint, followed by a grouting mix of water and cement. Leave an expansion gap between the skirting and floor tiles (or at the edge of the room). Make a concave shape in the grout, using a piece of hosepipe.

8 Clean off all the grout before it sets, using a damp sponge or cloth. Fill the expansion gap (which allows the floor to move in a centrally heated home) with caulking or a silicone-rubber compound. If recommended, apply one or two coats of a sealant, such as linseed oil, followed by floor wax.

PAINTING A CONCRETE FLOOR

If left untreated, a concrete floor in a playroom, utility room, workshop or garage can rapidly become dusty and dirty. The answer is a purpose-made floor paint, which will prevent dust forming and make the floor much easier to keep clean.

Floor paints are available in solvent-based and water-based versions. The solvent-based type is for heavy-duty floors (such as a garage) and can also be used outside. The low-odour water-based type can be used inside and has the advantage of drying quickly; it is ready to walk on after three hours. Specialist paints are also sold specifically for garage floors (they are harder wearing than normal floor paints) and for use on doorsteps (these contain a nonslip additive).

Leave a newly laid concrete floor for at least a month before applying floor paint; if an existing floor is dusty, treat it with a stabilizing solution before painting (see pp.48–49).

Floor paints are available in several colours such as blue, green, grey, black and white. Dark colours are more appropriate in a workshop or garage.

Where it is impossible to remove all the furniture from a room (for example, in a garage that doubles as a workshop), it may be possible to paint the room in two halves.

1 Before you start painting, remove all loose and flaking material from the floor. If flaking paint is left on the floor, the new paint will flake off.

2 You must clean the floor of dirt and debris – an "industrial" vacuum cleaner is ideal for this. If the concrete has been prone to creating dust, apply a stabilizing solution (see pp.48–49).

3 The floor does not need to be levelled, but you may have to repair any holes or cracks using a sand-and-cement mortar mix, pressing this well into any depressions and smoothing it level with the remaining floor surface (for more details, see pp.48–49).

4 The floor must be thoroughly clean and free of oil and grease if the paint is to adhere. If white spirit won't remove all the stains, you can use a proprietary degreasing agent to clean the floor.

5 You may need to dilute the first coat by 10 percent with water or white spirit. Make sure you mix it thoroughly – an attachment for a power drill that is specially designed to mix paint is the best tool for the job. Always turn off the drill before lifting the paint stirrer from the bucket.

6 Use a 100-mm- (4-in-) wide paint brush to apply a strip of floor paint around the perimeter of the room. If you don't have a steady hand, stick lengths of low-tack masking tape along the edges of the walls to protect them.

7 The best method for painting a floor is to use a shaggy nylon pile sleeve on a paint roller with an extension handle. Start in the corner farthest from the door to avoid painting yourself into a blind corner. After it dries, apply a second full-strength coat, starting at the other far corner and working your way toward the door.

PAINTING A BAND

The neatest way to finish the floor is to create a band along the walls at skirting board height. Measure up from the floor and use a spirit level to draw a guideline. Apply low-tack masking tape along the line, then paint up to it. Remove the tape before the paint is dry.

5

SHELVIMG AND STORAGE

SHELVING AND STORAGE DIRECTORY

SHELVING OPTIONS

PAGES 222–223

There are several methods for installing shelves, and a huge variety of materials available to meet any budget. You can plan shelves to suit your needs and tastes, using anything from one simple store-bought fixed shelf to a homemade stack of individually fitted, built-in alcove shelves.

PUTTING UP FIXED SHELVES

SKILL LEVEL Low
TIME FRAME Under 2 hours
SPECIAL TOOLS Spirit level, power drill plus masonry bit
SEE PAGES 224–225

The simplest fixed shelving arrangement involves putting up a single shelf supported on two shelf brackets. Longer shelves require more brackets, and you can fix shelves one above the other. The most important part of the job involves making secure fixings into the walls to ensure that the brackets support the shelf and its load adequately.

INSTALLING ADJUSTABLE SHELVES

SKILL LEVEL Low
TIME FRAME Under 2 hours
SPECIAL TOOLS Try square, hand saw or power saw, bradawl, spirit level, power drill, tenon saw, chisel
SEE PAGES 226–227

Adjustable shelves are an arrangement consisting of several individual shelves that can be easily moved to another position to vary the shelf spacing as your needs change over the years. The brackets usually fit into slots or channels in vertical tracks that are screwed to the wall.

ALCOVE SHELVING

SKILL LEVEL Low to medium
TIME FRAME ½ day
SPECIAL TOOLS Try square, hand saw, power saw, spirit level, bradawl, sliding bevel
SEE PAGES 228–229

Alcoves can accommodate shelves that are as long as the width of the alcoves; they rest on battens fixed to the walls.

The shelf positions are fixed on the walls, giving the appearance of a built-in unit. This type of shelving is the strongest one – the walls take the weight of the load.

STORAGE OPTIONS

PAGES 230–231

Turning unused space around the home into storage for everyday items – from linen to video tapes to pots and pans – is one of the most common home improvements today. The number of ways of creating storage is limited only by your own creativity. You can follow the techniques as described in this section or combine them to come up with your personal design.

BUILDING A FITTED CUPBOARD

SKILL LEVEL Medium to high
TIME FRAME 1 to 2 days
SPECIAL TOOLS Try square, spirit level, hand saw or jigsaw, power drill, mallet, pin hammer, profile gauge
SEE PAGES 232–233

Alcoves can be used for more elaborate storage needs than simple shelving. By adding a wood framework to the flanking walls, you can add cupboard doors and create enclosed storage either at low level or extending to the full height of the alcove. By adding glass doors, you can turn it into a display cabinet for a collection.

CREATING A MULTIMEDIA STORAGE UNIT

SKILL LEVEL High
TIME FRAME 2 days or more
SPECIAL TOOLS Try square, hand saw or jigsaw, power drill plus hole saw bit, drill stand or drill press, pin hammer, profile gauge, spirit level, mallet
SEE PAGES 234–235

Many homes now have an array of electrical equipment, from stereos, televisions and video recorders to computers and video games. They also come with space-taking

ROUTER

MASONRY DRILL BITS

HINGE SINKER BIT

CROSSHEAD SCREWDRIVERS

POWER DRILL

COUNTERSINK BIT

WOOD DRILL BITS

TENON SAW

STUD, CABLE AND PIPE DETECTOR

accessories such as CDs, albums, video tapes and manuals.

By starting with the step-by-step instructions for a fitted cupboard (see pp.232–233), you can build a media storage unit customized to your own needs. Take time to decide what should be stored together, and make sure you carefully plan and measure each storage unit before you start the job.

CREATING A WORK CENTRE

SKILL LEVEL High
TIME FRAME 2 days or more
SPECIAL TOOLS Spirit level, sliding bevel, tenon saw, panel saw or jigsaw, power drill, router
SEE PAGES 236–237

Whether you want a home office for your computer, a garden centre for potting up plants, an organized workshop or a kitchen island or breakfast bar, you can follow the principles here to create your own work centre, with custom-designed storage. This section instructs how to

build a freestanding cupboard and attach a worktop to it and the wall. Alter the design to suit your own needs: add legs to one end or extend the worktop from wall to wall and add extra cupboard units below (leave knee room if you want to sit while you work). To add storage units above the worktop, see pp. 234–235.

GIVING STORAGE UNITS A FACELIFT

SKILL LEVEL Low
TIME FRAME ½ day
SPECIAL TOOLS Paint brush, power drill
SEE PAGES 238–239

If you want to give a facelift to a room containing built-in cupboards or wardrobes, you may be tempted to strip everything out and start again. However, if there is nothing structurally wrong with the carcasses themselves, you can give the units a new lease of life by painting them or treating them to one of the many decorative paint effects, and by fitting new hardware such as handles and hinges. For the neatest results, remove the doors and drawer fronts to paint them.

REPLACING CUPBOARD DOORS AND DRAWER FRONTS

SKILL LEVEL Low to medium
TIME FRAME 1 day
SPECIAL TOOLS Try square, power drill plus hinge sinker bit, drill stand, bradawl or nail punch
SEE PAGES 240–241

Another way of making a dramatic change to existing built-in units in the kitchen, bedroom and bathroom is to save the carcasses, which should have years of life left in them, and to fit new doors and drawer fronts to them. You'll need to take careful measurements to get replacements that fit exactly.

REPLACING A WORKTOP

SKILL LEVEL Medium to high
TIME FRAME 1 to 2 days
SPECIAL TOOLS Jigsaw, power drill, circular saw, cartridge gun, router or laminate trimmer plus mitre template
SEE PAGES 242–243

Replacing a worn kitchen worktop is just another part of the process involved in updating your fitted kitchen. The job can be easy if it won't

involve cut-outs and the worktop is in a straight line. However, the presence of inset sinks and hobs and the need to make 90° joints between adjacent lengths of worktop at corners make the job more complicated. Careful cutting and the use of a router or special jigs can help minimize these problems.

MAKING GOOD USE OF CUPBOARD SPACE

SKILLS LEVEL Low
TIME FRAME ½ to 1 day
SPECIAL TOOLS Power drill, pin hammer, hacksaw
SEE PAGES 244–245

There is always a finite limit to the amount of storage space available in any home. Once that has been reached, all that you can do is to make the best use of the space you have. There are numerous clever space-saving fittings that you can buy and install to enable even the most inaccessible corner to be reached. In addition, some will allow for better airing of clothes and linen.

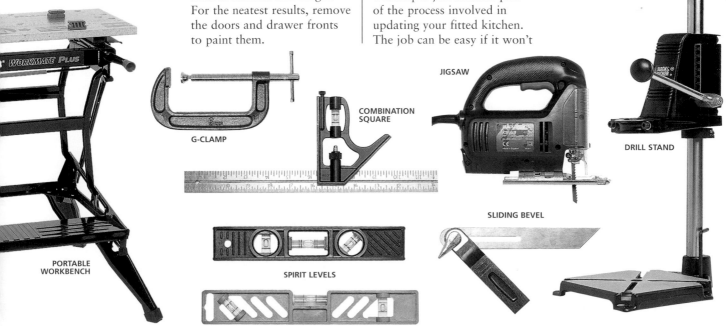

WORKMATE PLUS

PORTABLE WORKBENCH

G-CLAMP

COMBINATION SQUARE

SPIRIT LEVELS

JIGSAW

SLIDING BEVEL

DRILL STAND

SHELVING OPTIONS

POSSIBLE MATERIALS

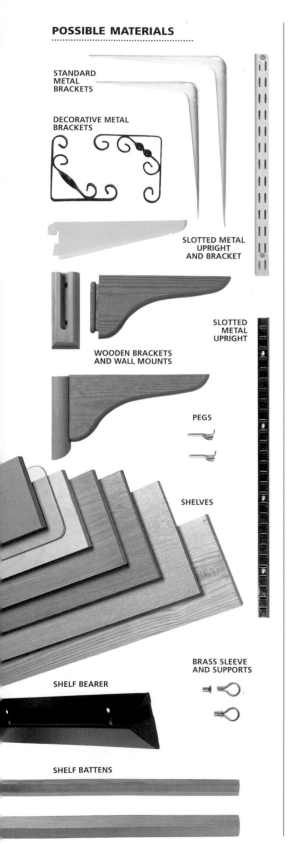

STANDARD
METAL
BRACKETS

DECORATIVE METAL
BRACKETS

SLOTTED METAL
UPRIGHT
AND BRACKET

SLOTTED
METAL
UPRIGHT

WOODEN BRACKETS
AND WALL MOUNTS

PEGS

SHELVES

BRASS SLEEVE
AND SUPPORTS

SHELF BEARER

SHELF BATTENS

After painting, putting up shelves is the one do-it-yourself activity that everyone tackles. Display and storage space is a necessity in virtually every room in the house, and there are several options you can choose to meet your needs. These range from open wall shelving to alcove shelving to freestanding units. Use different paint finishes and clever lighting to place your individual stamp on the shelves you choose to make, as well as on ready-made ones from stores.

▶ Colour is used here to blend in the alcove shelving with the rest of the surroundings. The combination of the shelves with the cupboards turns the shelving into a piece of built-in furniture.

◀ Built-in shelving makes efficient use of space and is inexpensive to install. These two units are fitted in the same way as traditional alcove shelving, but the top arches were custom designed. Because it's supported by walls on three sides, you can use this type of shelving to store large, heavy books. Store lighter items on high shelves to avoid removing or lifting up heavy objects above your head.

◀ Deep storage shelves can look dark. However, you can make them seem lighter by having no back on the unit (as long as it won't be supporting heavy items) and by painting bright colours inside the unit.

▶ High display shelves should be narrow enough for you to to see what is on them from below. These are suitable for items that you'll rarely need to take down.

▶ Downlighting your shelves highlights the items on them and casts mood lighting over the whole room. The same effect can be achieved by placing a table lamp on the shelf or a small light behind a large opaque item, such as a vase.

◀ Add a splash of colour by painting your shelves in a colour that contrasts with the colour of your wall. The curve of these shelves is not hard to achieve if you use the right material, such as MDF, and cover the edges with a veneer.

◀ Open shelving can be as simple as two brackets and a plank of wood – or as intricate and ornate as these, where the shelves are as interesting as the items on display.

▶ Enclosing your shelf space behind glass doors will protect the contents from dust, yet still allow the items to be displayed. Using glass doors instead of wood ones on a large arrangement of shelves will make the unit look less heavy.

PUTTING UP FIXED SHELVES

YOU WILL NEED

Tape measure and pencil
Try square
Bradawl
Screwdriver
Hammer (if required)
Torpedo spirit level
Power drill plus twist **or**
masonry drill bits

MATERIALS

Shelf
Shelf brackets
Wood screws
Wallplugs (for masonry wall)
or cavity wall fittings (for
hollow plasterboard wall)

SEE ALSO

Installing adjustable shelves
pp.226–227
Alcove shelving
pp.228–229

Using three brackets on this shelf is the best way to ensure that treasured relics are safe from a disastrous fall.

If you want just a single shelf, the simplest way of putting it up is to use individual shelf brackets. These are available in a range of decorative styles and finishes and are screwed to the wall and the shelf. A pair of brackets is all that is needed to support a short shelf, but longer shelves will require extra brackets. The spacing between the brackets will depend on what material is used for the shelf, how thick it is and the weight placed on it.

The maximum bracket spacing for 20-mm- (¾-in-) thick shelves made from solid wood or most manmade boards is 800 mm (32 in) for light-weight loads, 700 mm (28 in) for medium loads and 600 mm (24 in) for heavy loads such as stereo equipment and hardback books. For chipboard, reduce the measurements to 750 mm (30 in), 600 mm (24 in) and 450 mm (18 in) respectively.

With a hollow plasterboard wall, if you are not securing the brackets to wall studs, use cavity wall fittings that are strong enough to support the shelf and its load (see p.227). Check for wires and pipes hidden in the wall before starting any drilling (see p.228).

1 For long shelves that require three or more brackets, first determine the length and where you want the shelf. Measure the distance of the brackets and use a try square to mark their positions on the bottom of the shelf.

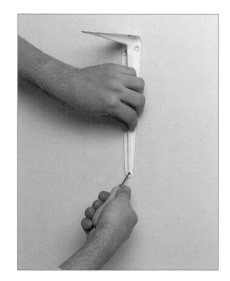

2 Place one of the outer brackets in position on the wall. The longest section should always be against the wall, with the shortest one supporting the shelf. Using a bradawl, mark the lowest screw position on the wall.

3 Drill a hole for the screw; use a twist drill for plasterboard or a masonry bit for a masonry wall. If the wall is masonry (see p.227), insert a plastic wallplug into the hole and use a hammer to gently tap it flush with the wall. With the bracket in place, drive the screw into the hole (or plug), leaving it slightly loose.

4 Set a level on the bracket; when the bubble in the liquid is centred, the bracket will be level. Mark the other screw holes, swing the bracket away and drill holes at the marks (insert plugs if needed). With the bracket realigned, drive in the remaining screws partway. Once all the screws are in place, tighten them.

5 With the first bracket on the wall, rest the edge of the shelf on it, with the level above the shelf, to align the top of the brackets. At the guideline on the shelf, mark the position of the other end bracket and fix it in place as you did the first one. Use this procedure to add any intermediary brackets.

6 Place the shelf on the brackets, using the guidelines previously marked on the bottom of the shelf. Drive the screws from the bottom of the bracket up into the shelf. The screws should be long enough to go two-thirds of the way through the shelf, but not any longer.

TWO-BRACKET SHELF

A short shelf that requires only two brackets is easier to install by first securing the brackets to the shelf with screws. You can use a straightedge or a strip of wood in a workbench to help align the back of the brackets to the back edge of the shelf.

With the brackets in place, hold the shelf the right way up against the wall, align it horizontally with a spirit level (as in step 5) and mark the positions for the screws. Drill the holes for the screws (see step 3) and screw the brackets to the walls.

Helpful hints

If you are putting up a shelf with just two brackets, position them one-quarter of the shelf length in from the ends to help prevent sagging. For more than two brackets, set the outer ones in from the ends by the shelf depth and set any further brackets at equal spacings between them.

You can drill pilot holes into the shelves to make driving in the screws easier. To ensure that you don't drill all the way through the shelf, use a depth guide – if you don't have one, wrap masking tape around the drill bit.

INSTALLING ADJUSTABLE SHELVES

YOU WILL NEED

Tape measure and pencil
Try square
Hand saw **or** power saw
Bradawl
Screwdriver
Spirit level
Power drill plus twist drill bit
or masonry drill bit
Tenon saw (if required)
Chisel (if required)

MATERIALS

Shelves
Tracks
Brackets
Woodscrews
Wallplugs

SEE ALSO

Putting up fixed shelves
pp.224–225
Alcove shelving
pp.228–229

Adjustable shelving is perfect for storing children's toys – the shelves can be moved up and down to accommodate new toys and other belongings as the children grow up.

A track shelving system is easy to install. It consists of two or more lengths of vertical metal track and a series of matching shelf brackets that fit into slots or channels in the tracks. They are available in white, bright primary colours and metallic effects.

The system can support shelves made of a variety of materials, including wood and MDF. You can use ready-made ones or cut and finish your own. Even with the shelves attached, the brackets are easy to reposition. Three or more tracks give greater flexibility in the lengths of the shelves and how you stagger them, allowing you to make the most of the space available.

The spacing of the tracks must be set as brackets on fixed shelves are: by the shelf type, thickness and load (see pp.224–225). The easiest way of putting up the shelves means that the tracks hold the rear edges of the shelves away from the wall. If you want them to fit flush with the wall, notch the rear edges of the shelves.

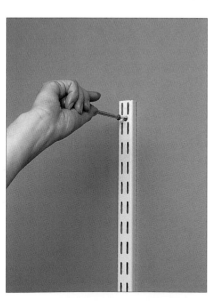

1 After you decide on the positioning and spacing of the tracks, hold the first end track against the wall and mark the position of its topmost screw with a bradawl. Drill the hole, and plug it if you have a masonry wall (see *Helpfuls Hints,* facing page). Drive in the screw partway.

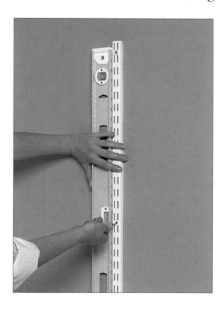

2 To get the track truly vertical, hold a spirit level against it and adjust it until the bubble is centred in the appropriate tube of fluid. Then mark the positions for the other screws, swing the track aside so you can drill the holes (and plug them, if necessary), then reposition the track and insert the remaining screws.

3 To position the other end track, slip a bracket into the same slot in both tracks. Standing a shelf on end on the bracket on the first track, with a spirit level on top to keep it horizontal, set the other end track in place and mark the topmost screw. Then repeat steps 1 and 2 to secure the track to the wall. Repeat for any intermediary tracks.

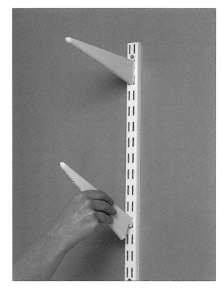

4 Slip the shelf brackets into place in the slots in the track, checking that they are level with each other – count the number of slots above or below the brackets. If necessary, cut the shelves to length (see p.229) – you can add strips of veneer to the ends to hide cut ends.

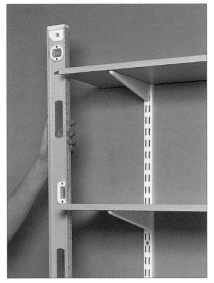

5 After you position the shelves on the brackets, you should use a spirit level or plumb line to align the ends of the shelves.

6 Unless the shelves are in an alcove and, therefore, captive, it is best to screw the shelves to the brackets. Drive the screws up from the bottom of the brackets, supporting the top of the shelf with your other hand. Make sure the screws penetrate only two-thirds of the shelf's thickness.

NOTCHING THE SHELF

Use a tenon saw to cut down the sides of the marked notch. Clamp the shelf securely, with scrap wood under it. With the chisel perpendicular to the depth line, firmly press the chisel down; then gently tap it with a wood mallet to increase the depth of the cut. Remove a thin layer of the waste by pressing the chisel, bevel side up, against the edge of the shelf. Continue these procedures until you remove all of the waste wood.

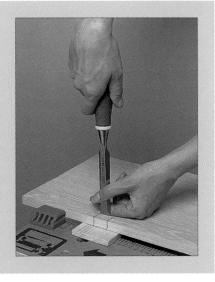

Helpful hints

Shelf brackets and tracks exert considerable force on the fixings securing them to the wall, so you must use the correct fixings. On solid masonry or plaster walls, use screws at least 38 mm (1½ in) long, and drive them into wallplugs inserted into drilled holes. On wood-framed partition walls, locate the studs (see p.229), which are usually 400 mm (16 in) apart, then drive 38-mm- (1½-in-) long screws into the plasterboard and studs. You can use cavity wall fixings such as spring toggles to mount shelves to plasterboard alone, but only if the shelves will be lightly loaded.

ALCOVE SHELVING

YOU WILL NEED

Tape measure and pencil
Try square
Fine abrasive paper
Hand saw
Power saw (if required)
Torpedo spirit level
Standard spirit level
Bradawl
Power drill plus twist bit
Masonry drill bit (only for masonry walls)
Gauge rods
Sliding bevel
Screwdriver

MATERIALS

Shelves
38 mm x 25 mm (1½ in x 1 in) softwood battens
Woodscrews
Wallplugs

SEE ALSO

Putting up fixed shelving
pp.224–225
Installing adjustable shelving
pp.226–227

Many homes have alcoves, often at either side of a chimney breast or a similar structure. They are an ideal site for built-in shelves or other forms of storage because the walls of the alcove can provide the support you need, especially for heavier loads.

The simplest method involves screwing wood battens to the side walls and resting the shelves on these. In wide alcoves, add a third batten along the rear wall to prevent the shelf from sagging. If you encounter uneven plaster on the alcove walls, trim each shelf individually to get a good fit. The shelves can be made from wood, plywood, veneered chipboard or MDF, which can be stained or painted.

If you are planning to fix a batten across the rear wall of an alcove, take care if there is a wall light installed there. The electrical cable running to the light will be buried in the wall, and a hole drilled in the wrong place could pierce it. Professional

A batten along the front edge of these shelves hide the ends of the side battens attached to the walls.

electricians always run buried cables vertically or horizontally, but an amateur may have run one diagonally across the wall. The best way to locate buried cables is to use a detector (see *Helpful hints*, facing page).

1 Start by deciding where you want the shelf to be (use a detector to locate studs, cables or pipes, see facing page) and what spacing you require if you plan to install several shelves. Then measure and mark each shelf position on one side wall of the alcove.

2 Using a tenon saw, cut as many battens as you need to support the shelves you are installing; sand the cut ends smooth. If you use a batten at the front of the shelves (see step 7), subtract its width from the width of the shelves to establish the length of the side battens; otherwise, cut the side battens to the width of the shelves.

3 Drill two screw holes through each side batten, about 25 mm (1 in) from the ends. Hold a batten at a mark and use a torpedo level to find a true horizontal; mark the position for the back screw with a bradawl. Drill the hole and plug it, if necessary (see p.227); drive the screw in. Secure the second screw as the first.

4 Once all the battens are in place on one wall, balance a spirit level on each batten and mark horizontal lines across the alcove to the facing wall. Use these lines as a guide to install the battens on the opposite wall, following the instructions given in step 3. For wide shelves, install battens along the back wall.

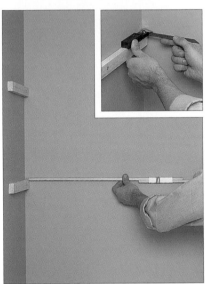

5 Measure for each shelf separately, using gauge rods – two pieces of batten held together with rubber bands – to find the width of the back wall (they are more accurate than a retractable tape measure). Use a sliding bevel (inset) to find the correct angle of each corner.

6 Transfer the measurements to each shelf and cut them to length. (At this stage, you can finish the shelves by applying stain and/or varnish or painting them, then letting them dry.) Carefully set the shelves on top of the battens; try to avoid marring the walls. To hide the ends of the battens, see the next step.

7 Cut a batten to fit under the edge of each shelf. Clamp it in place, using scrap wood to protect the surfaces of the work. Drive screws long enough to penetrate up through the batten but only two-thirds into the shelf. Use wood filler to fill the cracks between the battens and shelves. Once it has dried, apply a coat of paint.

Helpful hints

The best way to find buried electrical cables or water pipes or to locate wood studs behind plasterboard is to use a battery-powered detector. Some are sold strictly to locate studs, others combine this function with locating cable and pipes. To use a detector, simply hold it against the surface of the wall at the points where you want to make your fixings, following the directions from the manufacturer.

STORAGE OPTIONS

POSSIBLE MATERIALS

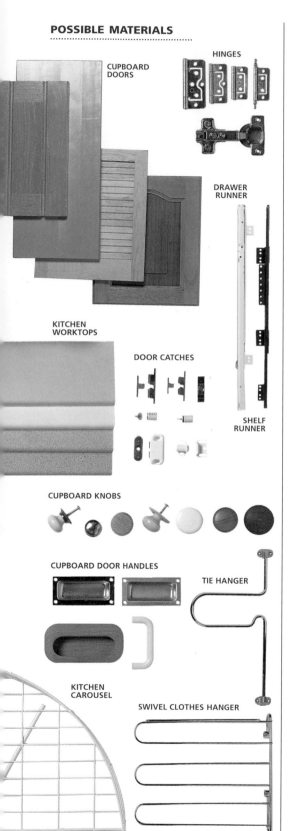

CUPBOARD
DOORS

HINGES

DRAWER
RUNNER

KITCHEN
WORKTOPS

DOOR CATCHES

SHELF
RUNNER

CUPBOARD KNOBS

CUPBOARD DOOR HANDLES

TIE HANGER

KITCHEN
CAROUSEL

SWIVEL CLOTHES HANGER

Successful storage means having a place for everything, and keeping everything in its place. Every home seems to have ever-increasing belongings to fit into it, yet new homes are often less spacious than those built in earlier times. With careful planning, you can make the best possible use of the space available by using any combination of the techniques described on the following pages.

You may be fortunate in having enough storage space, but you may still want a change of style. This is particularly relevant in the kitchen and bedroom, which often contain a lot of built-in furniture. They can be easily updated with little expense and effort.

▶ A fitted kitchen is an expensive investment. If your tastes change as time goes by, consider changing the way the units look. Use one of the many paint effects available; change paint for varnish or wood stain; or discard old doors and drawer fronts and fit replacements to the existing cupboards.

◀ Modular units are a hybrid between built-in and freestanding furniture. The open shelves allow you to display crockery, but be aware that the pieces will be exposed to dust.

◀ Louvre doors allow good ventilation, making them suitable for a clothes or linen cupboard. These doors have been made into a feature with a strong colour and distressed paint finish.

▲ When pressed for storage, there's no such thing as wasted space – you can create storage in the most unlikely places such as these steps to a platform area.

▶ When working from home, it is essential to separate living and working spaces. If you cannot convert a whole room to an office, create a work space in the corner of a room.

▲ Clothes that are properly stored will last longer, so make sure there is adequate room and ventilation by using a combination of shelves and hanging space.

◀ To work most effectively, your home-office storage space should be organized to allow you easy access to frequently used items. You can keep items rarely used on high, hard-to-reach shelves.

▶ When organizing storage for home entertainment, remember to allow for an ever-expanding collection of compact discs and video tapes, as well as to create room for your treasured albums.

BUILDING A FITTED CUPBOARD

YOU WILL NEED

Tape measure
Try square and pencil
Spirit level
Hand saw **or** power jigsaw
Power drill plus twist bits
and masonry drill bits (if
required)
Screwdrivers
Wooden mallet
Pin hammer
Profile gauge (if required)

MATERIALS

Softwood battens for the
framework
Dowels
PVA adhesive
Panel pins
Man-made boards for
shelves
MDF (medium density fibre)
board for plinth
Doors
Handles, hinges and catches
Woodscrews
Wallplugs (if required)

SEE ALSO

Fitting a bifold wardrobe
door pp.90–91
Alcove shelving pp.228–229
Creating a multimedia
storage unit pp.234–235
Making good use of
cupboard space pp.244–245

Start by deciding what sort of storage you'll need. For example, you can adapt a cupboard to store linen or toys, or you can turn it into high-level storage with hanging space for clothes below. With careful planning, you can even fit a storage cupboard under an open staircase.

You'll have to decide whether to fit the doors flush with the face of the protruding wall, to recess them slightly or, if the alcove is shallow, to build out beyond the face of the wall. Use ready-made doors if possible, adjusting the frame measurements so they'll fit. If you do make the doors, use dowel joints to make the frames and glazing beads to frame and support the panels.

BEFORE YOU START

Check whether the alcove is square and has truly vertical flanking walls (see pp.228–229). Out-of-true walls affect how you make the frame: insert packing between walls and uprights to

This cupboard may provide ample storage space in your living room, but you can increase its capacity by adding shelves or a glass-front display unit above it.

get the latter truly vertical, or scribe the wall profile onto the uprights and cut along the scribed line (see p.166).

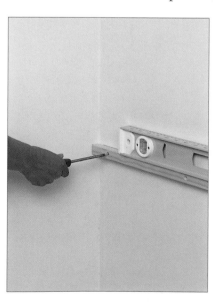

1 A top horizontal batten is needed to support the back edge of the top of the cupboard. After measuring the wall (see p.229, step 5), cut the batten to fit, using a tenon saw; then screw it to the rear wall of the alcove (see p.227, *Helpful hints*).

2 To support a flush-fitting or recessed front frame, mark the positions for the vertical battens. (For a protruding cupboard, see p.235.) Use a spirit level to align the top of each vertical batten with the top of the horizontal batten on the back wall. Fix the top screw, then align the batten vertically. End the battens above any skirting boards.

3 To make a front dowel-joint frame, use a tenon saw to cut each of the four lengths of wood to fit (with the vertical lengths sandwiched between horizontal ones). Clamp each length to a work surface; drill holes in the appropriate ends for dowels. Assemble the frame with dowels and adhesive; tap with a mallet for a snug fit.

4 Attach a fixing strip down each side of the frame so you can screw through this into the wall batten and not have any screws on show on the face of the unit. Add another fixing strip across the bottom to support the front edge of the lower shelf. Screw the frame to the vertical battens on the wall.

5 Cut a plinth made of MDF (you may have to scribe it to fit around the skirting board, see p.169); pin it to the bottom of the frame. Fit the bottom horizontal batten to the wall as you did the top, using the top of the fixing strip on the front of the frame to find its level. Add side and back battens for any middle shelves (see pp.228–229).

6 Cut the shelves to size after carefully measuring the width and depth of the alcove for each shelf. Rest the bottom shelf on the wall batten and the fixing strip on the frame (then, from the bottom up, any middle shelves on their battens). Glue the top shelf to the frame and batten; or screw joint blocks to the frame (see inset) and shelf.

7 To make your own doors, make a pair of dowel-joint frames (see step 3). Glue and pin thin lengths of wood to the inside edges at the back of the frames. Fit glass, plywood or MDF panels in place, then fix them in place by gluing and pinning glazing beads around the inside edges at the front of the frame.

8 To hang a door, attach hinges to the door with screws. Fix the hinges to the frame. Drive a screw in one hinge, then the other; add the other screws. Drive them in loosely so you can make adjustments as you go; once all the screws are in place, tighten them. Drill holes for the handles and screw them in place; add a catch.

CREATING A MULTIMEDIA STORAGE UNIT

YOU WILL NEED

See *Building a fitted cupboard* pp.232–233
Tape measure
Try square and pencil
Work surface
Hand saw **or** jigsaw
Power drill plus twist drill bits and hole saw bit
Drill stand **or** drill press
Screwdrivers
Pin hammer
Profile gauge (if required)

MATERIALS

See *Building a fitted cupboard* pp.232–233
Man-made boards
Sliders (if required)
Woodscrews
Pine strips
PVA adhesive
Pins

SEE ALSO

Installing adjustable shelves pp.226–227
Alcove shelving pp.228–229
Building a fitted cupboard pp.232–233

Most houses contain a range of home entertainment equipment, which can take over a room unless it is kept under control. Work out the best solution to your storage requirements by making a list of the equipment you own and thinking about how you use it. This will dictate whether you house everything in one large unit or create several storage solutions. For example, it makes sense to house the television and video recorder in one unit, along with the stereo equipment, tapes, CDs and vinyl. If you have a home computer, house it in another room if it is used for homework or business.

After deciding on the configuration, measure each component so you can include it in your design. Remember to provide enough depth for electrical and aerial connections at the back of each component, and to allow air to circulate. Make sure power points are accessible for the equipment; you may need to call in an electrician.

A home entertainment centre fits comfortably in this custom-made unit. Inside the cupboard there are shelves for a video recorder and cable or satellite decoder, and room for VCR and cassette tapes. Wires are hidden behind the CD storage columns.

1 If you don't already have a basic fitted cupboard, start by making one (see pp.232–233), then follow the steps here to adapt it. For wires and cables above the cupboard to reach equipment or power points below, bore a hole in a back corner of the top of the cupboard, using a hole saw attached to a power drill.

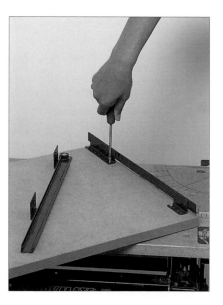

2 Sliding shelves let you pull out a video recorder or decoder to reach the connections, or can hold a computer keyboard. Cut a shelf to fit, allowing room for the sliders (see pp.228–229). Fit one slider at a time; fix one half to the shelf and the other half to the wall. The parts are easy to confuse, so do a test fit first.

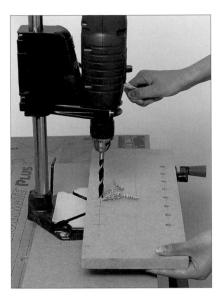

3 Begin to make a storage column for CDs or tapes. Measure and cut the four sides of the box. Mark the positions for two rows of holes (which will take shelf-support pegs) along the front and back of the two vertical sides of the box. Use a drill stand or drill press to make the holes (jigs are available to help drill the holes).

4 Assemble the sides of the box and secure them with screws; use screws long enough for one-third of their length to go into the far piece. Then attach a back to the box, using pins and a hammer – it will prevent items from falling out of the back.

5 Finish the face of the columns by gluing and pinning pine strips to the edges of the box. If you plan to paint the column, this is a suitable time to give it a priming coat.

6 Measure, cut and fit a shelf (or shelves) in place; follow the instructions on pp.228–229. If electrical equipment will be stored on the shelf, bore a hole in a back corner to correspond with the one in the cupboard below (see step 1). You can use adjustable shelves; however, the finished result will be less sophisticated.

7 Position the storage columns on the top of the cupboard; these two will be staggered to allow wires and cables to run down the shaft created in the corner. Drive a screw down through the front of the column to hold it in place. Fit sleeves for pegs in the holes, then the pegs and shelves. Fit a swivel bracket for a television if you wish.

INCREASING A CUPBOARD'S DEPTH

You can increase the depth of a cupboard in a narrow alcove so it can hold large equipment. Cut a piece of MDF to the desired width (scribe it at the skirting board, see p.169). Fix a batten to the wall 25 mm (1 in) from the corner. Butt the MDF against the batten; fix a second one over where the two meet.

CREATING A WORK CENTRE

YOU WILL NEED

Tape measure and pencil
Spirit level
Sliding bevel
Tenon saw
Panel saw **or** jigsaw
Power drill plus twist and masonry drill bits
Screwdrivers
Router
Hex key (if required)

MATERIALS

MDF for cupboard
Woodscrews and wallplugs
Hardboard for cupboard back
Nails
50 mm x 50 mm (2 in x 2 in) softwood battens for frame and wall
Ready-made door
Hinges and hardware for door
Worktop
Table legs (if required)

SEE ALSO

Alcove shelving pp.228–229
Building a fitted cupboard pp.232–233
Creating a multimedia storage unit pp.234–235
Replacing cupboard doors and drawer fronts pp.240–241

The work centre here is for a home office. However, you can adjust the design for other uses such as a sewing centre, kitchen island or even a breakfast bar.

A work centre can be created anywhere that you have available space. The one shown here is designed to illustrate several techniques, which you can then adapt to create your own customized centre. For example, you may choose to attach the work surface to battens fitted on two walls, perhaps in a corner. Or you can leave the battens out altogether and use a pair of the drawer/cupboard combination units – which can also be adapted, for example, by increasing the size of the cupboards and dropping the drawers or creating a stack of drawers. Yet another option is supporting one end with a batten on a wall and the other end with legs. If you position it high enough, you can store stools below it and use it as a breakfast bar.

It is important to decide exactly how you want to use the centre. Whether you'll be standing or sitting, make sure it will be at a comfortable height to work on, and also make sure it will be within easy reach of any necessary power points. Using ready-made doors and drawers will make the centre much easier to build.

1 For the sides of a base unit, cut two pieces of MDF to the depth of the drawer and the height of the door and drawer. Use a router to cut rebates for holding a shelf (the shelf also makes the frame more sturdy); make rebates along the back end of the pieces. Use a batten to guide the router; set it to cut at half the MDF thickness.

2 For the top and bottom, cut two pieces of MDF as deep as the drawer and as wide as the door. Drill three pilot and countersink holes at the back of the end rebates on the side pieces. Assemble the box, sliding the ends of the top and bottom pieces into the rebates on the side pieces. Use a power screwdriver to drive in the screws.

3 A back will help support the cupboard. Cut a sheet of hardboard for the back; nail it in place. To make a shelf, cut a piece of MDF the width and depth of the cupboard; insert it into the rebates. Drill pilot holes into the rebates from outside the cupboard; countersink them, then screw the shelf in place.

4 Mark the positions of the drawer runners on the inside of the cupboard. Drill holes for the screws, then fix the runners in place. Insert the drawer to ensure it opens and closes properly; then take it out and put it to one side until the work centre is completed.

5 Make a plinth so that the door can open: cut four lengths of wood 50 mm (2 in) shorter than the top's dimensions; butt joint and screw together. Screw the plinth to the bottom of the cupboard. Screw the hinges onto the ready-made door. Position the hinges against the cupboard. Mark and drill screw holes; fix the hinges (see p.241).

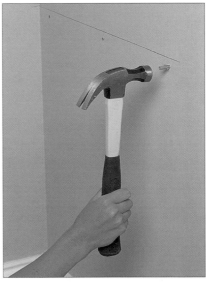

6 Cut a batten to the worktop's width. Move the cupboard to the wall, set the worktop on it and mark the height on the wall. Draw a horizontal line from the mark for the top of the batten. Drill holes in the batten; mark their positions on the wall. Drill holes at the marks, insert wallplugs and screw the batten in place.

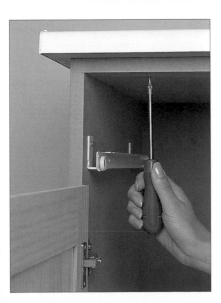

7 Cut the worktop to the correct length and place one end on top of the cupboard, the other end on the batten. Use white plastic corner brackets to screw the worktop to the batten. To fix the cupboard to the worktop, drill holes up through the top of the cupboard into the worktop before screwing it in place.

USING LEGS

If you want a freestanding end, turn the worktop over and position a pair of leg brackets on it. Mark and drill the screw holes, then screw on the brackets. Slip the legs onto the brackets and tighten them with a hex key. Turn the worktop over and fix the other end to the cupboard or wall batten.

GIVING STORAGE UNITS A FACELIFT

YOU WILL NEED

Screwdriver
Sanding block plus fine wet-and-dry abrasive paper
Workbench
Paint brushes **or** a spray gun
Power drill plus twist bit (if required)

MATERIALS

Paint
Sugar soap **or** detergent
Abrasive paper
Replacement handles **or** knobs

SEE ALSO

Painting basics pp.114–115
Using paint brushes pp.116–117
Using a spray gun p.121
Paint effects pp.122–129
Replacing cupboard doors and drawer fronts pp.240–241

Sooner or later you will tire of the look of your fitted furniture, whether it is in the kitchen, living room or bedroom. A coat of paint and new hardware can be all that's needed to create a modern look.

Updating the look of your fitted furniture, especially if it is still in good working order, doesn't mean replacing it. Instead, use the existing finish as the base for a new coat of paint (a primer and paint are available for melamine surfaces), whether it has a plastic or a natural wood finish.

Decide how extensive the paint job will be. You may want to tackle just the doors and drawer fronts – the parts that are visible when the units are closed up. Or you might decide to repaint the cupboard and drawer interiors too, but this is seldom necessary. Apart from all the extra painting involved, you would have to remove everything stored in the units.

Plan the job as a production-line operation. It is easier to paint doors and drawer fronts when they are laid flat on your workbench rather than attached to their units. You can apply the new paint with a brush or a spray gun. Store a small quantity of the paint you use in an airtight container, so you can touch up any chips and knocks to the units in the future.

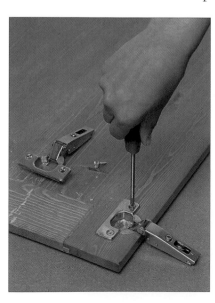

1 Take the doors off their hinges one by one, then unscrew any handles or knobs. In theory, all the door hardware should be interchangeable, but it's a good idea to keep the parts in separate, labelled piles just in case.

2 Wash the surfaces you plan to paint using sugar soap or strong household detergent to remove any dirt, grease and fingermarks. Rinse them in clean water and leave them to dry.

3 Sand the surfaces with fine wet-and-dry abrasive paper to give them a key for the new paint. Wipe the surface with a cloth moistened in white spirit or with a tacky rag to remove the fine dust the abrasive produces.

4 Paint the doors; if they are panelled, start in any recessed areas, move on to the panels, then finish off around the edges. When the base coat has dried, you can add a decorative paint effect if you wish. Re-attach the hinges and fit the doors back in their original positions (see pp.240–241).

5 Remove the drawers from their tracks. After pulling out a drawer to its full extent, tilt it down to release the runner on the drawer from the runner inside the unit. When you replace the drawers, tilt them to the same angle to engage the two runners. Make sure you put the drawers back into their original slots.

6 Remove the handles or knobs by unscrewing them. If the drawers have separate fronts attached to their carcases, unscrew them to release the front. The fronts are easier to paint if not attached to the carcases. (Screws from the handles or knobs may be holding the fronts in place.)

7 If you want to replace two-screw handles with one-screw knobs, or vice versa, fill the original screw holes with a wood or cellulose filler. Centre the new hardware on the fronts, mark the screw hole positions and drill the screw holes.

8 Set the drawer fronts on small pieces of cardboard or hardwood so that you can paint their edges without painting the work surface. (Clamp drawers without a separate front standing on their ends.) Apply the paint (and paint effect if desired); leave them to dry. Re-attach the fronts and handles to the drawers; fit them in the runners.

REPLACING CUPBOARD DOORS AND DRAWER FRONTS

YOU WILL NEED

Screwdrivers
Workbench
Tape measure
Try square
Pencil
Power drill plus twist drill
bits and 35- mm-(1⅜-in-)
diameter hinge sinker bit
(if required)
Drill stand (if required)
Bradawl **or** nail punch and
hammer

MATERIALS

Replacement doors and
drawer fronts

SEE ALSO

Giving storage units a
facelift pp.238–239
Replacing a worktop
pp.242–243
Making good use of
cupboard space pp.244–245

If repainting your existing storage units does not appeal to you, fit new doors and drawer fronts to the existing carcases. You can achieve a new look or style that you cannot create with paint – and it is less expensive than replacing the complete units.

The carcases, or the boxes, of storage units have no movable parts; therefore, they are not exposed to a great deal of wear and tear. There is little point in wasting both time and money replacing a series of perfectly sound carcases. Modern storage units are all modular in size, so buying new doors and drawer fronts to fit them is straightforward – as long as you take exact measurements. There is a wide range of materials, including solid and veneered wood and plastic laminates, and surface finishes include high-gloss coatings and decorative paint effects.

Both doors and drawer fronts are generally supplied as blanks. You'll need a standard 35-mm- (1⅜-in-) diameter hinge sinker bit to drill the holes in the doors to fit concealed hinges. Drawer fronts are usually attached to their carcases with screws.

1 Remove an existing door by releasing its hinges from the cupboard. If it has concealed cabinet hinges, as shown here, release the baseplates by loosening the screw in the centre of the cross. Hand-tighten the retaining screws back into the holes in the baseplates so they are not lost before the new door is hung.

2 Release the retaining screws securing the hinges to the door; if they are concealed cabinet hinges, prise the hinges out of their recesses. Put the screws in a safe place. Then use the old door as a template to mark the hinge positions on the inner face of the new door.

3 For concealed cabinet hinges, use a 35 mm (1⅜ in) hinge sinker bit to drill holes for the hinges at all the marks made in step 2. Use a drill stand to support the drill, and bore a hole to a depth that matches the thickness of the hinge bosses. For other types of hinges, drill pilot holes for their screws.

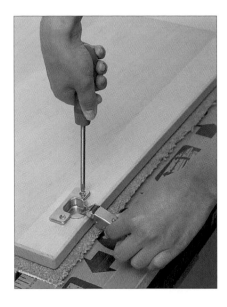

4 Fit the old concealed cabinet hinges in the blind holes. For all types of hinge, secure them with the retaining screws you had previously removed from the old door.

5 Hang a new door on its unit by attaching first the top hinge, then the others. For concealed cabinet hinges, use the adjustment screws on their baseplates to get the door to hang squarely. Make further adjustments to align the doors with each other when you have hung them all.

6 To replace a drawer front, undo the screws securing the old front to its carcase and set it aside. Lay the new drawer front face down and position the carcase over it.

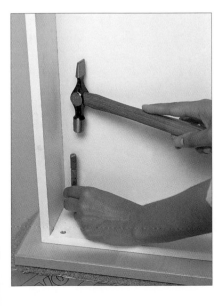

7 Insert a bradawl or nail punch in the screw holes to mark their positions on the inner face of the drawer front. Drill pilot holes, then attach the new drawer front to the carcase by driving in the screws. Check that it is fitted squarely, then slide the drawer back into the unit (see p.239).

Helpful hints

For a detailed shopping list, make a sketch of your units and number each door and drawer front. Measure each one and record its size on the sketch. Then count how many items you need in each size to make up your final order.

To change the exposed areas of the carcases, apply a veneer finish – a thin layer of wood. Trim the veneer (underside face up) with a veneer saw or utility knife, using a straightedge as a guide. Apply Scotch glue to the back of ordinary veneer. Edging strips have adhesive already applied; use a domestic iron to fix it in place. (Leave the bottom of the top units a light colour to reflect light onto the worktop.)

REPLACING A WORKTOP

YOU WILL NEED

Replacing a worktop
Screwdrivers
Tape measure and pencil
Jigsaw
Power drill plus twist drill
bits
Circular saw
Cartridge gun

Turning a corner
Router **or** laminate trimmer
plus mitre template (can be
hired)

MATERIALS

Replacing a worktop
Worktop
Retaining clips and
wood screws
Silicone sealant

Turning a corner
See above

SEE ALSO

Building a fitted cupboard
pp.232–233
Creating a work centre
pp.236–237
Giving storage units a
facelift pp.238–239
Replacing cupboard doors
and drawer fronts
pp.240–241

*The worktop in a kitchen
endures considerable
abuse, and one that is in
poor condition can make
a kitchen that is otherwise
in good condition look
tired and shabby. The best
solution is to replace it
with a new worktop.*

The worktop in the kitchen has to put up with more wear and tear than any other surface. It gets hot pans and dishes placed on it straight from the hob or oven, vegetables and other foods chopped and sliced on it and strongly coloured sauces spilt on it.

There are other materials available, but the easiest type of replacement worktop to install consists of a slab of chipboard covered with a durable layer of plastic laminate. The front edge is usually rounded off – a detail known as post-forming, where the laminate is shaped and bonded to the rounded-off board edge. It can be bought in a wide range of designs in two standard lengths – 2 m (6 ft 6 in) and 3 m (9 ft 10 in).

The same techniques can be applied to fit a top to a vanity unit in the bathroom or to create a work station.

1 If the worktop has an inset sink or hob, disconnect their supplies (see *Helpful hints)*; release the clips securing them to the worktop to lift them out. Undo the screws holding the worktop to the base units. Tape the screws you remove to the inside of the unit near the fixing position so you can reuse them to attach the new worktop.

2 Lift the old worktop off the base units – it may be in sections – and set it (or them) aside. Then clean away any old strips of sealant from the walls where the worktop was fitted against them.

3 You can use the old worktop section as a template to measure and mark out the new one. Mark any holes needed for inset sinks or hobs. Rest the worktop, underside face up, on a work-bench, with clearance below the inset. Drill a hole at each corner of the inset, making sure you bore the holes in the waste area.

4 Insert the blade of a jigsaw into one of the holes, and start to cut out the inset. Continue until all four sides have been cut.

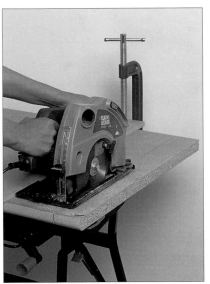

5 With the worktop underside face up, clamp a straightedge as a guide for a circular saw, and trim the end of the section to the correct length. If an end will be exposed, finish it off with a special-shaped metal trim, similar to one used for turning a corner (see box, below left).

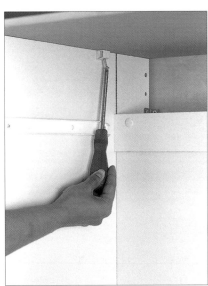

6 Lift the worktop into place, and secure it to the base units with screws and fixing clips. If you're using more then one section, join them with a metal trim as described in the box, below left. Seal the gap at the corner between the worktop and wall with a silicone sealant (see pp.160–161).

TURNING A CORNER

To finish a joint between adjacent sections at a corner, attach a special-shaped metal trim to fill the gap between the rounded front edge of one strip and the straight side edge of the other. A more complex method involves using a router or laminate trimmer with a special bit and template.

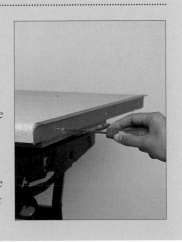

Helpful hints

If your worktop has an inset sink, first turn off the water supply and disconnect the taps and trap. If the sink is metallic, disconnect the earth link between the sink and the supply pipework.

If there is an inset hob, the gas or electricity supply has to be cut off. You can disconnect an electric hob after turning off the main cooker control switch; you must hire a qualified gas fitter to disconnect and reconnect a gas hob.

If there is more than a 10 mm (⅜ in) gap between the wall and worktop, scribe it, before fixing it, by holding a pencil against the wall and tracing the wall's shape onto the worktop. Trim along the pencil line with a jigsaw.

MAKING GOOD USE OF CUPBOARD SPACE

A carousel unit is the perfect storage device for corner units in a kitchen. It swings out or revolves to make items stored on it accessible.

E ven with the most ingenious use of space in the home, there comes a point where you can't fit in any more storage units. When you reach that stage, you'll have to make better use of your existing storage space. The kitchen and the bedroom are the main areas for storage, and there are many space-saving fittings available to make use of even the most inaccessible areas.

In the kitchen, some useful ideas include carousels to increase storage in corner base units, and wire baskets and racks in all shapes and sizes to fit in pull-out storage units and on door backs. In the bedroom, wire baskets come into their own as versatile organisers of storage space. You see at a glance what each basket contains and the clothes are better aired than in closed drawers. Other ideas include fitting split-level hanging rails and making use of space under beds.

Take time to research what is available in space-saving fittings. Apart from scouring high street home shops and DIY stores, look for advertisements in home interest magazines from mail-order suppliers.

FITTING A CAROUSEL UNIT

1 Start by deciding on the relative positions of the trays – this will depend on the height of the items that will be stored in them. Position the hinge bracket on the cupboard frame, mark the position of the screw holes, then drill the holes.

2 Screw the brackets into the frame, then continue with the other brackets until they have all been fixed.

3 Position the lower carousel tray on the appropriate bracket, making sure that the top flange on the tray goes on the top flange of the bracket. Insert the bracket pin and gently tap it down with a small hammer.

4 Fit a follower bracket to the door – it pulls the tray out when the door is opened. Pull the tray out so it meets the open door, position the follower bracket on the door with its hook over the tray and mark the screw holes. Take the bracket away, drill the holes, then screw the bracket in place with the tray under the hook.

FITTING A CLOTHES RAIL

1 To fit a clothes rail, measure and mark the position of the brackets on each side of the wardrobe. They should be in the centre of the side uprights and equidistant from the top of the wardrobe. Mark the screw hole positions, drill the holes and screw the brackets in place.

2 Measure from the inside of one bracket to the inside of the other. Cut a piece of rail to this length, using a hacksaw. Insert one end of the rail into one bracket, then fit the other end into the opposite bracket.

FITTING A SWIVEL HANGER

This hanger swivels outside of the wardrobe, so when you decide on its position bear this in mind. Mark the position of the screw holes, drill the holes, then screw the swivel hanger to the side of the wardrobe. You can buy a similar type of hanger designed to hold ties and scarves.

WARDROBE SYSTEMS

Ready-made storage systems are available to make the best use of the space in your wardrobe, with low rails for hanging short items and shelves above them for other items. To install one, follow the directions from the manufacturer.

GLOSSARY

ACCESS EQUIPMENT Ladders, platforms, scaffolding and any other equipment used to reach high, inaccessible areas.

AGGREGATE Sand and small stones mixed with cement and water to form concrete.

ARCHITRAVE The moulding that frames a door or window opening.

BALUSTER A post (one of a set) used to support a handrail along an open staircase.

BALUSTRADE The complete barrier installed along open staircases and landings. It consists of the balusters, newels and handrail.

BATTEN A thin strip of wood, typically of 50 mm × 25 mm (2 in × 1 in) softwood.

BEAD OR BEADING A type of moulding that has a half round or more intricate profile. It's often used for edging and as decoration.

BEVEL A surface that meets another surface at an angle of less than 90°.

BIND When a door or hinged casement rubs against its surrounding frame.

BORE To drill a hole greater than about 12 mm (½ in) in diameter.

BUTT To fit together two pieces of material side by side or edge to edge.

CARCASE The boxlike, five-sided structure that forms the base of certain types of furniture such as a kitchen cupboard or chest of drawers.

CHAMFER A narrow, angled surface, often at 45°, running along the corner of a piece such as a beam or post.

CONCAVE A surface that curves inward.

CONTOUR The outline or shape of an object.

CONVEX A surface that curves outward.

CORNICE A decorative moulding fixed at the junction between the walls and ceiling, often used to hide cracks.

COUNTERSINK A tapered recess made in the top section of a screw hole to allow the head of the screw to sit flush with the surface of the material.

COVING A prefabricated concave moulding, often used as a cornice.

CUTTING-IN BRUSH A type of brush with bristles cut at an angle to assist painting neatly at an edge such as at a cornice or architrave.

DADO RAIL A decorative moulding, also called a chair rail, installed on walls about waist height, originally to prevent furniture from marring the walls.

DAMP-PROOF COURSE Also referred to as DPC, an impervious material laid in the building foundation to prevent moisture from the ground spreading to the walls or floors of the building.

DAMP-PROOF MEMBRANE Also referred to as DPM, an impervious material laid under a concrete floor to prevent moisture seeping through it.

DOWEL A small cylindrical wooden peg, sometimes with grooves running the length of its surface. It can be used to plug holes or to form a joint by inserting it into holes in two pieces of wood.

EGGSHELL PAINT A paint that dries with a matt finish and is used for interiors.

EMULSION PAINT Used on interior walls and ceilings, a water-based paint with a matt or sheen finish. It dries quickly and is easy to clean off paint equipment.

END GRAIN The fibres in the end of the wood exposed after cutting across the wood.

FEATHER To dull or taper an edge to make it less noticeable, a technique often used in sanding and painting.

FILLET A small, often wooden, piece of moulding with a square cross section.

FURRING STRIP A thin length of wood fixed in parallel strips across a wall or ceiling, forming a framework to which cladding is attached.

GLAZING POINT Or sprig, a small triangular-shaped piece of metal for holding a pane of window glass in a rebate.

GLOSS PAINT A solvent-based paint that dries with a hard, shiny finish. It's suitable for painting interior and exterior wood and metal. This type of paint needs a longer drying time and is harder to clean off paint equipment.

GRAIN The direction of the fibres in a piece of wood.

GROUT A water-resistant paste used to seal the gaps between ceramic or other similar tiles fixed to walls or floors.

HARDWOOD Wood that comes from broad-leaved – usually deciduous – trees such as ash, beech and oak. This type of wood is typically hard; however, balsa is classified as a hardwood but is a soft, lightweight material.

HEAD The highest horizontal member of a window or door frame.

HEAD PLATE The highest horizontal component of a stud partition wall.

JAMB The vertical side member of the frame that surrounds a door or window.

JOIST A horizontal wood beam that is used to support a heavy structure such as a floor or ceiling.

KERF The groove created in a material when cut by any type of saw.

KEY To roughen a surface, often by sanding, to provide a better grip for a material such as paint or adhesive.

MASTIC A nonsetting compound that seals a joint between two surfaces such as a tiled wall and a worktop, bath or shower tray.

MATT FINISH A nonreflective finish on a material such as paint or quarry tiles.

MITRE A joint between two bevelled pieces that forms an angle, often a 45° angle.

MORTISE A rectangular-shaped recess cut into wood. It may be used to form a joint by combining it with a tenoned end. Alternatively, it is used to hold a striker box in a door frame for a lock or latch.

MOULDING A narrow, usually decorative, strip of wood or other material. It is available shaped in different profiles. Skirting boards and dado and picture rails are types of moulding.

MULLION A vertical dividing component of a window.

MUNTIN A vertical component between panels; they are used to form a panelled door or wall panelling.

NEWEL Part of the balustrade, the wider post at both the top and bottom of a staircase for supporting the handrail.

NOGGING A short horizonal component between studs in a partition wall.

NOSING The front, often rounded, edge of a stair tread.

PARE To use a chisel, bevel side up, to remove fine shavings from wood – often done to smooth a surface from which wood was removed.

PATTERN REPEAT The distance of a motif before it begins to be duplicated, or repeated.

PELMET A decorative wood unit used to hide the top edge of curtains or a structure such as the track of a sliding door.

PICTURE RAIL A type of decorative moulding that is normally fixed horizontally to the walls above head height.

PILE The fabric raised from a backing – often used to classify a type of carpet.

PILOT HOLE A hole drilled in a material to guide a screw. It should be smaller in diameter than the shank of the screw without its threads.

PLINTH A four-sided base on which a structure, such as a cupboard or chest of drawers, is placed.

PRIMER A liquid substance used to seal a material, such as plaster, plasterboard, wood or metal, before applying an undercoat.

PROFILE The contour or outline of an object.

PROUD When an object protrudes from the surface.

RAIL The horizontal piece of wood that joins vertical pieces in a frame or carcase.

RAISED GRAIN When the wood's surface is roughened by damping, which causes its fibres to swell.

REBATE A step-shaped recess in the edge of a workpiece, often as part of a joint but also used for exterior door frames to prevent the door from swinging through.

REVEAL The vertical side of a window or door opening.

RISER The vertical component of a step or stair.

SASH The structure of a window that holds the glass. It usually opens, either up and down or sideways, but it is sometimes fixed.

SCARF A joint between two pieces of material cut at matching angles – unlike a mitre, the faces of the pieces are flush.

SCRIBE To mark a line with a pointed tool, or to copy the profile of a surface onto a piece of material, which will be trimmed to butt against the surface.

SCORE A line that marks a division or boundary, or the act of making the line.

SECRET NAILING A method of securing components together, such as tongue-and-groove floorboards, using fixings at an angle and punched below the surface of the workpiece.

SHEEN FINISH Also known as a silk finish, the amount of reflectiveness of a painted or other surface, midway between matt and gloss finishes.

SILL The lowest horizontal component of a window or door frame or of a stud partition wall.

SHIM A thin piece of material, such as cardboard or plywood, used as packing to fill a gap between materials.

SIZE A thin gelatinous solution used to seal a surface, such as a plaster wall, prior to hanging wallpaper.

SKIRTING BOARD A wood moulding used horizontally along the walls where they meet the floor.

SPANDREL The triangular material that is used to fill the space below an outside stringer on a staircase.

SOFTWOOD Wood that comes from coniferous trees, including cedar and pine. Although softwood is typically soft in nature, yew is one type that is hard.

SOLE PLATE Also known as a stud-partition sill, the lowest horizontal member of a wood-frame partition wall.

STAFF BEAD The innermost strip of wood that holds a sash that moves up and down in the window frame.

STAIN A liquid that changes the colour of wood but does not protect it. It comes in water-based, oil-based and solvent-based versions.

STILE A vertical side component of a window sash or door.

STRAIGHTEDGE A length of either metal or wood that has at least one true straight edge. It is often used for marking straight lines or making a surface level.

STRINGER Also known as a string, one of a pair of boards that runs along the staircase, from one floor to another, supporting the treads and risers. If against a wall, it's called an inside stringer; if there is an open side, it's an outside stringer.

STUD A vertical member of a wood-framed wall.

STUD PARTITION WALL A wall constructed with a wood frame, usually covered with plasterboard.

SUBSIDENCE The sinking of the ground that occurs where land has been infilled or when it becomes excessively dry and shrinks. This may be due to a drought or to a large tree.

SUGAR SOAP A strong, alkaline-based liquid that is used for cleaning painted and other types of surfaces.

TEMPLATE Paper, card, metal or other sheet material formed in a specific shape or pattern to be used as a guide for transferring the shape to the workpiece.

TENON A projecting end of a wood component, which fits into a mortise to form a joint.

TONGUE AND GROOVE A joint between two pieces of material – such as floorboards or cladding – in which one piece has a projecting edge that fits into a slot, or groove, on the edge of the other piece.

TOP COAT The last coat of a finish applied to a surface. There may be several coats underneath it.

TREAD The horizontal part of a step that is walked on.

UNDERCOAT One or more layers of a paint or varnish to cover a primer or hide another colour before applying a top coat.

UNDERLAY A layer of material to provide a smooth surface for laying a decorative flooring. Rubber, felt or paper may be used under carpeting; hardboard or plywood may be used for other floorings.

UTILITY KNIFE Also referred to as a trimming knife or Stanley knife, a handle that holds a replacable blade, which may or may not retract.

VARNISH A liquid applied to wood materials, it hardens to form a protective surface. It may be clear or coloured.

WET-AND-DRY ABRASIVE PAPER A paper with silicon-carbide granules attached to it for smoothing surfaces. It may be used wet.

VENEER A thin decorative layer of wood applied to a less attractive base material.

USEFUL ADDRESSES

BOMBAY DUCK
231 The Vale
London W3 7QS
0181 749 8001
E-mail:
mailorder@bombayduck.co.uk
*Mail order of doorknobs and
other household accessories.
Catalogue available.*

**BRITISH GATES & TIMBER
LTD**
Biddenden
Ashford
Kent TN27 8DD
01580 291 555
*Woodworking tools and
accessories. Catalogue and
mail order service available.*

C.P. HART & SONS LTD
Newnham Terrace
Hercules Road
London SE1 7DR
0171 902 1000
*Decoration materials and
tools, wood, mouldings,
doors and windows,
flooring, plasterwork and
general accessories.
Catalogue and mail order
service available.*

CRAFT SUPPLIES LTD
The Mill
Miller's Dale
Buxton
Derbyshire SK17 8SN
01298 871 636
*Wood, tools, accessories
and finishing supplies.
Catalogue and mail order
service available.*

DALER–ROWNEY LTD
12 Percy Street
London W1A 2BP
0171 636 8241
Website address:
http://www.daler-rowney.com
*Whole range of artist's
materials, as well as
decorator's paint brochures*

*Catalogue and mail order
service available.*

FARROW & BALL
Uddens Trading Estate
Wimborne
Dorset BH21 7NL
01202 876 141
*Modern and traditional paints
and traditional wallpapers.
Catalogue and mail order
service available.*

FIRED EARTH
Twyford Mill
Oxford Road
Adderbury
Oxfordshire OX17 3HP
01295 812 088
*Handmade floor and wall
tiles, paints, fabrics, furniture.
Catalogue and mail order
service available.*

GREEN AND STONE
259 Kings Road
London SW3 5EL
0171 352 0837
E-mail:
greenandstone@enterprise.net
*Artist's materials, including
acrylic varnish, specialist
brushes, casein paints,
crackle varnish, gesso and
gesso paints, gum arabic,
linseed oil, powder colours,
shellac, stencilling materials
and transparent oil glaze.
Catalogue and mail order
service available.*

**INTERIOR DECORATORS AND
BUILDING CENTRE GROUP
LTD**
26 Store Street
London WC1E 7BT
0171 692 6200
Website address:
http://www.buildingcentre.co.uk
*Building information and
advice, and a comprehensive,
specialized bookshop on
building.*

ISAAC LORD LTD
185 Desborough Road
High Wycombe
Buckinghamshire HP11 2QN
Cabinet fittings:
01494 462 121
Architectural ironmongery:
01494 459 191
Website address:
http://www.isaaclord.s.com
*Cabinet fittings and handles,
kichen fittings, door and
window furniture and
fittings, locks and latches,
fasteners and fixings,
brasswork, black ironwork,
huge range of tools and
power tools, decorating
products, paint mixing.
Catalogue and mail order
service available.*

**JOHN BODDY'S FINE WOOD
& TOOL STORE LTD**
Riverside Sawmills
Boroughbridge
North Yorkshire YO51 9LJ
01423 322 370
E-mail:
info@john-boddys-fwts.co.uk
*Everything for woodworking
and wood finishing, including
tools, books and videos. Mail
order service available.*

**JOHN WILMAN LTD
(COLOROLL)**
Riverside Mills
Crawford Street
Nelson
Lancashire BB9 7QT
01282 617 777
*Wallcoverings, fabrics and
bedding. Catalogue and mail
order service available.*

JUNCKERS LTD
Wheaton Court Commercial
Centre
Wheaton Road
Witham
Essex CM8 3UJ
01376 517 512
Website address:
http://www.junckers.com
Solid and hardwood floors

*and worktops. Catalogue and
mail order service available.*

KEY INDUSTRIAL
35 Blackmoore Road
Ebblake Industrial Estate
Verwood
Dorset BH31 6AT
01202 825 311
Website address:
http://www.keyind.co.uk
*Over 30,000 items of
industrial and domestic
products. Ideal for storage
solutions. Catalogue and mail
order service available.*

**LASSCO
LONDON ARCHITECTURAL
SALVAGE & SUPPLY CO LTD**
Saint Michael's Church
Mark Street
London EC2A 3PA
0171 739 0448
Website address:
http://www.lassco.co.uk
*Bathroom and kitchen
furniture and fittings,
ceramics, doors, shutters,
flooring, metalware, door
furniture, panelling and
carved woodwork and
staircases and spindles.*

LIBERON
Mountfield Industrial Estate
New Romney
Kent TN28 8XU
01797 367 555
Customer services:
01797 361 136
*Wax polishes and finishing
products, colouring products.
Catalogue and mail order
service available.*

PAINTABILITY
9 Heneage Street
London E1 5LJ
0171 377 9262
*Stencils and paint effects sold
only by mail order.*

PARIS CERAMICS
583 Kings Road
London SW6 2EH

0171 371 7778
Website address:
http://www.parisceramics.com
Handmade and painted tiles, antique handmade terracotta tiles, reclaimed floors and newly quarried limestone floors. Catalogue and mail order service available; however, it is advisable to visit a showroom if possible.

PAUL FRICKER LTD
Well Park
Willeys Avenue
Exeter
Devon EX2 8BE
01392 278 636
Mosaic tiles and accessory materials. Catalogue and mail order service available.

ROMANY
52–56 Camden High Street
London NW1 0LT
0171 387 2579
Ironmongery, door furniture, hand and power tools and decorating accessories. Catalogue and mail order service available.

RUGBY JOINERY
Watchouse Lane
Doncaster BN5 9LR
01302 394 000
Website address:
http://www.rugby-joinery.co.uk
Largest range of doors in Great Britain. Catalogue and mail order service available.

RUSTINS LTD
Waterloo Road
London NW2 7TX
0181 450 4666
Finishing and restoration products, stains, varnishes and woodcare products. Information packet and mail order service available.

SPAZIO DOOR CO
Oaklands
Tenterden
Kent TN30 6NH

01580 763 593
Folding doors, folding walls and room dividers. Catalogue and mail order service available.

TRAVIS PERKINS
491 Battersea Park Road
London SW11 4NH
0171 223 4411
Website address:
http://www.travisperkins.co.uk
Timber and builder's merchants. Catalogue and mail order service available.

WINDSOR CARPETS LTD
For nearest store ring:
0800 731 2889
Website address:
http://www.windsorcarpets.com
Carpet and flooring specialists. Catalogue and mail order service available.

WOODFIT LTD
Kem Mill
Whittle–le–Woods
Chorley
Lancashire PR6 7EA
01257 266 421
Furniture fittings, doors and storage solutions. Catalogue and mail order service available.

FEDERATIONS AND ASSOCIATIONS

BRITISH BLIND & SHUTTER ASSOCIATION
42 Heath Street
Tamworth
Staffordshire B79 7JH
01827 52 337
Website address:
http://www.bbsa-uk.com
Information and advice on all matters concerning blinds and shutters.

BRITISH CERAMIC TILE COUNCIL,
BRITISH BATHROOM COUNCIL

Federation House
Stoke–on–Trent ST4 2RT
01782 747 123
Website address:
http://www.british-bathrooms.org.uk
Information and advice on all bathroom and tiling matters; free fact sheets available.

BRITISH COATING FEDERATION LTD
Website address:
http://www.coatings.org.uk
Information on paint available on-line; will respond to any queries.

THE BRITISH WOOD PRESERVING AND DAMP-PROOFING ASSOCIATION
Building Number 6
The Office Village
4 Romford Road
Stratford
London E154EA
0181 519 2588
E–mail:
bwpda@ukonline.co.uk
Trade advisers on all matters of damp-proofing and wood preservation.

BUILDERS MERCHANTS FEDERATION
15 Soho Square
London W1V 4LX
0171 439 1753
E–mail:
info@bmf.org.uk
Help and advice available on general building materials; also, lists of stockers and suppliers of building materials.

DESIGNERS ASSOCIATION LTD
(IDDA)
1/4 Chelsea Harbour Design Centre
Lots Road
London SW10 0XE
0171 349 0800
Website address:
http://www.idda.co.uk

Professional advice on working with designers and designing your own home.

DRAUGHT PROOFING ADVISORY ASSOCIATION, EXTERNAL WALL INSULATION ASSOCIATION, THE NATIONAL ASSOCIATION OF LOFT INSULATION CONTRACTORS, THE NATIONAL CAVITY INSULATION ASSOCIATION
PO Box 12
Haslemere
Surrey GU27 3AH
01428 654 001
Website Address:
http://www.nationline.co.uk/ceed
Information and advice on all aspects of home insulation.

GLASS AND GLAZING FEDERATION
44–48 Borough High Street
London SE1 1XB
0171 403 7177
Information on glaziers and retailers and general advice.

THE LEAGUE OF PROFESSIONAL CRAFTSMEN LTD
10 Village Way
Rayners Lane
Pinner
Middlesex HA5 5AF
0181 866 6116
Information and advice on professional craftsmen.

MASTER LOCKSMITHS ASSOCIATION
5D Great Central Way
Woodford Halse
Daventry
Northamptonshire NN11 3PZ
01327 262 255
General enquiries:
0800 783 1498
Website address:
http://www.locksmiths.co.uk
General information and advice; also lists of members and reputable suppliers.

INDEX

Note: **bold** figures show main references; *italic* figures refer to information given in boxes or picture captions.

ACKNOWLEDGMENTS

Photographic Credits

All photography by John Freeman, with the exception of the credits listed below.

Page **8** Robert Harding Picture Library/Ben Wright *bottom right*, Peter Willis *bottom left*; **9** Houses & Interiors *top*; **10–11** Houses & Interiors; **12** Peter Willis; **13** Reproduced by permission of Building Research Establishment Ltd; **110** Robert Harding Picture Library/Dominic Blackmore *centre* and *bottom left*, Tony Stone Images/Oliver Benn *bottom right*; **111** Robert Harding Picture Library/Homes & Gardens *top* and *bottom left*, Camera Press *top right* and *centre,* Robert Harding Picture Library/Bill Reavell *bottom right*; **112** Camera Press *centre*, Elizabeth Whiting Assoc *bottom*; **113** Abode *top left* and *centre*, Elizabeth Whiting Assoc *top right* and *bottom*; **130** Houses & Interiors *centre*, Camera Press *bottom*; **131** Camera Press *top* and *centre*, Robert Harding Picture Library/Homes & Ideas *bottom left*, Robert Harding Picture Library/Ideal Home *bottom right*; **150** Camera Press *centre*, Robert Harding Picture Library/Christopher Sykes *bottom*; **151** Houses & Interiors *top* and *bottom right*, Robert Harding Picture Library/Nick Carter *centre*, Camera Press *bottom left*; **162** Robert Harding Picture Library/Country Homes & Interiors *centre*, Houses & Interiors *bottom*; **163** Camera Press *top* and *centre left*, Robert Harding Picture Library/Jonathan Pilkington *top right*, Abode *centre right*, Robert Harding Picture Library/James Merrell *bottom left*, Robert Harding Picture Library/Dominic Blackmore *bottom right*; **178** Camera Press *centre*, Robert Harding Picture Library/Mark Luscombe-Whyte *bottom*; **179** Camera Press *top left* and *centre*, Elizabeth Whiting Assoc *top right*, Robert Harding Picture Library/Tom Leighton *bottom left*, International Interiors/Paul Ryan *bottom right*; **196** Robert Harding Picture Library/Simon Upton *centre*, Houses & Interiors *bottom*; **197** Robert Harding Picture Library/Dominic Blackmore *top left*, Camera Press *top right*, *centre left* and *bottom*, Robert Harding Picture Library/Tim Beddow *centre right*; **208** Camera Press *centre*, Robert Harding Picture Library/Flavio Galozzi *bottom*; **209** Robert Harding Picture Library/Dominic Blackmore *top left*, Elizabeth Whiting Assoc *top right* and *bottom left*, Camera Press *centre left* and *bottom right*, Robert Harding Picture Library/Brian Harrison *centre right*; **222** Robert Harding Picture Library/Trevor Richards *centre*, Robert Harding Picture Library/Ken Kirkwood *bottom*; **223** Robert Harding Picture Library/Bill Reavell *top left*, Robert Harding Picture Library/James Merrell *top right*, Robert Harding Picture Library/Christopher Drake *centre left*, Robert Harding Picture Library/Polly Wreford *centre right*, Robert Harding Picture Library/Ariadne *bottom left*, Robert Harding Picture Library/Jan Baldwin *bottom right*; **230** Camera Press; **231** Robert Harding Picture Library/Dominic Blackmore *top left*, Camera Press *top, centre* and *bottom*.

Illustration Credit

All illustrations by Amzie Viladot Lorente

Acknowledgments

The publishers are grateful to the following individuals and companies for their assistance in compiling this book: Abru Henderson Ltd, for ladders; Black & Decker Ltd, for power tools; Colefax and Fowler, for wallpaper borders; Cottage Flooring, for carpet and flooring demonstration; Daniel Platt Ltd, for quarry tiles; Farrow & Ball, for paint samples; Fired Earth, for flooring and wall tiles; Forbo Nairn Ltd, for vinyl floor coverings; GET plc (Rapitest), for stud, cable and pipe detector; HSS Hire, for hired equipment; Ideal Standard Ltd, for bathroom suite and mixer tap; Junckers Ltd, for woodstrip flooring; LASSCo London Architectural Salvage & Supply Co Ltd, for cast iron fireplace surround; LASSCo Flooring, for floorboards and flooring; Sheen Interiors, for wallcoverings; Stanley Tools, for hand tools; The Tool Shop, for hand tools; Vitrex Ltd, for tiling tools and accessories and safety gear; John Wilman Ltd (Coloroll), for wallcoverings and borders; Woodfit Ltd, for storage and sliding door equipment; Bob Cleveland, Barry Edwards and Martyn Judd, for studio assistance; and Simon Garrett, John McKeever and Jill Streeten for the loan of their homes.